Charles Hainsworth hails from Yorkshire stock. His family has lived [...] generations and he spent hi[s ...] sbury.

After a [...] up his pen to relate his [...] tor in this idiosyncratic [...] ars of the National Health Service.

He spends his time telling stories to his grandchildren, painting, reading, walking in Yorkshire … and writing.

Queensbury is a real place! It sits on the Pennine heights between Bradford and Halifax. Originally there was just a road: the packhorse track between Bradford and Manchester. An inn - the Queen's Head - was built adjoining the road at the summit of the causeway. There were farms on the surrounding moorland and a small settlement grew along the track and around the inn. The place became known as Queenshead.

In Victorian times, a woollen mill was established and the settlement developed into a large village.

A brass band was instigated at the mill: The Black Dyke Mills Band. This has triumphed in many championships over the years. It still practises in the original band-room in the village. In 1863, as a reaction to being named after a public house, the place was renamed Queensbury.

Other titles in the "Doctor" series:

It's Nobbut Snow, Doctor!
1960 – 1963

Kindly Oblige, Doctor!
1963 - 1966

CAN YOU COME, DOCTOR?

TALES OF A YORKSHIRE GP'S LIFE IN THE LATE '50s

1957 - 1960

Charles Hainsworth

Published by Gig Shed Books

Copyright © 2022 Charles Hainsworth

All right reserved.

No part of this book may be reproduced, or stored in a retrieval system, or transmitted in any form by any means, electronic, mechanical, photocopying, recording, or otherwise, without express written permission of the author.

Cover photograph: the view from Craig-na-Hullie garden looking north up the Dales. The Queensbury Triangle and station is in the valley below.

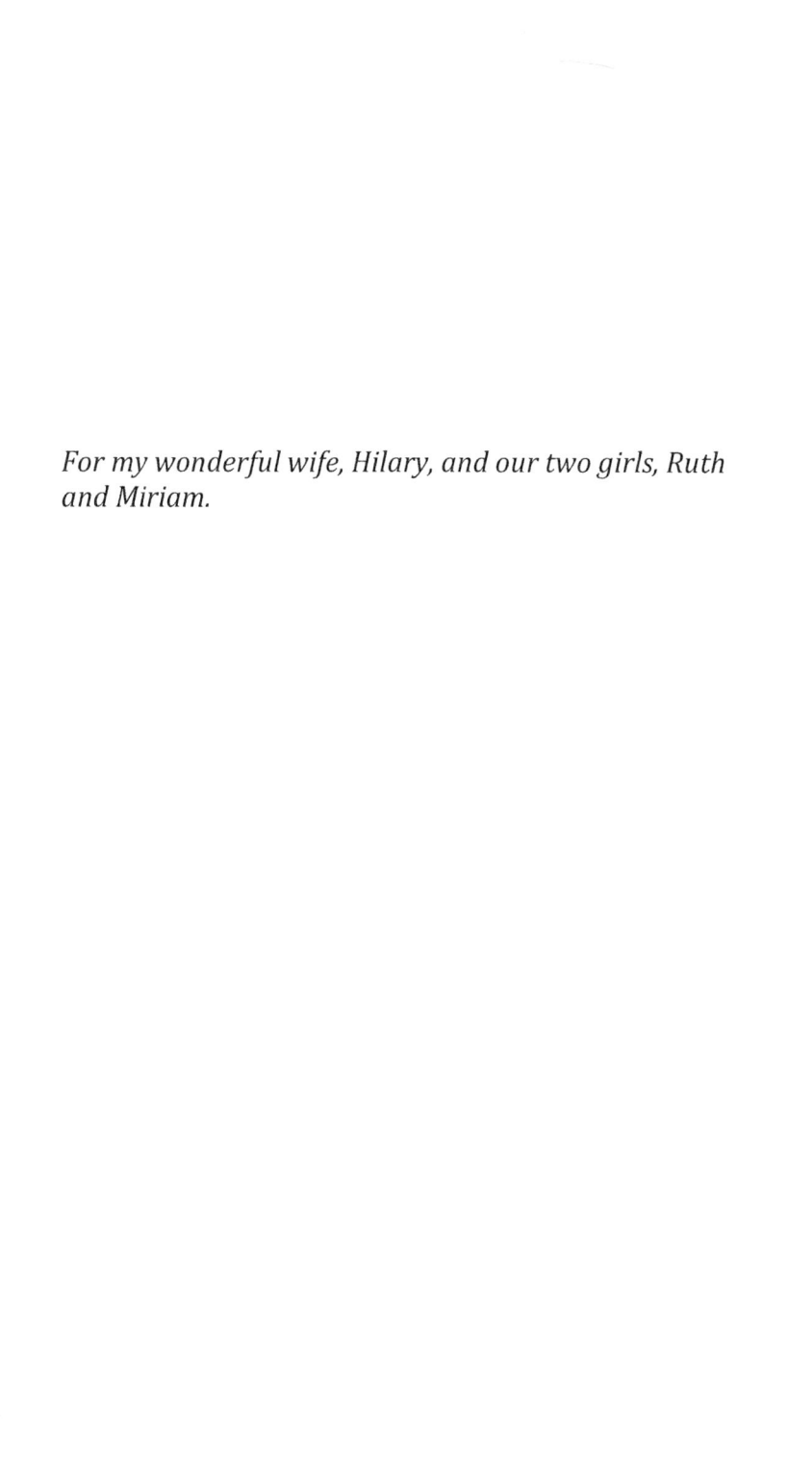

For my wonderful wife, Hilary, and our two girls, Ruth and Miriam.

An Explanation

Although this book is written through my father's eyes, he didn't write it. The stories enclosed within it, however, are all true. One or two came from other GP friends, but the majority are my father's. As a young boy, I first heard them, freshly minted that day, over the family meal table. They reappeared in the talks my father gave to various groups during his retirement. Many people encouraged him to make these reminiscences more permanent by writing them in book form, but he refused as many of his patients would then have still been alive.

He did, however, leave his notes, letters and photographs. On his retirement he also wrote a short book, 'The Doctors of Queensbury', which outlined the history of medical provision in the village as well as describe in detail the practice organisation when he was a partner there. I have used these and the recollections of my mother, extensively. She and I spent many happy moments, in the years before her death, talking about these early days. She was overjoyed when a fresh memory 'popped into her head', but, above all, she enjoyed just talking about Eric.

I have had to put flesh on the bones, however. I have used fictitious names and personal descriptions to hide identities. I have developed the narrative, dialogue and characters. Some people in this book are an amalgamation of a number of real folk. I have, however, used Dr Tom Akroyd's name and those of his family, with permisiion.

I might also have fictionalised, unintentionally, the village where my father was a GP. Queensbury is a real place and I decided I didn't want to hide it behind a false name. My father's patients were molded by the place and this story is part of the story of Queensbury in the late 1950s and early 1960s. I wanted to convey the essence of such a place in those times. Then it was self-contained in many ways as were many other communities. Such places have changed over the intervening years. The village and its development is part of history and part of this story. The third strand woven through the narrative is the story of the early years of the National Health Service. Modern doctors reading this book will hardly recognise it as the same organisation in which they serve: the consulting rooms in the doctor's house, the haphazard record keeping, the night calls, the lack of ancillary staff (except for longsuffering wives). The list is almost endless but I have tried to record the atmosphere of the time through these pages. I have made extensive research but I will have made errors. Please forgive them.

In writing this book I have been greatly helped and encouraged by many, but two people, in particular, have been alongside me throughout the project. Judy Francis helped plant the seed of the idea over a dinner table a few years ago and has read every word I have written since. Pat Schooling, my original agent, has been a rock. She has also been honest, but, without her guidance, none of what you are holding in your hands would have been completed. She was hoping to emulate her earlier success of *Call the Midwife*. Unfortunately, Pat died in early 2021 before this could happen. Thank you.

Since the first book was published I have been contacted by Frank Robertshaw, the nephew of Dr Alan

Glenn, who lived at Innisfree before Tom. He confirmed many of my facts and stories and gave me two more that I have added into this book. My thanks.

This, then, is the second edition of this book. The first had (to my shame) many mistakes in it. A friend from my childhood, Doug, read all the books carefully and edited them. I am deeply in his gratitude. He also provided me with a story about his father, Tom Akroyd, my father's partner. This appears in "Kindly Oblige, Doctor!" Thank you, Doug.

Chapter 1

It had been quite a night. After the evening surgery I had drawn the curtains to hide the glowering darkness outside as I got out my latest acquisition, a portable typewriter, to write up some letters generated by the day. The house became colder and the winter gloom seemed to accompany it.

Sometime later Margaret, my young wife, and I climbed the stairs to bed, driven by the dreariness and cold. In Craig-na-Hullie, the Scottish sounding name for our Yorkshire doctor's house, there were only two warm rooms besides the surgery: the kitchen and the bathroom. The latter was directly above the former, which housed the coal-fired range cooker. This heated both rooms. The bathroom boasted an oversized airing cupboard in whose comfortable warmth our children, Charles and Ruth, changed and left their clothes in piles, as far apart as possible at each end of the large cupboard, ready for the morning. They dallied over winter ablutions to delay the sprint into cold bedrooms and equally cold sheets.

Every morning they awoke to fascinating patterns of ice left by Jack Frost on the thin panes. As the cold deepened, the morning ice would thicken until the layer at the bottom of the window became over half an inch thick and wouldn't melt in the day.

Letters done, Margaret and I decided the warmest place to be was in bed. We dawdled in the bathroom. I rested against the cracked washbasin held up on cast iron art-nouveaux legs that Margaret had tried to make cheerful with pink paint, while she would invariably perch on the roll top edge of the bath, which had been installed when the house was built some fifty years previously. Now its enamel was sadly stained and worn into a depression where, over the years, doctors' bottoms had rested. We often wondered how we would get the thing out when we eventually could afford to do up the bathroom. At least we had managed to stretch our meager finances to a piece of cheap carpet that covered the cold, cracked lino.

I had been in the practice for two years and knew about the snow. However, this winter was going to be our first real test of coping in a place over a thousand feet above sea level as we had only taken up residence in Craig-na-Hullie in the previous summer. Fortunately, the snow hadn't arrived yet. The afternoon's clouds threatened to change this, though.

"Good grief, Eric. It's a cold one tonight. It hasn't been this bad since we got here." Margaret shivered.

I nodded. "I think it'll snow tonight. I just hope I can get the car out in the morning. I think I'd better get up early in case I need to clear the drive," I said with a sinking heart. The prospect was far from enticing. George Blunt who, alongside his wife, Bea, had lived in the house before us, had forewarned me of this extra burden to the usual doctoring duties here. It was a regular occurrence every winter and it looked as though we would meet it tonight for the first time. I didn't quite know what to expect, but I was imagining the worst. Margaret added to my miserable musings.

"You'll probably have to do the surgery path as well," she said. I nodded in despair. "And then there's the coal-shed," she added woefully. We had to get coal from the stone shed across the yard at the back of the house. Without coal to feed the stove in the kitchen, the house would soon be consumed by the cold.

We both started preparing for our nightly dash to the icebox of our bedroom. "I just hope there aren't any calls tonight. I don't fancy getting up in this weather." However, the vagaries of life were going to intervene. No sooner had I pulled the sheets and blankets tighter round my head to make a better cocoon when a shrill bell erupted into awful life by my ear.

The only telephone that was in the house when we had bought it the previous May was on a shelf in the hall by the door to the surgery - down the flight of stairs with its half-landing. Putting an extension telephone on the small table by my pillow was an obvious luxury, however unwelcome it was when it sprang into action. I reached my hand out and scrabbled for the handset before pulling it back into the warmth of the bed.

"Hello, Dr Hainsworth here," I tried to sound my usual cheerful self but, with heavy heart, I knew what was probably coming.

"Oh, hello, Doctor," a cheery female voice almost shouted as if the weather might somehow affect the telephone line and impede my hearing. "It's Florence here. You know, the midwife. I'm at the Firth's." Ah yes, I thought, Mary was due about now. She was one of my patients and I had kept a close eye on this, her fourth pregnancy. I was keen to do my own obstetrics and I was trying to build a good reputation in the practice.

"Yes, Florence. Is there something wrong?" I asked as I stirred out of my cocoon.

"No, no, doctor. Far from it. The Firths called me just over an hour ago. Mary always produces quickly and this time has been no exception. She's already in the final stages but I thought you might want to attend. She tends to tear and you might want to do an episiotomy to help her heal." The bed, just nicely warm was pulling me. It wasn't a real emergency and Florence Micklethwaite was very competent. The temptation was fleeting. Things could still go wrong though and I could never forgive myself if I had failed my patient because of my weakness for warmth.

"Right, Florence, I'll be there soon!" I flung the bed clothes off with resolve and tugged on my shirt and trousers over my pyjamas. I had done this countless times since my first ever night call and I knew many of my doctor friends did the same. It saved time and guaranteed warmth, which was essential if I was to function properly in the vicious cold of the winter night hours. I collected my bag from the surgery, making sure that I had some curved needles and suture material. At that time, I generally sterilized my own needles. Sterile scissors were also a necessity but I also took my other delivery instruments as well, just to be sure. I was ready. I was greeted by the snow as it danced round my face in large flakes as I left the house. It had finally arrived.

Sliding the old wooden garage doors back I thought I should close them again after I had got the car out. I could be some time and the snow might drift into the garage and have to be removed, as well as fromthose other places that

Margaret had so thoughtfully mentioned. Looking round I wondered if there was anything else I might need. Ah, the shovel – and thank goodness I'd had the tyres changed to ones with a tractor tread.

The snowflakes rushed towards the windscreen in manic flickers of white as I leaned forward to try and peer through and find my way. They were coming faster now and I slowed the car down to a walking pace. Thank goodness the Firths lived only just beyond the mill on one of the side streets of terraced houses that led off at right angles to the main High Street. I had no idea that I was being followed through the village. A black car pulled up behind me as I got out to retrieve my bag.

It was the car door slamming that brought my head up. A large figure was approaching through the swirling flakes and I instinctively stepped back. The man thrust his face closer to mine and then he brought his arm up so his hand could stroke the impressive walrus moustache. I recognised the uniform with a sense of relief.

"It's a strange time of night to be out and it's some night an' all, sir. Can I help you, sir?" the brusque voice pushed aside the flakes.

"Oh, thank you officer. I'm a doctor and I have a patient in that house there. The one with the lights on. She's in labour and I could do with an extra pair of hands."

The slightly aggressive look on the peering face changed to one of worried dismay. The face withdrew as the policeman backtracked on his offer, "Oh, I see, doctor. Labour you say. There'll be blood?" I nodded as he continued, "Well, I can't rightly give the time right now, doctor, I'm afraid. But I'm glad you're on legitimate business."

The policeman hastily retreated to his car and I banged on the Firth's door before opening it. My spectacles immediately steamed up in the humid warmth. "Is that you, doctor? We're up here!" Florence's voice shouted down the stairs.

I removed my mackintosh and scarf, and stamped my feet on the mat by the door. I was ready and fully awake. Two children in shabby nightclothes were standing quietly and shivering at the top of the stairs. They were listening outside a closed door, wide-eyed at the very strange and worrying noises that filled the house.

"Hello, you two," I said. "Don't worry, your mum's going to be just fine. I think you'll have a new brother or sister very soon. Why don't you go back to bed and get some sleep now? We don't want you to get too cold and poorly, do we?"

Mary was lying on her bed with a damp face, wet hair plastered to one side. She looked at me with unconcerned eyes, careless that the most intimate areas of her body were on full view of my gaze. She was panting slightly and had obviously just finished a contraction. "Hello, Mary. It's good to see that things are going well." Mary grunted a welcome.

"Oh, hello, doctor," Florence Micklethwaite, the midwife, straightened up to face me as I came in. She pushed her hands down the white apron that was covering the front of her pale blue uniform to smooth out any errant wrinkles. Florence was slightly dumpy and her round face never seemed without a shining smile. Her eyes twinkled. Her physique and personality radiated her ability to handle any situation. I was developing a very good relationship with her and we seemed to naturally work well together as a team.

Florence obviously had everything under control right now. "Thank you for coming, doctor. I knew you would like to be here, just in case. The baby's in a good position. The head's showing now but I think we need to do an episiotomy. It will help." I glanced down at the entrance of the birth canal and could see the damp mat of fine tangled hair of the baby's head. I knew that the end wasn't far away.

"I'll give you a small local anaesthetic, Mary, and you won't feel a thing. I can do it without but the anaesthetic means I can sew you up quickly afterwards."

"That's a'right, doctor. Do whatever yer think…"

I quickly attached a needle to a glass syringe and held it up to the light. Sometimes the end of the needle would get a slight burr on the end and this indicated a bluntness which could cause unnecessary pain. Once again, I was thankful for the portable syringe and needle sterilizer that had been developed by the doctors in my previous practice near Hull. It was regularly in use on our kitchen range at home and was needed in the days before disposable plastic syringes and needles.

Mary suddenly let out an almighty shriek as she experienced another contraction, but the anaesthetic had gone in. The cut was soon made and the baby emerged, head first in a perfect position and after one more push Florence could announce, "You've got a bonny girl, Mary."

"I'll do the stitching up, Florence, but I'd be so grateful if you could take care of the other things," I asked. "To be honest I should get back home and get some sleep. I can never tell if I'll get another call."

"No bother, doctor. Just leave it to me. There aren't any other babies due for a bit now. Ah doubt ah'll be out again tonight."

A bit later, Florence came to look at my handiwork. Mary was totally unconcerned about the fuss being made at her nether regions as she stared and cooed at her beautiful new arrival. I sometimes envied Florence over the next few years whilst she was still the village midwife. Her job was nearly always to do with the wonderful arrival of a new baby and the miraculous beginning of another life. My job so often entailed the gradual and unpredictable decline at the end of life.

"Well, doctor, ah'll say this for you. You've done a right good job there." She was right; I was proud of my stitching and pleased that once again my nimble fingers had helped. "But ah will say this, doctor, yer wear some interesting clothes!" I glanced down and saw that the bottom of my trouser legs had ridden up above my pyjamas, which produced a pale blue frill around my ankles. Had the policeman seen them? What in the world would he make of them? Surely, he hadn't been able to see them in the swirling snowstorm?

I soon found out what Mary thought of them though. She was leaning over the edge of the bed. "Fetchin', doctor. Aye, them's fetchin'! Ah'll 'ave to get some for my Alf."

It wasn't long before I had scraped off the clinging snow from the car windows and escaped home to bed. It had been a satisfying night, attending a successful delivery was one of the highlights of my job, and although I would be tired in the morning, I was content. As my wonderful wife vacated my side of the bed to roll over to her own cold half, she left a warmth in which I was soon basking. It was her very special contribution to the difficulties of night-calls. Welcome sleep over-whelmed my thoughts.

My dreams were taking on strangeness. There was a strident sound reaching me. I tried to push it away. It seemed to become stronger, more urgent. I turned my head. It was there, more so. "ERIC, ERIC!" Margaret shouted in my ear and shook me violently. At last I woke to the incessant, raucous nagging of the telephone bell.

I reached out my hand once again for the receiver, but before I could utter my usual cheery greeting, expressed however tired and miserable I felt, I heard a worried, "Is that you, doctor? Ah think we need yer!" There was an emphasis on the word 'need' that woke me up fully.

"Yes, it's Dr Hainsworth here. Who am I speaking to?" I had to concentrate to string coherent words together.

"It's Fred Riley 'ere, doctor. We're Dr Holdroyd's patients really but me Doris has had one of those ass, ass ... thingy attacks aggen, doctor, an' she's bad. We don't know what ter do."

"Has she had the attack long, Mr Riley?" I was sitting up now, fully alert.

"Well, it started last evenin'. She gets short o' breath a lot so we jus' sit in our chairs, like, until she gets a bit better. But this time she's just got bad like, an' she's strugglin' to tek any sort o' breath. Can yer come, Doctor?" I knew how these attacks went. They usually came on at night but the deepening cold yesterday afternoon must have triggered it.

"Ah, yes, Mr Riley. I'll be right out to you. Dr Holdroyd has told me about you. Can you remind me where you live?"

My mind was working feverishly as instructions were relayed. It was asthma and I knew it could kill. There wasn't a good treatment and, indeed, many in the profession still regarded it as one of the main psychosomatic illnesses and the treatment was likewise. However, I had my severe doubts and felt it was a medical condition that could be treated with medicines, but the first metered dose inhalers weren't widely available back then in the late fifties. I would probably have to get Doris into hospital if it was as bad as Fred had said.

"Oh, I know," I said, acknowledging Mr Riley's explanation, "that's just up beyond the Institute isn't it?"

"Aye, doctor. That's the one. Yer'll be quick. Doris is that bad like." Fred seemed to be sobbing as he rang off.

Once again, my clothes were thrown on over my pyjamas, this time with an urgency. The sudden blast of wind and brittle snow as I opened the back door shocked me anew. Flakes clung to my spectacles and pin-pricked my face with miniscule needles of cold. I turned my back on it to close the door and wipe the flakes from the lenses of my glasses. The wind howled and eddies swirled as I went across the yard, head down.

The garage door would have to remain open now – time was everything. The drive had been scoured by the wind, but there was a mound of snow alongside the main road - the residue of the snowplough's passing earlier that night. In the wind the small trees in our front garden were swaying manically over the wall by the drive as I sped along it. I knew I needed to take that mound of snow fast to make sure I got over. Tyres suddenly spun, scrabbling for a grip. But I was in the road and I was on my way.

The Rileys lived in Mountain, the aptly named highest part of the village. There the wind was at its fiercest. I had to fight the car door as it was nearly ripped from my grasp. The house was a mean two-up-two-down cottage in a Victorian terrace and I staggered across the pavement to reach the front door, which opened out onto it. I banged my arrival and marched straight in. Fortunately, Mr Riley had unlocked it in preparation.

There was only one room downstairs besides the tiny kitchen, which invariably housed the stone sink and cold-water tap. And there, in that front room, the Rileys were waiting. My arm was wrenched in greeting and relief.

Fred Riley pulled me forward. He was a small, thin man and was wearing an old pin-stripe suit a number of sizes too large for him. His face was lined with anxiety as he said to the figure sitting rigid by the meager gas fire, "Look, Doris, it's t'young doctor. E's come. It'll be jus' right now." Relief was in his voice.

Doris didn't reply but I could hear her. Short, desperate rasping sounds were struggling through her wide-open mouth. I crouched down in front of her and she looked at me beseechingly, eyes wide with fear. Her lips were tinged with blue. Her knuckles, gripping the end of the armrests, were white with exertion. It was an effort even to nod her head.

"Don't worry, Doris. We'll get you sorted out. I'm going to phone for an ambulance and they'll be up here in twenty minutes or so." As I said this in as cheery a voice as I could muster, my mind couldn't help wondering if the ambulance would get through the snow. Doris slowly nodded again and the rasps increased, exacerbated by that small movement.

I stood up and faced Fred. I had to appear calm. I looked him in the eye and said, "Doris needs to be in hospital, Fred. Do you have a phone?" Mr Riley had telephoned the call in, but in those days many patients used those of a neighbour or even asked a relative or friend to walk to Craig-na-Hullie to convey a message, which they would do at any time of night.

"Aye, we 'ave, doctor. When Doris got bad our Mary bought us it. It's right grand."

"Yes, yes, Mr Riley but where is it?'

"Oh, it's just 'ere in t'corner." I couldn't see it as I looked round.

"Nay, lad. It's 'ere," said Fred as he whisked off a piece of cloth that was draped over their prized possession to protect it.

I had quickly got through to the ambulance service and explained the situation and was just about to replace the shiny, black handset when I added, "By the way, the snow is quite bad now. You might need to be prepared…"

"Snow, Doctor? Are you sure?" The disembodied voice sounded disbelieving.

"Yes, it's been snowing since the evening. Haven't you got any?"

"No, doctor. Not so much as a flake. It's raining cats and dogs, though, but no snow. I'll pass the message on though. Thank you. We'll be with you in just over quarter of an hour."

I relayed the message to the Rileys and Fred's body relaxed in relief. Even Doris looked less frightened. "I'll stay with you until the ambulance comes, just to be sure. Is that all right with you?" I asked. I always did this, even at this time of night when my body and brain were crying out for bed and rest.

"Oh, doctor, thank you. Thank you." My hand was grasped in Mr Riley's. His was thin and warped by arthritis but the strength of the grasp conveyed his gratitude. "Sit yersen down. Sit yersen. Ah'll just mek a pot o'tea."

"No thank you, Mr Riley. I'll just have a cup of hot water, if you don't mind." Fred looked at me for a brief moment clearly wanting to query this strange request then disappeared into the kitchen to start the clattering process of boiling water in the tight space of the kitchen.

I sat down on a sagging armchair by Doris and held her hand. Her breathing had relaxed a little, no doubt now that she knew that help was on its way, and that she would be cared for.

Eventually Fred came through with my steaming cup. It was probably their best teacup and only slightly chipped. However, I was deeply grateful. As he handed it over to me, Mr Riley slipped something into the saucer.

"Is that enough?" he asked in a worried whisper. "We don't 'ave much but we want to do right by yer, doctor." I looked down and there, where a biscuit might nestle, was a screwed up and folded grubby ten-shilling note.

"Oh, Fred, what's this for?"

"Well, it's fer yer visit…an' t'amb'lance." Fred's voice conveyed the hope that this would cover all costs.

"Fred, you can put it away. All this costs nothing now. It's our National Health service…"

"What, even at night? Nah, that's a rum job." Fred's face was transformed.

"Yes, yes. Everything's free. Honestly." I placed the well-worn note back into the shaking hand of Mr Riley.

Even ten years after the start of the National Health Service I still found people who couldn't believe that they didn't have to pay a penny when they had called me. It made a refreshing antidote to the others who seemed to be taking advantage of this free access to everything to do with health and were taking it for granted. A couple of weeks before, I was made aware of one of my patients who seemed to be getting through a large amount of cotton wool. When I asked her what the matter was, I was told that she needed the cotton wool to stuff a cushion.

"But, Mrs Staines, cotton wool is supplied on the NHS for medical use …"

"But ah pay me taxes like everyone else, yer know," was the emphatic reply.

The ambulance soon safely arrived and pulled up behind my car. The peek-capped ambulance men soon wrapped up Doris against the cold and got on their way to Bradford Royal Infirmary. Doris would be all right.

I glanced inside the ambulance. Fred Riley was holding Doris' hands gently and gazing into her eyes. Suddenly, they both must have sensed my stare and turned to me. Tears of gratitude were whelming up in their tired, old eyes and they both smiled. As he closed the rear door of the ambulance, the larger of the two attendants grumbled to me. "Ah'll be glad ter be out o'this, doctor. Yer've got it bad. There's no snow down in Bradford, yer know!"

It had stopped snowing and my bed was luring me for the few short hours of rest before a new day started again. I started gratefully for home. I gripped the smooth hardness of the steering wheel as the car slid sideways a little, its tyres losing traction as they ploughed through a drift that had crept in the wind over the wall. The wheels spun and then held. "It'll be good to be out of this," I muttered to myself. And then I glanced sideways to my left.

Whether it was the momentary glimpse of a foreign landscape that had flickered into the corner of my eye, or was just from a blind impulse, I stopped the car and got out, entranced. The door clicked shut. The sensory blanket that immediately surrounded me was a rich mixture of intense, but strangely refreshing cold and an enveloping silence, all washed by the bright moonlight.

My stout winter shoes made the only sounds: a sharp whispered crunch, as the fresh snow compacted under my footsteps. I was drawn towards the tumbled dry-stone wall that obstructed the view beyond from the road. The scene suddenly opened out in front of me. The hued clouds that had oppressed the sky most of the previous afternoon and evening were gone. They had finally relieved themselves of their burdensome snow through the night. Later, the clouds had been dispersed as they were gradually tattered and scattered by the wind. Now this also was gone, leaving a wonderful sense of peace.

The field, now remolded into soft contours and strange mounds, fell away down the valley. The moonlight dazzled in the whiteness, which was etched by the black lines of walls as they wandered down to the railway into the valley floor. Way beyond, as the hills rose again, the orange-yellow strings of Thornton's streetlights twinkled and winked, pointing towards the greater orange glow from Bradford blushing over the far horizon.

The strange and unearthly beauty of the scene before me, made more intimate by the silence, was almost overwhelming. I looked around trying to absorb this before I had to turn away and leave for my bed. However, I was reluctant to break the deep contentment I was experiencing and my mind began to reflect on the past few hours. I was overcome by the memories of those Riley smiles.

The cold, now infiltrating every part of my being, snapped me out of my reverie. I looked again at the amazing frozen landscape before me. There was a soft sound and a fleeting shape passed overhead. I ducked down automatically before I recognised an owl's call. Suddenly, I had an overwhelming realisation that this place was where I was meant to be, the final rooting after all the struggles and wanderings of the last few years.

On impulse, to make concrete my intense feelings, I spread my hands out as if to embrace this place of which I was now a part. I declared in an earnest voice, made loud by the silence around me, which shocked me, "This is where I'm meant to be. I'm here…"

"Well, I wouldn't stay too long, doctor." A voice, gruff with certainty, stripped away the privacy of my reflections. "It's a mite cold."

I turned round, stung and embarrassed that someone had observed my unusual behaviour. Moonlight glinted off silver buttons and epaulette number. I knew who it was: the policeman who had pulled up in his black Ford Anglia police car as I had attended my first emergency call earlier that night. As he stepped forward, I could see his face again with the unmistakable walrus moustache that he stroked lovingly with a deliberate downwards movement of his hand. He ploughed through the snow towards me.

"Oh, hello, officer. Erm, you again," I stammered. "I'm afraid you've caught me good and proper now. I was just, erm, admiring the view." I jerked my head to indicate the scene that had so bewitched me, in case the policeman had any doubt about it.

He stopped by me and leaned against the wall gazing over the valley and said, "Aye, it's a good 'un, but you've chosen an odd time to be gawkin' at it." White breath clouds accompanied his words.

"Well, I was just on my way home…" my voice faltered as I realised how stupid the whole thing must appear to an officer of the law.

"Oh, has she produced then? Ah was wondering how things were going. I'm sorry I couldn't be any help."

"Yes, a girl … and mother and baby are doing well. That was my first visit. It was a quick job. Miss Micklethwaite was there, the midwife…"

"Oh, I know Florence," The policeman interjected, grinning at me. "We all know Florence. She delivered my sister's boy. I think she has delivered most of the kids in the village." He paused. "Oh, she must have been here fifteen odd years now. She lives in the village an' all." I nodded.

The policeman and I leant on the wall and gazed over the peaceful scene before us. We retreated into our own thoughts as we allowed the silence to embrace us.

I smiled as I reflected on the bizarreness of the situation: I was frozen solid but still persisted in leaning over the wall, admiring the landscape, and chatting away about the nocturnal adventures to a policeman as if it was the middle of a summer's day. I said, "and do you know, officer…"

"Oh, doctor," he interjected with clouds of freezing breath. "Call me Alfred, Alfred Clarence. You must."

"Well, Alfred. For some strange reason all this," I paused and swept the view with my open hand, "this, has made me feel really at home. This is where I'm meant to be."

Alfred looked at me and said firmly, "I know. I know what yer mean. It's a strange place this. A bit cut off like. An' we're not posh. We call a spade a spade and life is tough. Yer can tell by the landscape." He paused and looked around. "It's hard, like we are. But the people are grand. We all pull together an' make it work. Yer won't be one of us for another twenty odd years but I'd like to welcome you, doctor. Oh, an' I'll tell yer somat fer nowt. Yer need to put somat heavy in yer boot ter mek the back wheels grip if yer going to go round in the snow."

"Thank you, officer…er, Alfred. I will, first thing."

I smiled. I had just realised something else. When I had arrived at the Rileys I was greeted as the 'young doctor', an appellation I had attracted when I was taken on to help Dr Blunt out nearly three years ago and it had stuck. However, during my visit it had changed. When I left Fred Riley shook me by the hand and said with gratitude and relief, 'Thank yer, doctor. Thank yer."

Chapter 2

It actually seemed amazing that I should be back here in Queensbury, after such a circuitous early career that could have ended anywhere. It was through this village that I travelled as a student in the war years to Bradford Technical College to take my Higher School Certificate in the sciences that I needed for medicine. My own school did not cater for these so I had to endure this journey from my home in Halifax in the clapped-out bus, which wheezed its way up the hill to Queensbury.

Despite being a rather shy schoolboy, I eventually got to know one or two of the regular participants in this laboured journey. One rather dumpy lady, whose age I could not even guess despite much effort, shared with the bus its wheeziness and cough. She took me in hand and sat next to me on every trip from Halifax before alighting at a bus stop just past the gaunt church in Queensbury. Its Victorian stone walls were blackened by the smoke that had pervaded the air for years. Eventually, after a few weeks of acknowledging each other's presence in the world with nods, we added a salutatory grunt. After months, this greeting had taken on the form of words and it was through them that my companion discovered my name.

" 'Ainsworth, did tha' say?" She grabbed my arm in some sort of mysterious rapture.

I was taken aback, in my shyness, at this forthright development of our relationship, but managed to reply, "Er, yes. Eric Hainsworth. Why?"

"Well, yer mus' be famous up 'ere!" she carried on enthusiastically.

"Oh, I don't think so. I've never stopped in Queensbury. I go on all the way to Bradford."

"Well, the've called a moor after yer family. It's just before t'church on t'right. That bit's 'Ainsworth Moor. Jus' fancy that!" my fellow traveller had become transformed; her eyes lit up as she looked at me.

"I don't think it was us. It must have been another Hainsworth," I managed to mumble in my adolescent shyness.

"Oh…oh,' she replied, obviously disappointed. Thereafter my attraction to her was somewhat diminished, but she still would sit next to me and watch the passing countryside and various buildings as we ground past. She lost some of her volubility but still managed to relate stories of various points of interest in our journey. I accepted these tales with a pinch of salt having discovered her gullibility over Hainsworth Moor. However, from her I became aware of Percy Shaw's factory.

One day, when our relationship had progressed beyond the disappointment of Hainsworth Moor not being named after my family, the bus had started its grinding climb out of Halifax. Suddenly, the lady dug me in the ribs with her elbow. This was her usual indication that she was about to say something of great interest and from which I couldn't escape, being trapped by the window.

"There it is!" she exclaimed as she jabbed her gloved finger at the window. I looked to see a low factory beyond a wall. A tree seemed to be growing out through the middle of the roof. "That's Percy Shaw's factory! 'E's famous, 'e is!"

Percy Shaw was indeed a bit of a local celebrity, of true fame. He had developed the reflecting road stud, known as 'cats'eyes'. My father had told me the story behind this feat. He had been born into a farming family in 1890. When he was two years old the family moved into a slightly larger house on the outskirts of Halifax, by the Queensbury road. Percy left school at thirteen and tried different occupations before hitting on the idea that was to transform his life and roads the world over.

I was fascinated by the fleeting sight of his factory that seemed to have been built in the garden of the blackened stone building that was still his home. More wondrous was the top of the tree that was poking out through the roof of the factory. It was intriguing and I broke my self-imposed rule not to ask the lady any questions that might elicit a long lecture of a reply.

"Why is there a tree sticking out of the middle of the factory?" I asked.

Even the inventiveness of my female storyteller would not stretch to explaining this. "Ah don't rightly know," she replied with words that she probably hadn't used before.

After she had alighted, I was more able to observe the passing scenery and wonder about the day ahead. Sometimes I read or revised. I became vaguely aware of a stone house, just before a bus stop, on the side of the road just before the summit of the last rise out of the village. Once over this, the journey was downhill all the way to our ultimate destination, and the bus, including its grateful passengers, could experience gears other than first or second. I would have taken much more notice had I known then that this house would be my home for most of my career and would be where my own family would grow up.

I have no idea why I was so determined to become a doctor. It certainly wasn't in my blood. My own father had clawed his way up from the grinding millwork of his own forebears to owning his own factory, but business didn't attract me. Visitors to our Halifax terraced house would often ask me what I would like to be when I grew up, a question often used by adults when trying to get children to talk. My response from a very early age was that I would be a doctor. This produced suitable admiration and occasional advice. I remember one of my father's friends looking at me sagely, when he had heard my ambition, and saying, "Eric, your father is in business. In business you can make a lot of money, but you can also lose a lot. You are going into the professions. You won't be very rich but you won't be poor either." I recollected this wisdom years later when I was a GP and my father lost everything.

As a boy I was becoming more aware of how doctors got paid. As in any family, my brother and I had our illnesses and accidents. The doctor was visited or called and money was handed over in payment. My mother would make sure that she had the necessary two and six (twelve and a half pence) in her purse before setting off for a consultation at the surgery. If the doctor had been called for a home visit, the three shillings and sixpence (seventeen and a half pence) would be carefully placed in a pile on the hall table. This also covered the cost of a bottle of medicine. We were well off then and such amounts were not hard to find.

Outside our comfortable door others struggled, however. Lloyd George, as Chancellor of the Exchequer, proposed the National Insurance Act in 1911. It only applied to wage earners who had to pay a small amount out of their wage packets into the scheme to gain some medical benefits, including 'sick pay' when off work due to illness. However, many still had to pay for treatment and it was the National Health Service that introduced the idea of being free at the point of need for all. This relieved the stress and anxiety, caused by the bill that would inevitably follow, that had accompanied any consultation with a doctor.

However, how doctors were paid, or rather how they received pension benefits, in this new service was to have a deep effect on my early career. The State established a very good Superannuation Scheme for doctors. To obtain full benefits, though, a doctor had to have paid into the scheme for ten years or more. The National Health Service was formed in 1948, whilst I was training, so older doctors couldn't really retire until 1958 in order to obtain a full pension. Up to this date they just had to keep working and so, consequently, partnerships were very scarce. Practices took advantage of this and took on young doctors as Assistants at a much lower level of pay. However, these were the least of my concerns when I started the second half of my training at St Thomas' Hospital in London. The first half was at Cambridge but it was at 'Tommy's' that theory became reality.

Medical students were extremely aware of the nurses who worked with them in the care and healing of their patients. Nurses not only sometimes helped out with their greater experience and saved many bumbling students from potentially embarrassing situations resulting from lack of proficiency, but also provided lively female company outside the hospital walls. They were the only female company we managed to meet. A shared 'calling' and experience of the rigours of medicine deepened any social contact. This joint encounter with intense and serious circumstances produced an earthy humour and a bubbling vivacity, when we were 'off duty'.

In my bespectacled studiousness, I hadn't indulged in this lighter side of student life too much but was very conscious of pretty well all the young nurses and midwives at St Thomas' Hospital. They were great fun, but none had particularly grabbed my attention until my training involved me taking a course on Obstetrics and I found myself involved in a childbirth alongside a young, but obviously experienced midwife.

We exchanged pleasantries and I hastened to join in the activity and add my new-found expertise. However, I soon realised that the midwife was more than capable, so I stepped aside and watched her as she worked. The baby was well presented and labour seemed to progress without any problems.

Most popular images of midwives are of comely faces under curls or a tight bun on a sturdy frame. However, I was strangely moved by the slightness of this midwife's body that not even the uniform and 'sensible' shoes could disguise. Her sparkling eyes contained a soft yet assured determination as they commanded the room from a beautiful face. How was it that I hadn't noticed her before? My eyes that should have been concentrating on the mother-to-be in the bed were fixed on this young lady attending, and only looked away in self-consciousness when she returned my gaze. No doubt she was becoming aware that this slightly gawky student was of no help whatsoever and seemed to be looking at her rather more than at the patient.

I decided that I would try and strike up some sort of conversation between contractions. I was rather inexperienced in this and couldn't exactly ask, "Do you come here often?" Eventually, I managed to stammer rather nervously, "Erm, you seem to be very good at this."

The reply came from our patient, "AGHHHH!" as another contraction came. I also felt this, as I had decided my contribution to the proceedings would be to hold the mother's hand. I could tell the intensity of the contraction by the pain in my hand. "AGHHH!" I echoed. I started breathing deeply. Maybe a bit of gas and air would help me? I decided not to ask the midwife.

The pain from my hand subsided and the midwife, a Miss Geissler, said, "You've got a Yorkshire accent, Mr Hainsworth?" That was it. The floodgates of conversation seemed to have opened only to be rapidly closed with the arrival of another contraction. I extracted my hand quickly.

It was only in the final stage of labour that I was able to start a fumbling conversation. My elation at being in the presence of such a wonderful being was tempered by our patient. As Miss Geissler, Margaret, handed over the carefully examined and wrapped new son to her, the mother mused, "Oh, I'd like ter name 'im after yer, doctor. It's been such a good labour, me best yet."

I beamed. That was the icing on the cake. I had met the most enchanting girl and she hadn't taken an instant dislike to me, but I was to give my name to a baby. "It's Eric," I said.

There was a deflated silence. "Eric, yer say?" the mother asked in a similarly deflated voice.

"Yes, Eric. Is anything wrong?' my voice was also tainted.

"Well… Eric. Imagine someone calling a li'le sprog tha'!"

I almost jumped in with a defensive, "Well, my own mother for a start," but I decided to play the 'glorious history' card. "It's a Viking name you know. Eric the Red was a Viking king of York…"

"I'm not 'aving no Viking in are 'ouse! Anyway, my milkman's called Eric, an' what would people think?"

Fortunately, Margaret loved my name, or at least professed so, and our relationship started and grew despite the ribald comments from both of our groups of colleagues once they knew where we had met. Our rapport was helped along by Ivor Novello in the back rows of cinemas, when we could afford it.

Our relationship grew and deepened despite the caprices of our respective duties and my studies. I was still two years away from my finals and yet I knew without a doubt that I wanted to spend the rest of my life with Margaret. I thought I had been in love at various times in the past, but my feelings for her surprised me in their intensity. I had many things medical to squash into my overflowing memory, but it seemed that every time I sat down before my books and notes, my erstwhile disciplined and motivated brain soon drifted to thoughts of love – things

I would definitely not be examined on. I caught myself with a glowing smile on my face having wasted yet another half hour of revision time.

Our future plans seemed so much more attractive now than the intricacies of gynaecology. Through our enthusiastic conversations, which were always in spate when we were alone together, we started to get to know each other. She, in turn, wanted to find out about me – surprisingly, as I thought I was totally uninteresting.

"I grew up in Halifax but all my family have lived around Bradford for generations…"

"Since Viking days!" Margaret smiled. "You can tell by my name, Geissler, that some of my family were from Germany, so you could say we are both immigrants! My parents are elderly and I'm their only child."

"Didn't they want any more children? I asked.

"I don't know. I haven't asked. Mummy's a bit of a dry stick really. She's really old and I have no idea how in the world I was eventually conceived. I sometimes think she doesn't quite know either. Mummy was over forty when she had me and she probably found the whole business too messy. Daddy was wonderful and we had a lovely relationship when I was growing up."

"They must have found it hard to let you go to London in the war to train as a nurse," I mused.

"Yes, Mummy relied on me a lot and Daddy was losing the one thing that made life a bit more fun. I was desperate to get away though. I was just nineteen. We didn't know that the doodlebugs - you know, the flying bombs…" I nodded. I knew. Margaret seemed to have experienced the world in a much deeper way than I had done.

"It was wonderful, Eric. The group of students I joined - my 'set' - were wonderful. We're still good friends. Initially, we were trained in a place outside London, near Godalming. Part of the St Thomas' had moved there in the Blitz." Margaret went on to tell me about the training and the life of the students when they had returned to London. They were quartered in an annex to the St Thomas' Hospital nurses' home. Apparently, even the trip to the bathroom involved a dash in night-gear along a London street, with much hilarity, and this seemed to epitomize the young nurses' attitude to the situation.

I tried steering the conversation back to her parents. With an ulterior motive in mind, I particularly wanted to find out about her father. I needed to get some idea of the man to whom I hoped to be asking the most important question of my life.

"Well, poor Daddy. He was such a patient man; and I loved him deeply."

I was sensitive to the tense Margaret had used. "Was?" I said. I didn't know how to continue.

"Yes, Daddy died last year. On November 11th. It was two days before my own birthday as well." Margaret's eyes watered.

I mumbled, "Oh, Margaret. I'm sorry. I really am. I shouldn't have mentioned it."

"No, it's all right really. I like talking about him. In his own way, he was a great man, a true gentleman. And he was my friend as well. He seemed to know how difficult it was for me, growing up an only child with an elderly mother." She paused. "Well, she seemed old!"

"What was he called?'

"George. George Robert..." Margaret glanced at me.

"Can I ask what he died from?" My medical training barged into the conversation with its curiosity.

Margaret paused before answering, "It was his heart. He'd had rheumatic fever, oh, ages ago. However, it was only when he joined up in the first war with a group of friends from the village that they found in the medical that it had damaged his heart. They wouldn't let him fight at the front. When he had his last illness, I had to nurse him at home; mummy couldn't cope. It was the most difficult thing I've had to do. Watching Daddy die. And helping Mummy. She seemed so lost and helpless. Daddy was her life and strength. And mine"

My hands cradled hers as she related this. Behind the brave words I sensed the sorrow. This was probably the reason for the strength in her character, which I had detected underpinning her bubbling sense of humour and fun. The difficulties she had encountered in her early life had given her abilities to cope with whatever life might throw at her.

In the end, I proposed on the train up to my parents in Workington in Cumberland. My father had moved his textile factory up there after the Second World War in response to the government's appeal for industry to move into 'depressed areas'. Margaret had still to meet them. My secret prayers were answered as we entered an empty compartment and no others joined us. However, my romantic dropping onto one knee was rendered humorous by the sudden lurching of the train and Margaret's subsequent exclamation, "Eric, what in the world are you doing down there?" By the time we alighted to be greeted by my father with his embracing jocularity, we were pledged for life, even though I hadn't managed to buy a ring for her as yet. From now on, whatever happened in our lifetimes, we would face them together. I knew that my life would be transformed by the love and strength of my young fiancée.

Three months later, in the May, I had saved up enough to take Margaret out for a meal. It was a place in Soho that I had heard about from one of my medical student friends, Angus. He was as much an extrovert as I was introvert, but we seemed to have found an open friendship almost instantaneously. We provided a balance for each other. We were opposites in a number of other ways. He was tall and slim and his face, which had a classical ruggedness, was topped by a blaze of carefully styled blond hair. He wore his fringe long and had assumed a languid habit of combing it back from his face with his fingers. Girls loved him. He carried his good looks with the same ease with which he approached everything in life, especially his relationships with everyone he met. I wondered if this was the product of an upbringing of quiet wealth.

Angus could have overshadowed me with my gawky ways, slightly thinning hair and owl-like spectacles without which I was lost in a blurred world; but I never felt belittled in any way. Margaret, the most wonderful woman in the universe, had, after all, chosen me! This was something that never ceased to amaze me and I was looking forward with relish to this meal together.

Angus had told me about this place, James's. Apparently, his family always dined there when they were in town. I was more used to Lyon's Corner Houses so the expense of James's had delayed our celebration whilst I saved up. On the afternoon beforehand, Angus offered to help me achieve an appropriate 'look' for this momentous occasion. I felt a tinge of unease at this. Did I need a 'look'? However, Angus' enthusiasm swept away my nervousness. After all, I did have a rather smart dinner jacket that I had had tailored from some of my father's best cloth and some patent leather shoes, which I had worn precisely once, four years previously. I was sure I wouldn't stand out too much.

Unfortunately, during those four years I seemed to have changed my body shape – outwards. This has always been a bit of a battle for me but this was the first occasion when I was made aware of the problem. My top fly-buttons and the main ones on the waistband just wouldn't reach the required holes, despite hilarious efforts. Eventually Angus rigged up elastic loops that did the job but looked awful. My heart sank. "Never mind, Eric. I've got a rather dashing cummerbund that will cover that mess up. Just the job," Angus reassured me.

Finally, with the bright red cummerbund in place, Angus approved my appearance and said I looked 'dashing'. "You'll sweep her away, Eric!" he enthused. However, I had never worn a cummerbund before and I felt very self-conscious. I also felt rather like a trussed chicken … and I had to pull my stomach in to prevent too much strain on material wrapping my stomach. However, I was deemed ready to escort Margaret into James's.

Angus, extending his largesse, had offered to take me to James's in his rather smart Riley coupe, a lovely car when any vehicle was a rarity amongst students. I think he knew that I would be stretched to pay for a taxi in both directions. We would pick up Margaret on the way.

Unfortunately, getting into the Riley's passenger seat highlighted the tightness around my abdomen. I could hardly breathe. I was entering new levels of discomfort as we drew up outside Margaret's digs. I think Angus knew that I was suffering. He had been humming cheerfully as we had driven along in the late evening traffic. He stopped and said in a reassuring voice, "Never mind, Eric, the food will make up for it. It's truly delectable. Margaret will love it at James's! You'll see!"

Margaret was stunning. I wish I could say that she took my breath away, but that had already disappeared, squeezed out of my body by my clothes. She wore a dark crimson evening dress and had a simple gold chain necklace, which was all that she needed. She had managed to borrow a very short fur jacket. I was glad that I hadn't donned my battered, but comfortable, tweed jacket after all. Margaret looked rather pale though and her smile was a little forced. She was obviously nervous. I knew that I was and my heart started sinking at the thought that the evening would descend into an embarrassed silence. Why didn't we just go to the Cornerhouse? We felt comfortable there.

The entrance to James's was very understated. Gold lettering on the faded black paintwork announced the name of the place and 1827, the date it had been established. Angus shot round from the driver's side of the car and opened our door. He rather fancied himself as the gallant companion. He opened the restaurant door with a "Have fun you two love birds! This will be memorable, just see!"

A butler sort of chap met us inside. He looked positively ancient in his black tail-coat. His wrinkled face looked to have been washed, and then washed again. Not a hair was out of place. I nearly asked him if he had been there when the place opened. I thought better of it.

The man took our coats with deliberate slowness. "This way, sir," he announced in a mellifluous voice and preceded us over the undulating floor. His shoes squeaked as he walked. Normally this would have sent Margaret into giggles. The whole thing was becoming slightly ridiculous. However, she remained silent. I glanced at her reassuringly and smiled. She returned the smile but it seemed forced. I became worried.

As we took the menus in their leather bindings delivered like rare antiquarian books by a doleful waiter, Margaret said quietly, "Eric, I'm really sorry. I don't feel very hungry today."

"Are you alright?" I enquired; my doctor's hat that I had thought was left well behind in my digs had suddenly appeared.

"To be honest I don't think I am. I've been feeling a little off-colour for some time, but I have tried to just get on as normal. My energy has gone and I have a loose tummy. It's been like it for a few days now." Margaret looked at me with a tinge of concern in her eyes. She toyed nervously with a strand of her hair that had escaped the beautiful brunette waves. These adorned her head and framed that now familiar, wonderfully open face. This was now clouded with concern.

I was aware of a slight cold grip on my heart. It could be all or nothing with that description, but it had lasted a few days. "Have you got any other symptoms?"

"Not really, I don't think, Eric. But I'll let you know if anything changes. I think I'll just have a piece of toast tonight, just to be on the safe side. I don't want to spoil it for you," she said in a forlorn voice.

"Oh, Margaret, are you sure?" I asked.

She smiled, "That's rich, coming from a Yorkshireman! I would have thought that you would have been pleased at the cheapness of my choice. Come on, let's enjoy the evening at least. It's so nice being together."

"Yes, it is. It's lovely." I looked round at the surroundings that spoke of a faded luxury. The walls were panelled and painted in a Georgian green. In fact, as I looked closer it seemed as though they had been painted just once in their lives. Dark wood tables, endowed with crisp white cotton tablecloths and starched napkins, were placed at discrete distances apart. Only a few other tables were occupied at this early hour, but the slightly hunched diners provided a low murmur.

"But you will let me know if you notice anything else or you don't get better, won't you?"

"Yes, Eric. Of course, I will. Now stop being a doctor for once and order some food."

I opened the tome in front of me and glanced down the offerings. Starters that would normally have enticed me by their very names now seemed just expensive. Maybe this was because they were entitled 'Entrees'. I noticed that a few were accompanied by toast – Melba Toast. That was it! I wouldn't cause embarrassment by eating a large meal in front of my poorly fiancée. And it would be cheaper that way.

I glanced, beckoning, at the hovering waiter who came over, order pad ready. His slightly red face with a glowing nose was the only colour on his person. Dressed in a black formal dinner jacket with matching black hair greased down in combed furrows over his head, he stood with a spotless white napkin draped over one crooked arm waiting for this new order from the delectable food on offer.

"Erm, I see that you do toast. Just here," I pointed to one or two starters.

"That is so, sir. Melba Toast. Freshly prepared just before the dish is served." The waiter licked his dry white lips as a further advertisement.

"Would you be able to serve toast without the rest of the starter… erm, entrée?"

The waiter looked a little askance. "That is a bit irregular, sir, but I cannot see why not. Would you like some Melba Toast to accompany another dish?" He bent down at his waist and his silver pencil hovered over the pad.

"Well, in that case we'll have two helpings of toast, please."

The pencil still hovered but then was retracted. "And what entrée would you like to supplement your toast, sir?"

"Nothing. That would be just perfect." I beamed at the poor man.

"And for your main course, sir?" the waiter had resumed his normal line of inquiry.

"Oh, that's all thank you. Just two helpings of toast. That is all we want." I looked at the man. A strange look had come over his face. I asked in my medically concerned voice, "Are you feeling well? I'm a doctor, you know. Well, almost."

"Just a little discomfort, sir." And then his face brightened. "What wine would you like to go with your toast? We have an extensive list and I could recommend some lovely whites to go with your … erm…toast."

I looked across at Margaret who for some reason seemed to be taking great delight in this whole ordering process and its effects on the seemingly imperturbable features of our waiter. "Oh, I think I'd better stay with water, Eric."

The waiter somehow wilted and shrank inside his penguin suit as I turned to him and said, "We'll have two glasses of water, please."

It became a lovely evening. The toast was delivered, over-seriously, by two waiters and the water poured with due care. I was tempted to add to his woes by saying that I thought it was corked. He left us alone, no doubt pondering about our sanity, as we celebrated and wondered what our lives together would bring.

A week later Margaret was diagnosed with Crohn's disease. This is a debilitating illness of the bowel that my young, vivacious wife would have to face. But she would not have to face it alone. I was with her and we would confront this together.

Margaret was referred to a Mr Wilson. I had heard a bit about him. He was a colorectal specialist with a weighty reputation, despite his relatively young age. He had just come back from the States and I had no doubt that he would know the most advanced and up to date treatment for Crohn's disease. I was to meet him the first time with Margaret. We entered his consulting room and, as we did so, he stood to greet us. He was tall and slim and his hunched shoulders made him look like an elongated question mark. His eyes shone with a warm confidence though.

"Sit down, sit down you two. I'm glad you could come along Mr Hainsworth. I heard that you were engaged and that you had a hand in Miss Geissler's diagnosis."

"Yes, a little," I replied. "Margaret first told me her early symptoms when we went to celebrate our engagement."

"Ha, that sounds like a good medical way to start your lives together. I had heard on the grapevine that you are a dab hand at diagnosis, Mr Hainsworth. So, you've got your finals next year?"

"Yes, and if all goes well…"

"Oh, should do, should do by all accounts."

I carried on, wondering how in the world he knew so much about our situation and realising that the hospital, large though it was, was actually a small world and the staff looked out for each other. Margaret would be well cared for. "If I don't need to retake anything, we'd like to get married in September..."

Margaret interjected, "What sort of treatment is available?" She had sat in silence until now, but longed to know the therapy and prognosis. "I've heard some awful things about Crohn's." The look on her face was calmly determined but I could tell from her voice that she was concerned.

Mr Wilson responded with a grim voice, "Yes, it is a serious disease that lasts for life and can end in premature death. The immune system, for some reason, attacks the bowel wall and inflammation occurs. Crohn's was only described as a separate illness in the 1930s so there is no medication that can really address it at the moment. Fortunately, you, Mr Hainsworth, picked up on the early symptoms but it seems that your bowel is much more inflamed now. I'm truly sorry, Margaret."

Margaret quickly interrupted, "But does that mean I'll just have to live with it, there's nothing anyone can do?"

"No, no," Mr Wilson quickly replied. "I have just returned from the States where I helped in a pioneering surgical procedure a number of times. It looks very hopeful. It means entering the abdominal cavity and bypassing the inflamed bowel section. The secret seems to be to bipass just the right amount before joining up the bowel again otherwise the bowel gets attacked again at the join." Mr Wilson's enthusiasm was encouraging.

I asked, "What is the prognosis after such an operation?"

"Well, it seems good but it is very early days yet and obviously we haven't been able to observe patients who have been treated in this way for any length of time, but the Crohn's hasn't returned, at least in its former intensity, for one or two patients. We have learned a great deal from those that haven't responded well." Mr Wilson looked at Margaret. "It seems that your colon is quite inflamed now in one section, although we shall have to see the actual damage when we open you up. To give us the best chance we need to get the inflammation down and that means bed rest for three weeks, total removal of stress, absolute bed rest…"

Margaret was aghast, "You mean not getting out of bed for anything? And I'm on duty tomorrow!" Her resolve had been shaken.

"I'm afraid that you will have to put your career on hold certainly for the moment, and maybe for quite some time, Margaret. And, yes, you will be totally bed-bound,

I'm afraid. We can't put the bowel under any stress whatsoever and we will give you a careful diet to get the inflammation down as much as possible. After three weeks I will operate and then you'll be in bed for another two weeks. And then you'll have to take it gently for quite some time to make sure you recover as well as possible." Mr Wilson was apologetic as he spoke these words. He knew that it meant Margaret would be giving up her midwifery and that we would have to continue our courtship in a hospital ward. But then he added with a smile, "However, if all goes well, you should still be able to get married in September."

Margaret and I looked at each other. I couldn't speak. We were experiencing what it was like on the receiving end of medical care with a potentially life-changing illness to deal with. Eventually Margaret said, "Well, Eric, this all sounds remarkable really. There can't be many people with Crohn's who have this opportunity and you'll be able to see me anytime you like with your doctor's coat on…And you'll have more time to revise!" Then she looked fiercely at Mr Wilson, "But I will be getting out of bed to go to the toilet. And that is that!"

So began one of the strangest chapters of our lives. It was a mixture of hospital work, frantic revision and visiting a frustrated fiancée to hold hands and talk about life after the operation, all squashed into long, tiring days and relieved by short nights and snatched catnaps. I was determined to do well for Margaret.

One Sunday morning I turned up unexpectedly in Margaret's ward. She was out of bed and playing the piano for morning service on the ward. Apparently, Sister Burnett had decided that the musical requirements were of more importance than Margaret's stress levels. Actually, when I looked at my fiancée's face, I thought the whole thing was very beneficial to her - as long as Mr Wilson never found out.

He didn't and the operation was a remarkable success. Margaret's long period of convalescence coincided with my last days of revision and then finals, so there were days when we didn't see each other at all. However, all was rewarded when in June I joined an excited throng of fellow medical students by the Examinations noticeboard in the medical school.

I rushed round to the nurses' home bursting with my exciting news. Margaret jumped up from her chair and flung her arms round my neck. I looked down into her beaming face through my awry spectacles. Did she know?

"I've got some great news darling. Mr Wilson's signed me off. I'm fit again…" she beamed.

I gave her her an almighty hug. "Darling, I'm so pleased. And do you know what? I've passed. You'll have to call me Doctor now!"

"Oh, Eric! That means…"

"Yes, I know. We can get married in September.

Chapter 3

"Eric, it's just too much. This place is getting on top of me a bit now. It feels so cramped and we'll soon have a new baby..." Margaret's voice, forlorn, tailed off into unspoken thoughts. I had just popped up to our tiny flat above the surgery to say a quick 'hello' as I was passing on my round of home visits. I knew Margaret would be home as it was afternoon naptime for our two-year-old son, Charles.

I entered the stark brick building that had all the design features of a shoebox, by our doorway at the bottom of the staircase up to our abode. The surgery, waiting room and dispensary, which were under our flat, were accessed by another door. At the foot of the stairs, opposite the door, was the patients' toilet that had been commandeered by Margaret as soon as she found out the size of our accommodation – the kitchen had been made out of a walk-in cupboard. "Honestly, Eric. The patients have more room here than we do and you're the doctor. The refrigerator's going in there!" There was no arguing.

I had taken the stairs two at a time to find Margaret huddled in a chair. Her slim figure was starting to show signs of her pregnancy but it was her general demeanour, communicating 'fed up', that held my attention. This was most unusual for her. Since getting married I had been amazed at how Margaret coped with the difficulties and discomforts of life. She faced everything without complaint and always found something to laugh about.

Margaret looked at me through tired eyes. "Do you know what happened today? Charles sat down in our kitchen and found he had just got tall enough to put his back against the wall and his feet could touch the cupboard doors under the sink. He's never done it before but he's not that big – he's only two for goodness sake!" I decided not to make light of the situation and say that he was tall for his age. I looked sympathetic. "It's getting a bit much, Eric. I'm sorry. It's just after all this moving round the country and then to end up here. It's probably because of the baby coming…"

"Darling, I'm sorry. I thought you liked it here." I muttered, embarrassed that I hadn't noticed before that my wife was feeling like this.

"Oh, I do. In many ways. It's lovely to be able to go out for walks especially now the weather's getting warmer. I take Charles down the road to see the trains, which he loves. And then there's the Fox's farm across the road. He loves going to see the billy goat being fed. The wives of all three partners pop in now and again and we are becoming really good friends now. It's just…" I could tell: with a new baby on the way the flat was starting to feel small to me and it must be far harder for Margaret as she contemplated trying to get all the baby things squashed into the space, with its single cabinet to store anything in. All this whilst trying to cope with a toddler, however perfect he might be!

I sat back and contemplated possible options. "I think I'll go and see Philip and see if there's any chance of a partnership." Philip was the senior partner of the practice and I knew I could talk things through with him even though I knew the financial situation in his practice here.

Margaret's eyes brightened, "That would be wonderful! Do you think they would make you one? Their wives all say good things about you and the patients love you."

I didn't want to encourage my wife's hopes too much; I knew the realities of the situation. None of my Thomas' friends that I was still in contact with had managed to become a partner in a practice yet; some hadn't even gained my heights of being an assistant general practitioner. They were resigned to waiting until those due for retirement could do so. Those older doctors, working out their final ten years before then, were causing real problems. Their energy levels were low and they prevented the necessary new blood and ideas coming into the profession.

"And if they can't offer anything, I'll start looking in the BMJ. We'll be all right." I tried to put some optimism in my voice.

"Thank you, Eric, you're right. At least you've got a job. Can you remember our first home in Burton-on-Trent?" Margaret was back to her usual self now. It was one of our favourite conversation points: reliving those early days of marriage. It somehow relieved the pain of present difficulties.

It hadn't been a great flat but we had to accept it without seeing it first. I had managed to get a Junior House Physician post at the hospital in Burton-on-Trent when I had qualified. This I had managed to do as the two consultant physicians there were both St Thomas' trained. We went straight to Burton-on-Trent on our return from our honeymoon.

We moved in with our few possessions – mainly our wedding presents. The hospital couldn't let us have any accommodation on site so we had to find a place for ourselves. We arrived on a grey, drizzly evening when people had started putting on the lights in their warm homes. We virtually used up the last of our cash to pay for the taxi. We stood close together both for warmth and encouragement, our possessions starting to get wet at our feet.

I said, "Oh, it doesn't look too bad after all!" We hadn't had a chance to see it and had spent ages speculating on what our first home would be like. Our imaginations had run wild. Before us was a semi-detached house, typical of the pre-war building boom. It looked tatty and forlorn but was better than we had expected.

"I wonder what Mrs Frobisher is like. She sounded a bit bossy on the 'phone and was a bit short with me," Margaret expressed my own thoughts in her words. "Anyway, there's only one way to find out."

We seemed to have been standing under the dripping eaves for a number of minutes after ringing the bell, and then knocking loudly, before a light came on in the room beyond the door. The door opened to reveal an elderly lady. She was looking at us through a pair of spectacles that had diamond encrusted wings on either side where the arms were attached to the frame. The eyes behind them were not welcoming. Her highly permed and lacquered white hair had a faint blue tinge, which really didn't match her pink outfit knitted with fluffy wool. She said nothing. I was at a loss but I could sense Margaret starting to giggle.

The woman turned her malevolent gaze onto Margaret and then pushed her lips together and forward as though inviting a kiss. We declined the offer. Margaret, though, snorted and hid it with a cough. I quickly intervened, "Erm, Mrs Frobisher, I think?" I stammered. "It's Dr and Mrs Hainsworth. Erm, I think we were expected… the flat…"

"You're a bit late, aren't you? I was expecting you this afternoon. Come in, now you're here. Don't drip anywhere!"

Margaret and I managed to get all our stuff out of the drizzle and onto the hall floor. "You can clean up the floor when you've finished!" Mrs Frobisher commanded. "Your flat's through here." A door led off the hall. We went through it.

The front room, with the bay window was quite large but made smaller by the addition of a small kitchen in a quarter of the room, and a grand piano in the bay window.

Mrs Frobisher's demeanour didn't invite any conversation as she led us silently around but Margaret had to ask about the piano. After another invited kiss, Mrs Frobisher said, "That's MY piano from when we had the whole house to ourselves. The men couldn't get it upstairs to my flat, so it's had to stay here."

"Oh, can I play it, Mrs Frobisher?" Margaret asked enthusiastically.

Our pink landlady turned around and stared as if we had asked to be waited on hand and foot during our stay. The lips pushed together and she barked, "IF you must! But only when I'm out. I'll do the same when you're out."

The rest of the flat comprised a bedroom at the back and a toilet under the stairs that could only be accessed from the hall. "You haven't shown us the bathroom yet, Mrs Frobisher," I bravely ventured after she had given us a key.

"Oh, that's upstairs in MY flat!" Mrs Frobisher declared. "If you want a bath, you must arrange it with me and you pay extra for the hot water. You get one free bath every month, though." She said this as though she was shocked by her own generosity.

When we were by ourselves, we looked at each other. Tears were welling in Margaret's eyes. We hugged. She then looked at me and smiled weakly. "But at least I can play the piano!" she said.

We had to beg Mrs Frobisher to use her bath whenever we needed one. However, if Margaret asked for one and Mrs Frobisher considered, for a reason only known to herself, that she had had too many already that month, the lips would be pursed.

Margaret smiled and when we were alone, she imitated Mrs Frobisher's look exactly and mimicked, "ANOTHER bath! That's the second one this month AND we haven't even got to the END of it yet."

It had been a tough time as houseman because of the hugely long hours and sleep grabbed in catnaps. I loved it though and it confirmed my deep desire to go into medicine. One or two things relieved the constant workload. Margaret would come in by bus and have an evening meal with me in the doctors' dining room. I was under a wonderful illusion that this was because she wanted to see me, but she had an ulterior motive: "Darling, my grocery bill came to ten shillings last week so I'll be popping in to the hospital a bit this week," she declared in an unguarded moment.

Now and again, we indulged in the luxury of a trip to the cinema. We could only do this if I had time off duty and I had signed a cremation form recently, for which I got a fee. This was about the only way I could get extra money on top of my meager wage, so this was a real treat.

Margaret was still recovering from her Crohn's operation and rested as much as possible, especially in the afternoons when she sat and made a rug, painstakingly attaching each woollen strand with a rug hook. Whenever I came home the resulting progress was proudly shown and dutifully admired. It worked though, and she never really suffered from symptoms of the disease again.

We also saved money on transport. Margaret could walk to local shops and spend her valuable shillings. I acquired a heavy black bike that was probably pre-war – pre-Great War – and I could cycle under a raised walkway alongside the River Trent to the hospital. This walkway was out of bounds to cyclists but when the ground underneath was flooded this rule was routinely broken.

We even managed to enjoy our first home as a married couple. Mrs Frobisher thawed and nearly smiled one or two times, but I never got to kissing her!

But now the imminent arrival of our second child was forcing us to make decisions. Margaret smiled at me again, "You know, Eric, you were much fitter in those days when you used to cycle in Burton. I think you're getting a bit of a tummy."

"Well, I can't cycle round the practice. I know, I'll have to give up potatoes or chocolate…"

"Yes, and I know which one you'll choose!"

I gave Margaret a quick kiss on her forehead as I resumed my rounds. I had spent much longer at home than I had intended but I left with a new resolve to find a partnership. I was aware that this could be anywhere in the country and I was reluctant to leave my native Yorkshire, but, as I argued with myself, needs must. I would telephone Philip that evening and arrange a chat. It would be marvellous if they could offer me something here. We had settled in and the other doctors and the patients knew me. Maybe this discussion would force the issue a little. This East Yorkshire countryside lacked the hills of my native West Riding, but this also was positive in some respects, especially for my car.

As I drove off in our battered but much-loved Ford Prefect, I carried on reflecting on our hectic and unpredictable early-married life. The houseman job in Burton-on-Trent had to finish when I joined the RAF as a Medical Officer in January 1953 for my National Service. Because I wanted as short a time as possible in uniform, I elected to serve for two years. This meant that I knew exactly when I would leave, something that was not possible if I had elected for a three-year stint, but it also entailed being posted anywhere and I would have no choice in the matter at all, even if a posting was to last a very short time. Poor Margaret, I don't think she realised that she had signed up for this when she had repeated 'for better, for worse'.

However, we had a happy time and had made many good friends round the country. At my first posting at RAF Full Sutton near York, we discovered that Margaret was pregnant. It was there that we had huddled round the small black and white television in the Officers Mess to watch the Coronation in June 1953. Part of the garden at the Hall where we were quartered was covered in strawberries and Margaret traded these with a farmer's wife for cream so, not only did Margaret and I have a delicious summer, but also we were able to celebrate this momentous occasion in style with strawberries and cream. The day after the Coronation I traded all our savings for our first car. No child could have been more excited over a new toy. It felt like freedom despite its well-used crank handle and three gears.

After our time at Full Sutton, we found ourselves on our way to Scotland, Margaret was seven months pregnant and we were sure our baby would be born there. We actually moved on our first wedding anniversary to our third home in that year. We had a flat in another converted house, this time in Nairn. Margaret had managed to buy one or two electrical gadgets for the home with carefully saved pennies from her housekeeping, and her heart sank when she realised that there was no electricity in the flat - just gas. At least the wringer on her new washing machine could function. It was turned by hand.

It seemed hardly a moment had passed when Margaret's due date came … and went. A week passed and despite repeated trips in the car over bouncy roads the baby didn't seem to want to put in an appearance - probably due to the Scottish weather, we joked. As a doctor I was concerned, but our GP reassured us that Margaret had probably just got her dates wrong. I had taken her blood pressure and discovered that it was high. But then that didn't indicate anything really as quite a few women experience high blood pressure in pregnancy. However, there was a niggle at the back of my mind. If only our GP would test for protein in Margaret's urine.

I said nothing, knowing that I would not like another doctor pestering me, if I was in a similar situation. Nearly another week went by, a week in which I knew of Margaret's discomfort especially at night and growing frustration, before I was met by an excited wife as I came off duty. "Eric, I think I've started. I've been having contractions regularly this afternoon and they're nothing like my Braxton Hicks ones."

I gulped - this was it, at last. My niggles, and Margaret's occasional contractions pushed my foot closer to the floor as I drove Margaret with her suitcase, carefully packed and repacked for the past two weeks, to the hospital. There I said a quick goodbye as another contraction clouded the excited face of my young wife. She was taken away in a wheelchair and my last sight of her was a languid hand waving.

The nurses and the midwife made it very clear that they would be taking over from now on and that I was not required in the process. This was one situation that Margaret would have to face without me. It was emphasised by a rather burly Scottish nurse. She was nearly my height and her uniform dress had short sleeves that accentuated her muscular arms that were folded across an ample chest. She barred my way. "Ye can go home now, Mr Hainsworth…"

"It's doctor, actually. Doctor Hainsworth…" I started.

The arms tightened and the bust rose. "Well Doctor, I'm sure you know that your wife is in good hands. I'm sure that you will have things to do at home. Just leave us your telephone number and we will let you know when anything happens."

I felt helpless, suddenly alone. The feeling deepened as I reached our flat back in Nairn. As I opened the door a wave of emptiness washed around and engulfed me. I was now experiencing, first hand, what it was like on the receiving end of medical treatment. I knew that sleep would not relieve me this night as I waited for the telephone to ring. It didn't. The night was long, made longer by the realisation that the next day would be the fourth anniversary of Margaret's father's death. I couldn't stop myself wondering, totally illogically, if this was some sort of omen.

By the next morning I still had not heard anything from the hospital and the niggles had become a storm cloud of concern. I decided that I would go to the hospital rather than telephone, as my duties on the base were light: RAF Dalcross was being decommissioned and would close in a month to become a civilian airport. My hands gripped the hard steering wheel of the car as I tried to keep its speed lower than that demanded by my surfacing panic. I tried to convince myself that no news was good. I would probably find that Margaret had temporarily stopped her labour. She was probably smiling and drinking a cup of tea in bed right now as I pulled up in the car park.

I resisted the urge to walk unbecomingly fast but as I approached the labour ward my medical sixth sense picked up a frisson of panic. "Oh God, don't let it be Margaret. Please don't let it be Margaret," I prayed under my breath.

The double swing doors flapped impatiently open and a young doctor in a white coat and crowned with tousled black hair emerged, barging into my body. His eyes stabbed into mine, equally impatiently. "Yes? Can I help you?" he barked, daring an answer.

"Well, yes, actually. I'm Doctor Hainsworth and my wife is having a baby. I was wondering how things were going."

The aggressiveness in the doctor's eyes disappeared and he looked down, unable to meet mine. His hand crumpled his hair further as he paused before talking again, this time in an apologetic voice that emphasized his slight Scottish burr, "That will be Margaret Hainsworth?" I nodded, coldness clawing my heart.

"She's just had a convulsion…"

"What? An eclamptic fit?" I was agitated and my voice was raised.

"Yes, I'm sorry." The doctor finally looked me in the eye. "We're doing all we can…"

"Is the baby all right? Is Margaret?" Panic was seizing me. I knew the dangers of eclampsia for both the mother and child. They involved the possibilities of death for either, or both. Surely that wave Margaret had given me was not one of goodbye? "I mean…" mumbles reduced to nothing.

"Doctor Hainsworth, we are dealing with the situation. Your wife was in coma for a short time, but is awake now, and we are preparing to deliver the baby."

"Caesarian?" I managed to ask, my training controlling my panic.

"No, the delivery is too advanced for that. We're going to use forceps. The consultant obstetrician is in charge now but I must be getting back. If you could just wait in that room down there." His pointed indication was more of a command than an invitation.

The room was bleak in its unhomely décor and atmosphere, heavy with clinging stale cigarette smoke that I found suffocating. Clearly this was the room where soon-to-be fathers waited, wondering, desperate for any news. I joined my invisible fellows and slumped on a decrepit chair opposite the open door, watching helplessly as nurses and the junior doctor left and then re-entered the labour ward pushing the swing doors open with their shoulders. It was then that I resolved to develop my obstetrics and gynaecological skills and to treat expectant parents with more openness and care than Margaret and I were experiencing. It would be the first thing I would do on leaving the RAF in just over a year's time. I started planning. I would contact a friend at St Thomas' – a senior 'Obs. and Gynae.' consultant and talk through my plans. My musing and new resolve took me away from those stark conditions.

My thoughts were interrupted sometime later by a gentle knock on the door. I looked up to see a new face, smiling this time. The man, in white coat and with a white mask around his throat like a goitre, had a mess of white hair and spectacles with large lenses that added to his friendly gravitas. "Umm, Doctor Hainsworth? You have a bonny son. It was a bit bumpy at one time with the seizure but everything is fine now. There should be no organ damage, but we'll keep Mrs Hainsworth in for a while to make sure. You can come through now and see her…oh, and your new son, of course."

It was my turn now to push the swing doors open and greet my son and my wife. I looked at Margaret propped up in bed with a white, slightly haggard face and hair in a shambles, smeared over her forehead with the sweat of hard labour. Her eyes though shone strongly and undefeated into mine. She smiled and looked down into a small cot on tall legs by the bed. In it I could just make out a bundle…and then the tears came.

Over the next three days I kept driving over to the hospital to admire our new son through a window let into a wall of a small room dedicated to a number of these tiny cots, each holding a sleeping baby. Although they all looked so much the same, I cooed suitably through the glass especially after Charles was pointed out. Thank goodness he was alive. I was becoming aware about how close death had prowled when I heard snippets of information about the labour. As soon as Margaret was admitted she noticed her ankles had swollen, a sign of pre-eclampsia. She then developed a searing headache that became almost intolerable during contractions. However, the hospital usually only had two eclampsias a year and their second one had been the day before, so the signs were initially disregarded. They just couldn't believe that there was another case so soon! Every time I saw Margaret she was sleeping, but alive. She didn't see me or Charles for those three days. The resolution I had made whilst waiting by the labour ward hardened.

Any thoughts that we might have a time to relax a little, as we settled into our new state of parenthood, were dispelled with a new order to become a medical officer at RAF Kirkbride near Carlisle. This was much nearer my parents' house near the woollen mill in Workington that my father had established in those hard years after the war. I knew that he was finding the going very tough: the workers had, on the whole, lost the work ethic in the years of unemployment and working in the mill required skills they didn't have, the supply route for wool was tortuous, and getting the finished pieces to the market place in the West

Riding was equally problematic. However, I knew they would help us out with the move and the new baby, Charles. Margaret, however, might find the relationship with my mother strained after she had taken her first look at Charles and pompously declared in her 'posh' Yorkshire accent, "Huh, it should 'ave been a girl!" Poor Margaret didn't know how to respond.

We managed to find a comfortable furnished house in Bowness-on-Solway, west of Carlisle, where Margaret happily settled into motherhood with the help of good, newly-made friends in the village. There my role as medical officer was hardly irksome and I had time on my hands to help a GP in Carlisle on a sort of unofficial basis. The one really challenging medical situation, when a pilot activated his ejector seat whilst his aircraft was on the ground and killed himself, happened when I was away in a recruiting office in Carlisle. The rest of the time I spent counting down days and planning my future career.

The flat above the surgery in Yorkshire was tiny compared to the Bowness house and I realised this drastic reduction of space was at the heart of Margaret's present state. Philip was the senior partner of the practice. I liked and admired him a great deal. He listened well and the practice was well run. I had learned a great deal from him. Although he was older than the normal retirement age and his full head of hair was a respectable grey, he looked far younger. His skin was just slightly florid but was unlined. His eyebrows and jutting chin spoke of his earnestness but his eyes revealed his slightly wicked sense of humour that he brought to most situations. He could tell a good story.

When I telephoned him later and explained our situation, he invited me over the following evening, after the surgery, to talk things over. Neither of us would be on duty so we could be sure of a good, uninterrupted discussion.

As my car scrunched up his drive, he opened his front door with a flourish. He boomed, "Come in, Eric! Come in, do!" and spread his arm wide in welcome. Philip led me into the capacious sitting room with its tiger skin rug, a relic from his childhood in India. Despite the magnificence of such a creature being displayed in disrespectful death, it causing him little embarrassment. Charles made for it, every time we visited as a family, and put his fingers into its glass eyes challenging a response. Fortunately for him, none came.

Now Philip shepherded me by my elbow to a lovely old leather armchair, whose comfort had been tested to tattiness over the years. "I'm afraid Ann is out at the WI tonight, Eric, but can I get you a drink of some kind. Beer…whisky?"

"No thanks, Philip. I'd better keep a clear head for driving home." I somehow didn't want to admit my dislike of most alcoholic drink. I seemed to have spent my RAF career pouring obligatory officers' alcohol into convenient plant-pots, much to the dismay of the Dalcross Station Commander who loved his plants and couldn't understand their demise.

Philip poured himself a good measure of whisky before sitting opposite me. He crossed his legs encased, as they always were, in corduroy trousers. He saw me gawping at his drink, "Oh, I'm having yours as well. Can't let it go to waste, can we? Anyway, Ann's out!"

He leaned back, closed his eyes luxuriously and sniffed the whisky before taking his first mouthful. "Ah, my favourite Islay malt. You should try it sometime, Eric. Nothing like it. You can smell the moors." Suddenly, Philip sat bolt upright, "Oh, I do apologise. Got a bit carried away. You've come about a possible partnership, I think you said?"

"Yes, Philip. I know it's a tall order but now that we have another baby on the way we're finding the flat a bit small…"

"Know what you mean, Eric. Know what you mean. It could easily fit into our sitting room. Er, probably twice." Philip looked expansively at his acres. "It was designed for a single chap," he explained.

"Well, Margaret is a bit fed up actually. When we were up in Cumberland we had a lovely house. It wasn't on this scale," I indicated our surroundings with my hand, "but we could live in it and enjoy it there. I think we just exist at the moment. It got to Margaret the other day when Charles sat in the kitchen with his back against one wall and his feet touching the cupboards on the other side…"

"Good grief, Eric. I had forgotten it was that small. Haven't been up there for some time…"

"No, we can't have people around for meals, it can only manage two chairs. We'd love to have you and Ann around of course but…"

"Don't mention it, Eric. Know the problem."

I decided that I had to get to the heart of the matter, "Margaret always faces every situation well. She has amazing determination but this has really got to her. I really can't see any way out except by finding a partnership. I'd love to stay here." I left the thought hanging.

Philip leaned back again and closed his eyes. I thought he was reflecting on the Islay moors again, but then he muttered, "Umm. It's that damned superannuation scheme. I should have gone two years ago, but I have to keep going now for another two-and-a-bit years. Buggered my plans, I can tell you. Oops, don't tell Ann I said that!"

"Well, what do you think? Is there any chance?" I kept the conversation on track.

"I wouldn't want to lose you, Eric. Between you and me, you've done dashed well here. You work hard and the patients really like you. I've been here for years and it's a bit galling when the patients want to see the new doctor…"

"Except Mrs Colman!" It had been one of my early calls just days after we had arrived. The telephone had rung at 9.30pm one evening and Margaret answered it. She immediately held the receiver away from her ear. I was party to both sides of the conversation as a voice boomed out, "Is that the doctor's? The NEW doctor's?"

Margaret answered gently, "Yes, it is. Doctor Hainsworth's…"

"Well, it's Mrs Colman here. I'm sure he knows that I am a private patient and I have an emergency that needs his IMMEDIATE attention."

"Oh right, Mrs Colman," Margaret continued. "What seems to be the problem?"

"It doesn't SEEM. It IS. I have a headache. Please tell the doctor NOW. I think he needs to visit me IMMEDIATELY!" The receiver boomed as Margaret put her hand over the mouthpiece.

"It's Mrs Colman!"

"Yes, yes. I know. I heard it all. Tell her to…" I had a flash of mischievous inspiration. "Tell her to take an asprin and drink lots of water."

Margaret hadn't finished repeating this to the first private patient I had come across when an eruption happened. I could see the receiver vibrating. "Take an ASPRIN? Tell the doctor that he is an IDIOT!" The line suddenly went dead.

Philip and I chuckled as we relived the call. "Did you know that her family firm makes Dispro?" Philip asked.

"Er, yes," I replied, a little sheepishly.

"And you advised she take asprin, made by the opposition?" I nodded and Philip thrust back into his seat. He laughed. "I'd loved to have seen her face. Fortunately, she didn't leave the practice. The next nearest one's miles away anyway. Well, maybe Mrs Colman won't be sad to see you go! Ha!"

I brought the conversation back to the problem in hand; we could be discussing patient stories all night. "About a partnership then, what do you think are the chances, Philip?"

"Well, Eric. I have to be honest, I don't think we can stretch to that just yet. I will have to work out the finances and have a chat with Ken and John." He paused, "Remind me, when's the baby due?"

"The beginning of October and I know it will be on time this time, they are keeping a very close eye on Margaret after the problems with Charles. Really, we would like to know as soon as we can and, if possible, have something in place by the end of September."

Philip and I chatted for quite a long time, aided by Philip's whisky intake. We rambled over the frustrations of some of our patients, but also the hilarious stories they often engendered. We had had some good times together and I had learned such a lot about general practice in a relatively short time. We touched on Philip's early struggles in his career, and this brought us back to my own present problem. I became increasingly aware that, however much Philip wanted me to stay, there wouldn't be any sort of relief for our plight in this practice.

I had just carefully avoided yet another offer of a whisky when I glanced down at my watch. I gasped, "Goodness, Philip, it's nearly ten o'clock and I have to take the early morning surgery. Margaret will be wondering where I am…"

"Eric, don't go just yet; Ann should be home soon and I know she would love to see you," Philip beamed at me lopsidedly.

"No, Philip. I must go. Please give my best wishes to her." I got up and went to the door. Philip swung it open theatrically and grasped my hand in both of his before pumping it and exclaiming, "Don't go, Eric. Don't go!" Whether it was an entreaty about my immediate departure or the next stage of my career, I did not know.

"I'm sorry, Philip. I must," was my equally obscure reply. I managed to extract my hand and climbed into the car.

The night was dark and the headlights, despite their size that added an owlish quality to the box-like styling of the car, were not up to penetrating the gloom. No matter, I knew the highways and byways intimately. My mind drifted back to the evening's conversation. It had been very good of Philip to give me so much time. However, I now resolved to search through the ads in the next BMJ. I started wondering where Margaret and I would eventually end up. Would we be prepared to go anywhere in the country?

Soon I reached the home straight: I just had to negotiate the bend underneath the railway bridge. My thoughts wandered … too much. I turned the steering wheel. The dim lights lit a stone wall shooting towards me. It flared in the headlights and then there was a dull metallic thud and scrape as I was flung forward onto the hard wheel. There was a painful silence as the engine died. There was a sharp pain in my chest as I sat daring a quick self-examination. No head wounds. No other pain, no blood. I hadn't been going that fast, thank goodness. I started breathing again. I found it hard to see, though, and a moment of panic struck me before I realised that my spectacles must have flown off in the jar of impact. I fumbled around in the darkness, but couldn't find them – I'm extremely short-sighted.

I tried the door. It opened with no trouble but on turning to get out the pain in my chest turned into a shriek of agony. With infinite care I managed to extract myself and stand. In the light of the one unaffected headlight, I could see that I had hit the stone pillar on the left side of the bridge. The nearside wing was a crumped mess and the headlight had totally smashed. Looking closer I could see that the damaged wing was squashed onto the wheel.

With my chest screaming I got back into the car. I pressed the starter button… the engine fired. At least I hadn't damaged that! Carefully I put the gear into reverse. The car juddered back, the dented wing stuttering angrily on the wheel.

Despite the sharp agony in my chest, I once again got out and pulled the wing off the wheel. The car could be driven! Margaret's annoyed criticism of my late return died on her lips when she saw the pain reflected in my face. I looked different, almost strange, without specs on anyway. I quickly explained, trying to be as reassuring as I could. "Oh, Eric!" Margaret said with an equal mix of alarm and sympathy as she helped me out of my overcoat, "You could have killed yourself…"

"No, darling. I wasn't going that fast. It was so dark. I just wasn't thinking," I replied. "Aghhh, that's painful. I'd better get to bed. I've got the early morning surgery."

Margaret looked me in the eye. Her face had assumed the steeliness that I was beginning instantly to recognise the longer I lived with her, "You will do no such thing, Eric. You'll stay in bed until you've had your chest seen to. I'm going to telephone Philip right now whilst you get ready for bed. Do you think you can undress yourself?" I nodded. I was starting to feel sorry for myself but grateful that Margaret was in control of the situation. She was a wonder.

Sometime later I had just managed to get my pyjamas on when Margaret returned. "That's all arranged then. Philip sounded distraught and sends his best wishes. He'll do the surgery and Ken will come round as soon as he can in the morning to have a look at you. He was most emphatic. No work tomorrow!"

"Oh, I'm sure it's nothing, Margaret. I'll be…"

"No, Eric. NO work tomorrow! You can spend the day looking through the BMJ." Margaret smiled.

"We've got a new one?" I asked.

"Yes, it came this morning."

The next day I was relaxing, propped up in bed with three pillows and the BMJ. I had been amazed that there were two interesting partnership jobs going that I had circled ready for a further chat with Margaret later. I was perusing the rest of the magazine when Ken banged on the outside door. He was one of the partners and was obviously in a bit of a hurry. Judging by the sounds he was making he seemed to be falling up the stairs. His bald head, devoid of any hair except a rim that went from ear to ear above his collar line, appeared round the bedroom door. "Ah, Eric. Bad luck old chap. Philip has told me what happened. Could have been me, could have been me, any number of times."

Ken came in and examined me. He manipulated my arm until the pain grew in intensity. Ken seemed rather perplexed. "Oh, bad luck, Eric. I think it's a disc…"

"A DISC!" I exclaimed.

"Yes, you will need a proper examination to find which one, you know." Ken smiled. However, I was unsure about his diagnosis - he liked working with disc problems and he regularly diagnosed them only to discover later that the pain had another cause altogether, much to the amusement of his partners. I was obviously his latest victim.

"It can't be. Surely, it's my clavicle or a rib…"

"No. I've checked all those. The only one it could be is your first rib but that never breaks. Everyone knows that!"

"Well, could I get it checked? Have an x-ray? I'll need one if it's a disc anyway," I asked.

"I'll see what I can do. I know someone at the infirmary and they might do it today, if I ask nicely. Margaret doesn't drive, does she?"

"No, and anyway the car's a bit of a mess."

"Don't worry, I'm sure Ann or Jean will take you over. Anyway, must rush. I'll 'phone at lunchtime and let Margaret know."

Luckily the x-ray confirmed that the first rib had, in fact, broken, probably due to a severe muscle spasm when the car crashed to a sudden halt. It was very unusual for this to happen so I forgave Ken his pet diagnosis. At least I would be back to work with a healthy and intact vertebral column.

The next morning, after a slightly better night's sleep, I produced the BMJ and opened it to the graffitied page before passing it to Margaret casually. She looked down, "TWO, Eric!" she gasped. "TWO!"

"Yes, darling. And they're both in Yorkshire!" I beamed. "One in Guisborough, you know, up near Middlesbrough. But it's this that really has caught my eye."

We both looked down and read: "Queensbury, Bradford, Yorkshire West Riding: Full time Assistant post with a view to a partnership in an extensive, part urban, part rural practice. Would suit young doctor with some experience. Further details and applications: Dr G Blunt, Craig-na-Hullie, Queensbury, Bradford, West Riding. Tel: Bradford 157."

Chapter 4

"Goodness, Eric, I don't think this road will ever stop going up!" Margaret and I had spent most of the journey in a nervous and self-absorbed silence. Although she knew the roads around Huddersfield well, Margaret had never ventured this far and the experience of these hills was both a little disconcerting and invigorating as we pulled away from the smoke blackened sandstone houses clustering round the crossroads at Hipperholme.

The road just kept going up, bordered by fields occasionally populated by cows and sheep, the fleeces also greyed by the smoky air. Fields and animals were kept in check by dry-stone walls that looked to have been carefully thrown together and which, now and then, tumbled, losing their constant effort against gravity and wind. "It's good to be back in the West Riding though. Do you think you'll get it?"

"Oh, eerm," I repied, as my own secret thoughts were pushed aside. Two things were vying for my attention. The first was the car. After the accident we had decided to buy a new one, a Ford Anglia. It was similar to the Prefect in many ways: it had three forward gears and no synchromesh between first and second, it had bizarre vacuum powered windscreen wipers that slowed as the car speeded up and even stopped when overtaking, and was a colour that blended in well with mud. All-in-all it made for an interesting, if camouflaged ride.

However, its shape was more modern. There was a rounded box in the middle in which passengers sat, there was a smaller one at the front for the engine and a similar one at the back for the boot. It became the car shape that all children loved to draw from then on. But, like all new cars, it needed to be 'run in' – driven slowly and carefully. I was worried about the constant climb up the hill, especially after the drive over from Hull the day before. In our minds buying the car was a sort of statement of faith that I would get the Queensbury partnership. I hoped we were right. The repayments would severely stretch us on my present salary.

I spent the journey nursing the car and listening for any signs of distress from its engine. However, thoughts of the day ahead interrupted for my attention. I had telephoned the two practices that were advertising partnerships in the BMJ immediately after I had shown them to Margaret. I had expected them to be filled already, but was pleasantly surprised when both senior partners had responded positively. I asked Henry Smith in Guisborough about the sort of practice he ran and the expectations that he had of their new appointee. He made cursory enquiries about my medical career and about my family. He didn't seem at all interested in me and gradually seemed to run out of conversation.

The response on telephoning the other practice could not have been more different. "Dr Blunt here," a deep and genial voice had boomed from the receiver when I had telephoned the Queensbury practice. "What can I do for you?" I immediately took to the owner of the voice as a picture popped into my head of a 'hail-fellow-well-met' giant of a man. He sounded as though any request would be willingly met.

"I'm Eric Hainsworth and I'm enquiring about the post that you advertised in the BMJ…"

"Oh, yes, yes," the genial voice encouraged.

"I'm very interested in applying and I wondered if it had been filled yet?" I went on.

"Oh no. We've had one or two enquiries – early days yet, you know – and no firm applications. I suspect that people are trying to find out where Queensbury actually is on the map. Ha!" Dr Blunt seemed highly amused at the idea.

My hopes were raised so I decided to jump in with both feet, "Well, I have to say that I'm very interested. I know the place well, Dr Blunt…"

"Oh, goodness. Call me George. And you are?"

"Eric Hainsworth…"

"So you know Queensbury, Eric? Goodness, how is that?"

"Well, I grew up in Halifax and I used to come through Queensbury on the bus," I continued, my rising hopes reflected in an emerging smile.

"Thank goodness, Eric. The other enquirers had no idea of the place. Had to explain at length. So, you're interested in the job. Assistantship at first. My heart has told me to retire - two attacks - but I've still got some years to go so I need to give someone most of the load. Be a good way to hand over though."

I had started to imagine the situation as I asked, "Is it a large practice? Queensbury didn't seem very big when I went through."

"I know, long and thin – strung out along the main road. We cover quite a number of outlying villages as well. Altogether we have just over six thousand three hundred patients. Dr Akroyd, Tom, is the other partner. Tell you what, Eric, why don't you pop over and we'll go into all the details then?"

"You mean an interview? Don't you want to know a little about me?" I was controlling my excitement at this sudden invitation.

"Oh, we can go into that when you come over. Where are you now?" it sounded as if that evening for him would be just fine for the interview.

"We are in Yorkshire, but over near Hull. It makes popping over tricky but I'll have a chat with the senior partner here. I'll have to take three days off, I think. We have a young son so we'll spend the nights with my wife's mother. She's near Huddersfield…" I was thinking aloud.

"Splendid, splendid!" George bellowed. "Give me a call when you know. Must dash now, Eric. Time waits for no man!" With that George rang off leaving me in a haze of hopes.

Surprisingly, my enquiries about the Guisborough job also resulted in an interview but my heart, and hope, was really in Queensbury. Fortunately, this latter was the first interview and, after a brief consultation with Philip, I arranged it all, but I had to take the time off as holiday. We had three days away towards the end of August, the middle one being the day of the interview. Margaret and I were going to meet Tom Akroyd for the formal part as he would be taking over as senior partner when George retired. George and his wife would then show us around the doctor's house that we were expected to buy from him when he retired in 1959 in just over two years' time.

The journey across Yorkshire was a gift from the county itself. After loading the car with our smart clothes, freshly dampened and dabbed with a cloth for the occasion, and Charles, now just over two and a half years old, we set off under a cobalt blue sky of rare intensity. There was just a tickle of a breeze and soon the air, wafting through the open windows, was heavy with warmth and scent. It was soporific and Charles was soon asleep. He was unaware of the passing countryside, first the Humber flatlands then the welcome hills as we went into the West Riding. I was being drawn home by subtle strings, and was being greeted by the land itself.

We had spent the night at Margaret's mother's house in Kirkburton, a village near Huddersfield, and left Charles there for the day.

My nervous thoughts about the interview ahead were now interrupted when I saw a darkened woollen mill at a road junction to the right. Stone terraced cottages hunched around it. A memory emerged from George's telephone instructions to me. I looked at the finger post: Shelf.

"We're nearly there! George told me to look for the mill. Shelf is part of the practice. They have a surgery there. Queensbury is the next village." I settled back into silent musing. The road was still going up.

"What do you think they're like, Eric?" Margaret voiced my own thoughts. "Did George tell you much about Tom?"

"No, not really. He's older than me. He and Chrissey have got three boys. The youngest is Charles's age."

"That sounds promising, Eric. It will be good to have people about our own age with children in the practice already. Did you say they live at the other end of the village?"

"Yes, apparently it's another doctor's house with a surgery. It's just past the church."

A few minutes later Margaret exclaimed, "I can see a mill chimney over there, Eric!" and pointed.

I looked, "Ah, yes. That'll be the mill at the crossroads. I think I can remember it. We turn left there to get to Tom's"

We passed stone mill buildings, starkly Victorian, and made dirty over the decades. At the crossroads we stopped and glanced around: 'The Stag's Head' across the road, a glimpse of a strange cupola peeking over to the right, small purposeful shops bustling with women and young children and, just by us on the corner, a proud memorial - the only piece of ornamentation. The buildings were all from the same era and of similar colour as the mill; they stirred my memory and I had a flashback to my adolescence.

We turned up the High Street still climbing up hill, past more shops and the ornate wrought-iron mill gates protecting the village from the activity and noise within. The church, Victorian Gothic, seemed squat as if it had sunk into the ground but embellished with a high tower as some sort of compensation. We had arrived.

As Margaret and I stood outside 'Innisfree', Tom Akroyd's house and surgery, our hands touched briefly. We both knew the importance of the next few hours and we were glad to face them together.

Following the usual practice of Yorkshire folk, we approached the back door and announced our presence with what I hoped sounded like a 'polite' knock. It was immediately opened by a small, sprightly lady with black hair. Her face smiled behind her slightly too large spectacles. "Ah, come in. You must be Dr and Mrs Hainsworth." She stood back and beckoned us in. She shook our hands profusely and introduced herself. "Tom, they're here!" she bellowed behind her.

We waited in the kitchen surrounded by piles of washed children's clothes waiting for folding and sorting. A door opposite opened and a man entered. It was obviously Tom, smartened in a dove grey suit. His face was faintly tanned and faint lines ran down each cheek. His hair was prematurely grey and swept back from his forehead. He looked about ten years older that I was, I thought. His smiling eyes and handshakes welcomed us warmly.

"Eric and Margaret?" he asked in a pleasantly resonant voice. We nodded at his enquiry. "It's good to see you. You've met Chrissey. Come through and we'll have a coffee and then we can get down to business. Have you had a good journey? George said that you live near Hull – quite a way…" Preliminary niceties followed and I was impatient to start talking about the practice and what I could bring to it in terms of skills, ideas and energy.

However, when we were all together in a slightly over full sitting room, the ritual opening remarks about the height of Queensbury on its Pennine summit, and the countryside that surrounded it, enabled me to sense what sort of person Tom was. He lounged back, one leg carelessly draped over the other and held his cup and saucer in thin fingers tinged with yellow. The smell of cigarette tobacco was embedded in the fabric of the room and now I knew the culprit. I was always amazed at colleagues who smoked. A large number did and all seemed to have developed a carapace of excuses, despite the mounting and damning evidence of the harm caused by the habit.

Margaret obviously found it very easy to talk to Chrissey and they were chatting away by themselves, whilst Tom and I discussed our respective training and experiences, especially the progress of the NHS, which was only just eight years old. He suddenly looked at me, "By the way, is your mother May Hainsworth?"

"Yes, why?"

"She's living up in Cumberland now?" I nodded. "You wouldn't believe it but my mother knows her. I told mother you were coming the other day and it was the name Hainsworth which she recognised. I won't hold it against you though!" Tom smiled and winked.

The next, more serious stage was announced when Chrissey stood up and said in voice that I now identified as having a Scottish lilt, "Well, Margaret and I are going to look around the house and we may pop down to the village centre for a while whilst you two have a good natter. We'll be back for lunch though. Around one o'clock. Is that alright, Tom?"

When our wives had departed, Margaret with a secret wink of encouragement, Tom pushed the cups back and produced a silver box. "Cigarette, Eric?" he said as he pushed the box over the coffee table towards me.

"Er, no thanks, Tom. I don't." I held up my hand.

"Mind if I do, Eric?" It wasn't really a question. "I find it helps me to think."

I watched as a cigarette was fished out of the box, tapped twice on the table and then held over a silver lighter. Tom leaned back and blew out the first smoke luxuriously. "Chrissey doesn't like me smoking when she's around," he explained.

"Right then, to business," he continued in a cloud of smoke. "I imagine that you would like to know something about the practice. Well, it covers a large area. We've got patients in Clayton, quite a few actually, and in places on the edge of this side of Bradford. There are a large number in Shelf and I hold a lunchtime surgery there four days a week. All in all, we have six thousand, three hundred and fifty patients between the two of us. It's a lot but they're an uncomplaining folk up here. We only get to hear about serious things and, sometimes, not even then."

"Probably a left over from the days when visiting a doctor needed to be balanced with other financial needs," I suggested.

"You're right, Eric. Most of them are not well off and we only have one or two private patients. Many still seem to want to give us payment in kind though. Amazing. We have to take it. Source of pride to them." I nodded. I had experienced this in the practice near Hull.

"You probably know that there is a lot of farm-land around Queensbury," Tom went on, exhaling another cloud at the same time. I nodded. "Most of our patients work at the mill or in small industries near here, but we have a good smattering of farmers."

"Do many have telephones?" I was starting to imagine the problems.

"Ha, no! They get round it though. People send someone to walk to the surgery or borrow a neighbour's phone. They manage. They're a hardy lot. Bit blunt at times, mind you."

Tom continued to talk about the practice management as if I might be joining any moment. I tried to suppress my hopes, which were getting a bit out of hand, in case my wishful thinking was leading me astray.

I asked why there was a vacancy.

"I don't know what George has told you," Tom replied. This new topic of conversation was accompanied with a new cigarette, lit in a well-rehearsed ritual. I was fascinated by Tom's ability to let his cigarettes burn down to leave a bent grey cylinder of ash, which somehow managed to hold on to the glowing tip. Occasionally, grey flakes would break away and float down onto his suit. They were well camouflaged there, but he would lazily brush them away with a slow stroke with the back of his 'non-smoking' hand.

"Well," I explained. "He said that he had had two heart attacks, and that he now had to share the load before he retired."

"Yes, that was last year. We got an assistant, Dr Angus Morgan, to share the burden. He has a house just down the road towards Bradford. You'll…erm… whoever takes over will be able to use it. Bit small I'm afraid and it looks as though your family is growing."

"Yes," I said. "Margaret's due at the beginning of October. Our second. Can I ask why Dr Morgan is leaving?"

"Certainly. He came from a hospital job and has discovered he doesn't like general practice. He's due to leave at the end of the year." My mind was buzzing. My present contract finished at the end of September. I would have three months… "George will have done his ten years in May 1959 and he'll probably go a month later." We carried on talking for a while longer. We were both finding out about each other with gently probing questions. It must have been one of the gentlest of interviews and we both seemed to be enjoying it.

"By the way, Eric, do you want to see my set up? It's just downstairs." Tom led the way. The stairs were steep and ended at a door. "We have to come down here to get to the garden as well. Bit of a faff!"

At the bottom of the stairs, Tom led me into what looked like a play-room – toys were strewn around. Ahead there was a French door which seemed to lead out into the garden. There was also a door on the right. After going through this door, Tom switched on the light to reveal a small room with chairs around the edge. It was tidy – it was obviously a waiting room. I wondered what the one at Craig-na-Hullie would be like.

Tom laughed. "Patients come in at most strange times to wait for the surgery. I try and keep it warm in winter. It is a bit strange discovering someone at odd times. Dr Glenn, the previous doctor in this house, and his wife had their nephew living with them sometime before the war. One of the lad's jobs was to switch on the light and put the heater on. However, he didn't come in – just put his hand round the door to find the light-switch. One time, as he put his hand round, he felt a very strange smooth object. It was the bald head of a patient who had come early and was sitting in the dark! Must have given the poor lad a fright!"

75

Our reverie was interrupted with the return of Chrissey and Margaret. Their animated chatter also indicated another successful time

After a quick ham-salad lunch, Margaret and I walked to our car for the next part of the proceedings. We were both bubbling with excitement. I felt that this job was perfect for me. I would have the chance to work alongside two experienced GPs for a bit longer, and get to know the practice well, before taking on a partnership. I thought that Tom considered that I would fit in well. Margaret was very happy about the village, which was so much closer to her mother's house, as well as getting on well with Chrissey. The village just seemed 'right' as we drove back through it, past the mill and crossroads.

Shortly after, on the left, we saw the rather grand building with the cupola which we had glimpsed earlier. Beyond was the second doctor's house, Craig-na-Hullie. More memories were stirred of those adolescent bus journeys. Following instructions, I pulled up on the side of the road and we approached the front door of this solid and proud house, down a short path that pushed its way over a small lawn. There was another path to our left leading to a less imposing door that proclaimed, in etched letters on the glass above it, that it was for the surgery. In between the two doors was a curved bay window that must have been very grand at one time but now looked forlorn; its dark green paintwork was peeling and faded,

Holding hands once more for reassurance, Margaret and I approached the grander door in the centre of the front elevation. I pushed the large bell button. After a few moments the door opened and once again we were greeted, this time by a 'well-upholstered' lady, as Philip would have described her. Large necklace pearls and a slight blue hair rinse added to the simplicity of her attire. A white and worn face welcomed us and a cheerful voice chirped, "You must be Eric and Margaret about the job?" We nodded. "Well, come in, come in. It's lovely to see you." We felt warmly welcomed again.

We stepped through a small, tiled and aspidistra-adorned porch and then another door before halting in the hallway. It was an imposing room with a lovely staircase rising out of it. The overall impression, however, was brown: the woodwork was a dark brown and had a matching carpet with a fussy pattern of different shades of brown. The walls were also brown, but tending towards yellow as if to acknowledge that there might be other colours in the palette. Margaret and I were slightly overwhelmed by our surroundings, but our host rescued us.

"It really is lovely to see you. Have you had a good journey? You've already spent some time with Tom and Chrissey, haven't you?" Before we had time to answer either question, the lady held out her hand for us to shake and continued brightly, "I'm Bea. George said you'd be coming about now. He's just had to go out on an urgent call so he has asked me to show you around a bit."

She glanced round and seemed to notice the surroundings for the first time. "Oh dear, it is a bit shabby. We've never got round to decorating. It hasn't been one of George's things. I imagine you young people will want to change it." She led us up the generous stairs, which doubled back on themselves at a half-landing. I could see that Margaret was intrigued by the 'art nouveau' design in coloured glass in the half-landing window.

I wanted to find out as much as possible and asked, "So you and George have been here some time?"

We had reached the main landing and Bea turned, "Yes. It seems like a lifetime – well, it is really. We came in 1924 when George bought the practice from Dr Shields. He had the house built in 1909, you know." She smiled at me. "But we have changed the carpet though. We wanted something a bit more modern that would complement the paintwork. I think that was in the 1930s."

Margaret interrupted, she was looking up another flight of stairs that went up from the landing, "Do you use up there? Are there more bedrooms?" There was a wonder in her voice that betrayed her amazement at the size of the place compared to anything we had experienced before.

"Oh, those are the maids' rooms..."

"Maids?" Margaret gasped.

"They're not there now, of course. We had maids before the war. We use the three rooms up there as storage rooms now. Well, junk rooms really. One of our children, when he lived here had the middle one." Bea's face clouded, "But that's another story. Let's look at the bedrooms down here." Four doors led off the landing and another three from a short corridor that led off the main landing.

The bedrooms were similar in décor: brown with thick, peeling wallpaper. Heavy brown Edwardian furniture finished off the effect. We just glanced in each room but Bea led us into the largest. It was the only one at the back of the house, facing North. Immediately we went across the threadbare carpet to the sizeable window. The view was magnificent and claimed our whole attention. The blue skies of the previous day were now embellished with lazy, white clouds, which, if anything, added to the scene in front of us.

I was looking down the valley that fell away from the back garden. I could just make out a railway line that seemed to form a triangle in the valley floor. A train, its engine betrayed by a procession of miniscule white puffs, was approaching from the north.

"Goodness," Bea said. "You can see Ingleborough today. It's a good forty miles away and you're very lucky to see it." Margaret and I followed her pointed finger up towards the blue horizon. There was the distinctive limestone outline with its totally flat top. We were both captivated. "George and I used to go cycling up there before the war. We had a tandem, you know."

'That sounds rather fun. Did you have to stop when the war came?" Margaret asked.

"No, no. It was when we were out, going through Burnsall, so we hadn't gone far. I was on the back seat, as usual, when someone called out to George that I wasn't pedalling. I often didn't! However, George had never noticed!" Bea simpered at the memory. "I helped up the hills of course but George decided to sell the bike and get a caravan."

"Oh lovely. Eric and I have thought about doing that. Did you take it up the Dales?"

"Well, no, not really. We had it in the garage just down there." Bea pointed to the building across to our right. "Every holiday, and weekends when George was off duty, we would open those green doors." We could just see some large doors in the gable-end wall of the garage, over a tall wooden fence. "That fence is moveable. We just pushed the caravan onto the lawn."

I looked at the lawn more closely. I could see a rectangle in the middle of it, paved with flagstones. I had noticed them but now the mystery of their use was solved. "And that's where you had your holidays?" I was amazed.

"Erm, yes. George made sure that we weren't disturbed by patients. Wouldn't see them or even talk to them when we went up the village. He was very strict about our holidays down there on the lawn." Bea laughed to herself at the memories. "If I had left anything in the house by accident, we couldn't come back to fetch it. Ha!"

A loud whistle shrilly interrupted the story of the Blunts' holiday arrangements. We all swung round to find the culprit. Another blast pierced the air. It came from the corner on the other side of the bed. This latter, like all the others in the house, was based on a sturdy black iron bedstead with shining brass spheres topping each post. It impressed with its size. The hollow between the bed head and the railings at the foot was filled with shapeless mounds like a turbulent sea.

"Oh, that's just the speaking tube. It's here," Bea indicated a cloth covered tube sticking out of the wall. There was a brass attachment on the end. Bea held it up, for inspection. 'It's like on a ship, you know. The captain speaks through it to the engine room, you know."

Bea pulled off the end of the attachment and held the tube to her mouth. "HELLO … HELLO!" she bellowed.

"It's the DOCTOR speaking…" a voice wailed from the tube.

"Oh, it's only George. GEORGE, DO BE SENSIBLE. ERIC AND MARGARET ARE HERE!"

There was a final ghostly "Woaa!" from the strange instrument and then silence.

Bea looked at us. "I'm sorry about that. It's his toy and he enjoys joking around with it. The other end's in the surgery porch. People can talk to us when they come in the night for an emergency. George doesn't even need to get out of bed to talk to them."

I was rather doubtful about this contraption but I managed to mutter, "That's wonderful…"

"Well actually, it sounds good but none of the patients seem to understand how to use it. Sometimes they can blow down it to get the whistle working but then there's always silence. George only uses it to frighten patients coming to the surgery. We once heard a conversation going on in the surgery porch through the tube." Bea giggled. "It was a courting couple and they had gone in there to keep warm. They must have thought it was nice and private. We listened to them for a bit and then George did one of his 'woaas'. They ran off in a hurry. It's great fun for that sort of thing and George loves it. Ah, I can hear him coming now." As Bea looked towards the door, I glanced briefly at Margaret. I wondered how she was coping with this strange interview. It was totally unlike any that I had experienced or even imagined. But Margaret had a smile on her face – she was taking it in her stride.

At that, the door was flung open. My expectations about George being a jolly giant sort of chap were dashed when a diminutive man with a wiry frame stormed in. His white hair was an untidy mass that had been swept to one side and there it remained as if blown by a perpetual storm. His laughter, though, resided in his eyes.

"Did you like THAT?" he boomed. His voice had outgrown the rest of him. "GREAT FUN, isn't it?" He then extended his hand to both of us and shook them vigorously.

"Eric and Margaret, isn't it?" We nodded. "WELCOME, welcome. I hope Bea has made you feel at home."

"Yes, I have George. They thought we had maids and they love the view. You can see Ingleborough today!"

"SPLENDID, SPLENDID! It is good, isn't it? Let's look at the surgery whilst Bea puts on the tea. Fancy a cup?"

Margaret and I both answered in the affirmative. I don't drink tea but I felt that accepting was the easiest thing to do. George led the way down stairs and along the hall away from the front door. We stopped at the arched entrance to another narrow corridor going off to the left. "That's the surgery…my door," George pointed to the brown door to the right of the corridor. "But we'll start in the waiting room down here. In Dr Shields'day, the patients used to ring the bell by the surgery door and a maid would come along this passage to the door to let them in."

At the end of the dimly lit corridor were two doors on the right. Opposite these was a door to the outside, on our left. George opened it with a struggle. It had jammed slightly. The surgery porch was where the other end of the speaking tube emerged. "When I used to do my own dispensing, I used to leave the made-up packages in here to be collected. I had to take the Clayton ones down to the station and put them on a train. A chap picked them up in Clayton and took them to our calling-place. Did Tom tell you about them, Eric?" I nodded. "Bit of a bother really. Don't do much dispensing now, thank goodness."

George slammed the door and opened the one to our right that declared itself the Waiting Room. We stepped inside and Margaret gasped. The room was in darkness as the window still seemed to have blackout curtains shrouding them from the last war. "Patients used to watch Bea in the garden, watched the children as well when they were little. So, we put the curtains up. We've got a light though!" and he switched it on. The green gloss paint was curling in the corners and were covered in faint cracks like roads on a map. An assortment of wooden and cane chairs, of indiscriminate age, lined the room.

"We've also put in a heater. Not much else I'm afraid. Just haven't got round to it. The next man will do something I expect. Cushions, that sort of thing. Modernise. And through THIS door is the sanctum, the surgery." George indicated yet another door.

"Can't the waiting patients hear through the door though?" I asked.

"Oh no. NO! Totally soundproof! Not a THING. And when they have finished the consultation, they go out through the other door in the corridor so they don't have to come back in here. SPLENDID system. One way!"

"And how do you call the next patient?" I asked.

"I'll tell you what. I'll pop into the surgery and you can be my patient." George disappeared. TING! A bell sounded.

"Did you hear that?" George's voice sounded distinctly from the next room, through the 'soundproof door".

"Yes, no problem," I replied.

"Well COME THROUGH, COME THROUGH." George appeared excited.

Margaret and I looked at each other, smiled in resignation and went into the surgery. George sat, beaming, at an old roll top desk to the left; papers were strewn about and bulged out of drawers. A vacant heavy wooden corner chair, its seat needing some radical surgery, was between the desk and the door we had entered. Behind George's chair, underneath the window that overlooked the garden, was a chaise longue. George could see us looking at it.

"Oh, that's the examination couch. Rather splendid, don't you think? Came with the house. I'm sure you could find something a bit more up to date but I just haven't got round to it. It works though."

Cardboard boxes, including a number advertising Bronco toilet paper amongst other things, lined the rest of the walls. They were stuffed with patient records in their manila folders. The filing system relied on letters, written in pencil on the front of the boxes, to help arrange the records in the correct box.

George stood and lovingly stroked the top of his desk. "I'll just show you the dispensary before we have tea." He walked past us and through another arch in the corner.

It was a tiny space lined with glass-fronted cabinets. Bottles of various shapes were housed within, containing their magical powders. Handwritten name labels, sometimes in Latin, were a reminder of their contents. In front of the window at the far end, a small table held a pill making machine, surely a museum piece, and another that compressed powder into tablets. Underneath, two cardboard boxes held clear and brown bottles of different sizes, waiting to be used.

"I haven't done much in here. Hardly use the place now. The next man will modernise it…Ah there's Bea." We could just hear Bea's voice outside the hall door.

The sitting room was redolent of another age. I looked round and saw a brown water stain by the edge of the curved bay window. I was aware of the faint odour of damp and dust. Stuffed furniture vied for space. "Goodness," I said as I looked at the imposing surround to the fireplace. "Are those bells to call the maids?" There was a small handle each side of the fireplace.

"Yes, Eric." Bea exclaimed. "Do you like them?"

"Yes. Erm, yes. It's just that I imagine they're a bit superfluous now."

George nodded, "I know what you mean. We were going to get rid of them when our last maid went. That was during the war but we just haven't got round to it. Next man will do it I expect."

A telephone rang from the hall. "I'll get it, George. You finish pouring the tea and you can carry on talking."

We heard Bea's voice and then she reappeared. "It's Tom, George. He'd like a word with you." As she said this, Bea looked at us. I knew the subject of the conversation. I glanced nervously at Margaret and touched her hand. She smiled back, encouraging. Our futures would depend on the discussions in the hall.

Bea tried to keep us cheerful by prattling away. Her voice drowned George's voice, just discernable through the closed door, to an indistinct murmur. The hot tea was almost welcome.

Silence in the hall smothered our conversation. George came back in, his face glum. My heart, and my head, sank – Guisborough next week.

"Oh, George! Don't be such a tease!" Bea exclaimed.

I looked up. George, smiling, stomped towards us with his hands out. "We both think you'd be perfect here. We'd love to have you. What do you think?"

Our strange trial by the unexpected had been successful.

Chapter 5

I turned up in good time to wait before taking my first surgery in the practice; it was to be the introduction to my future. Bea showed me into the overstuffed sitting room, redolent with memories from that first visit when George had held out his congratulatory hand which had decided the course of our lives.

Margaret and I had accepted the job, and the prospect of taking on Craig-na-Hullie, despite the apparent enormity of the work needed to get the house out of its pre-war state; pre- Great War, we had joked. The partners in the practice near Hull had kindly allowed me to continue in my post until after Ruth was born. She had arrived on time, induced to prevent any recurrence of the problems of Charles' birth.

This had meant that we only had two months to wait before I took over from Angus Morgan. We lived with Margaret's mother and I filled the time helping at a local hospital, which helped eke out our meager finances. We popped over to Queensbury once or twice a week to discuss the practice organization, and the details of the supporting role I would initially play. George and I held these chats in the dining room, which was across the Craig-na-Hullie hallway opposite the sitting room, so we could benefit from the large table and the warmth of the coal fire in the grand inglenook fireplace.

Doctor Blunt took a morning surgery every day of the week, apart from Sundays, from 8.30 to 9.30 and an evening surgery on Monday, Tuesday, Wednesday and Friday from 5.30 to 7.00pm. He had a 'half-day' on a Thursday.

Tom Akroyd had a similar pattern of surgeries, taken in Innisfree, but with a 'half-day' on Wednesdays. These 'half days' started when all the home visits were completed for that day. The off-duty time lasted until 8 o'clock the next morning. Tom also took a surgery in Shelf on four days a week.

As we sat planning at his dining table, George asked me if I would take over the second part of his evening surgeries, from 6 o'clock to 7 o'clock and the whole thing on a Wednesday. I could have Tuesday as my own 'half-day'. I also agreed to take some of Tom's surgeries.

"SPLENDID, splendid!" George always exclaimed at any decision, as if it was momentous, and we celebrated with a slurp of coffee or hot water. This was the usual response to all our plans. Talking with George was always jolly despite the mundanity of the topic.

"I don't want to take any calls after half past five, Eric. If you don't mind, you'll take those and deal with them. Doctors' orders, you know. Must have a rest every afternoon as well. What a bind. Damned doctors, eh?" George smiled and winked.

"That's fine, George. That's why I'm here." I had just agreed to take all George's evening and night calls. Each doctor was on duty every night of the week, for emergency calls from their own patients, except on their half days and weekends off duty. There would be an 'on-duty' weekend every three weeks as we shared these with another, single-man, practice in the village. George wouldn't have any weekend work at all. The 'off-duty' time started after the Saturday surgery and any home visits that had to be made.

It was a heavy workload, but I had known this when I entered the profession. Each practice in the country covered every minute of every day with at least one doctor on duty.

"SPLENDID, splendid!" We had slurped again.

George was sitting opposite me across the fireplace with its redundant bell for summoning long-departed maids. We spent a few minutes amicably chatting before the surgery started.

A few minutes later, Bea came in and interrupted our musings and told George that he was late already. "Well, I must be getting on, Eric. All the best!" George said as he stood to leave for the first half of the surgery. Bea playfully pushed him out. She then left me to my thoughts to make me a cup of hot water, my preferred drink in the afternoons. The room was getting colder. I could just feel a faint glow from the paltry electric fire placed in front of the fireplace. It was fighting a lost battle against the winter cold.

I looked around. The stain by the window had grown since the summer. It had produced a deep brown cauliflower shape embedded in the browned wallpaper. What had we taken on with this place? It could be a lovely house; it had a real solidity and strength. However, everything needed attention. George planned to retire in two and a half years, and this would give us enough time to think things through: what we wanted to do with the place and how to finance it. However, they seemed impossible questions to face just then. I couldn't imagine that we would be able to do work on anything more than the surgery at the start.

I hadn't even looked at the kitchen yet, but I imagined it to be in no better state than the rest of the house. I was sure that Margaret would want that tackled as a priority.

It would be a great house for the children, however. They wouldn't mind the rooms being left in a raw state, they would just be a succession of playrooms to them. And then there were the attic rooms – the maids' bedrooms. My thoughts rambled all over the place.

On her return from the kitchen, Bea rested for a time on the arm of the sofa whilst I sat on the same chair as on my previous visit, holding my water nervously. We talked about our new home, which was a small semi-detached house a few miles down the road towards Bradford.

"So, you've settled in well, Eric?" Bea asked. I felt that she wanted to return to the kitchen but her curiosity, and desire to make me feel welcome, had raised the question.

"Yes, thank you Bea," I answered. "The house is pretty well sorted out now and Margaret loves having more space, especially having a separate room for Charles and the baby. Having a garden is wonderful. She can't wait for the better weather when she'll have somewhere to dry clothes any time."

"It must be nice not living on top of Margaret's mother, as well," Bea went on. I nodded in vigorous agreement.

Sometime later, Bea looked at her watch and said, "Nearly six, Eric. Don't worry, the patients are a funny bunch at times but have hearts of gold when you get to know them. They won't accept you for ages, but don't be put off. I can see that you'll get on well with George. I think he must be on his last patient now, then the rest are yours."

I smiled at Bea. "Thanks for the water. I'm really looking forward to working with George. It's a great way to ease into the practice." Suddenly George stomped in. He was looking distinctly pale and drawn after the exertion of the surgery, but he still seemed to take life at a gallop. He was being treated by a wise doctor, who knew George well, but he had only managed to restrain him a little. I hoped that my presence would make all the difference.

"Right then, Eric. Your turn. Quite a few in tonight. It'll be good for you ... and for them, for that matter. There's Mrs Bartholomew there, I think. I could hear her voice. Comes for nothing much usually, but I suspect that she just likes a chat in the waiting room. Bit of a busy body and I bet she wants to meet the new doctor!" He stood aside with a smile. "Well, good luck, Eric!" He patted my back as I passed.

I went through the hall door into the surgery. I took a deep breath as I looked around. It was an antiquarian muddle and I knew it was always difficult working in someone else's surgery. But this was my first step towards a partnership. I had been working towards this moment for the past eleven years or so, the culmination of all the hard graft and sacrifice. In this room I would meet male and female, old and young - but all at their most vulnerable. Although they didn't know me, yet at least, they would put their trust in me with their lives. There would be hope and tears, fear and elation. I would have to meet them all with dignity and professionalism.

I decided to go through to the waiting room and introduce myself, rather than just ring the bell for the first patient. As I walked across the surgery, past the boxes of records, I heard the distinctive slam of the outside surgery door. I entered the waiting room with my smile of welcome ready, only to find an almost empty room. I looked around somewhat puzzled as the sole occupant stood up.

It was a lady with a double chin and a figure to match. Her eyes and faint moustache were formidable. She was dressed in a thick woollen coat, in assorted brown checks, and a felt hat that looked as if she had sat on it sometime in the past. Stout, wrinkled stockings encased equally sturdy legs. I went towards her. "Hello. I'm Dr Hainsworth and…"

"And ah'm Mrs Bartholomew. Dr Blunt knows me. An' you must be t'young doctor." Mrs Bartholomew's shrill voice, somewhat at odds with her build, brooked no argument.

"Yes, yes," I muttered, trying to inject some warmth into my voice. "I'm sure I'll get to know you as well, Mrs Bartholomew. This is my first surgery. I'm sure that Dr Blunt said there were quite a few in tonight."

"That's right, there were. But they want ter see t'old doctor so they'll be back termorrer."

"Oh, right then. And can I do anything for you?" I was sure that if I made a good impression with Mrs Bartholomew the news would spread quickly.

The lady in question leant towards me and in almost a whisper said, "Ah'm not going yer know!"

"Oh, I'm very pleased to hear that, Mrs Bartholomew. And you can come through to the consulting room right now." I smiled broadly at her. I thought I was winning with her, but her eyebrows had come together and she looked at me as if I was deranged.

We went through and I indicated the solid corner chair whilst I sat on the wooden swivel chair for the first time. This was more like it. "Now that there are no other patients, we've got time to get right to the bottom of the problem."

Mrs Bartholomew sat bolt upright and looked shocked, as though I had insulted her. I went on quickly, trying to sound jolly. "And what seems to be the matter?" I asked, sure of my ability to diagnose.

"Well, ah'm bunged. Right bunged up." Mrs Bartholomew challenged some sort of response from me with her look. As she said these words, she produced a white, starched handkerchief and dabbed her nose. I was sure it was her non-verbal way of telling me the problem. It seemed strange that she was so embarrassed about a blocked nose. It couldn't be bad as her speech seemed normal, but I remembered that George had told me that she often just came to socialise in the waiting room.

I attempted to express sympathy and said, "Ah, a blocked nose, so you're finding it difficult to breathe?"

"Does it affect that as well? Well ah'll be."

"You don't sound too bad at the moment…"

"But ah am, doctor. Ah might'a left wi' t'others but ah had ter see yer. Ah 'aven't gone fer three days an' ah've

93

got this bad pain just 'ere." Mrs Bartholomew rubbed her lower abdomen with her hand.

The whole thing made sense now. "Mrs Bartholomew, you've got constipation!" I exclaimed triumphantly.

"Ah know that, young doctor. Ah've been tryin' ter tell yer ah'm comsitated. Ah just don't like ter say it. All these big words."

"Well, Mrs Bartholomew, we can sort you out. I'll give you some tablets. Fortunately, I have some here. I wouldn't take them tonight though. Take them tomorrow morning. I would have a good cup of warm water before going to bed tonight. Put a bit of baking soda in as well, if you've got some. Or some lemon juice. Have you got any prunes?" She nodded. "They're good as well. Have some for breakfast."

"If it doesn't get better, or comes back quickly, come and see me again. And if you notice blood in your…"

"There's no need ter go into details doctor. Ah know what yer mean." Mrs Bartholomew, smiled for the first time. "And ah was thinkin' you'd be examinin' me, and that would'nt do wi' a young doctor. Ah'll be back if there's blood in ma …ma…"

"It's alright, Mrs Bartholomew. You don't need to say it." I smiled as well.

My first patient looked around at the mess of the consulting room. "Well, ah'm glad that yer 'aven't changed anything! We don't like change here, tha' knows. It worked well for Dr Shields and Dr Blunt."

"Oh, Dr Blunt hasn't left yet. This is his consulting room, but I will be taking some of his surgeries to help him out a bit."

Mrs Bartholomew, her session now over, had resumed her brusque manner. "Well, don't ferget it, young man. We don't like change 'ere. Ah'll be seein' yer."

At that she went out through the door to the passage and I heard the outside door slam. I reclined into the curved wooden back of the antiquated swivel chair and smiled. It had gone well despite the rather embarassing opening. It had been touch-and-go, but she had said that she would be seeing me again. And she had smiled.

I looked for the correct Bronco box, smiling at its appropriateness with the diagnosis, and found the brown manila envelope made plump by a wodge of record cards. I wrote up the notes of this consultation on the latest of these and glanced at her name. Mrs Bartholomew was forty-seven. If she had lived in Queensbury all her life, she would have known Dr Shields. I glanced at the earliest cards in the pack. Yes, there was his handwriting. In fact, I mused, she was the same age as this house.

I reached forward to the bell on the top ledge of the desk. It was a noble thing; the large, brass dome with a brass knob on the top was imperious. It reminded me of ones I had seen in hotel reception desks on the few occasions I had frequented them, mainly with my mother and father. I was pretty sure that there was no one else in the waiting room, but the surgery didn't officially end until seven o'clock and there was no appointment system of any sort. Patients just turned up whenever they wanted during surgery time and, if there were others there already, they just waited their turn. It seemed that the patients had their own queuing system. They sat on the assortment of chairs, the next one in to see the doctor on the one by the surgery door. The others went in order round the room with the last to arrive at the end of this line. As the next patient left for the consulting room, the others would all move around one chair.

I struck the knob with a flourish, announcing to an empty waiting room with a resounding ting that I was open for business. I listened and leaned back. I could see a major problem with this system: I could be sitting here until seven with absolutely nothing to do, waiting for the possible arrival of a patient. I started thinking about what my life here would be like and what changes I would like to see happen despite the supplications of Mrs Bartholomew.

I was sure now that when I took over the house, I would have to remodel the whole surgery. I glanced at the boxed piles of records, evidence of lives sketched out in illnesses. That they were there in the cardboard boxes was testimony to our calling, to heal the sick and, by so doing, help them through their lives. Dr Blunt had served his patients well and I wanted to do the same. The boxes would have to go, though. I would devise a new storage system. As soon as possible, I would also introduce an appointment system. I wondered how I would propose this. Tom would be the senior partner then. Would he accept ideas from me?

I stood up and wandered around. There were one or two sepia prints of the Lake District and a map of New Zealand, for some reason. I straightened them. I carefully opened the door into the hallway. The one light bulb on, in the central fitting, was just enough to define doorways but didn't penetrate much more of the gloom. There were faint, muffled voices though and it sounded as though they were coming from the dining room.

I gently knocked and George's "ENTER at your peril!" invited me in. George had been sitting at the head of the table but now stood to greet me. Bea was placed to his right, facing the blazing fire, which made this room alive and cosy with its dancing glow. They were just going to eat their meal by the look of things.

"Hello, Eric. Don't tell me you've finished already…"

"Well, actually I have. There was only one patient in when I got to the waiting room. The others will be back tomorrow to see the old doctor!"

"Ha! I should have guessed," George said forcefully. "I'm sorry, Eric. They take some time to accept anyone new here. And I bet the one was Mrs Bartholomew?"

I related the whole consultation to George and Bea. They roared when they heard I had promised Mrs Bartholomew to get to the 'bottom' of her problem. George observed, "You won't have done yourself any harm there. She will tell everyone who cares to listen in great detail. She isn't liked much because she's such a busybody but her story will give everyone a good laugh. You'll be reminded of it for weeks to come, you'll see."

Bea was looking round at me with her warm smile, "Why don't you sit down for a time with us? You can have some more hot water. It will while away the time until the end of the surgery."

"Yes, and I want to go through your lists for tomorrow," George added.

I had one port of call before I could take them up on their offer, "Do you mind if I use your toilet before I sit down?"

Bea stood. "Oh, I am remiss. I should have shown you them when you came before. You have a choice. There's the downstairs one or ours upstairs."

A downstairs toilet! That would be convenient - and patients wouldn't need to go upstairs, whenever they needed to use one. "I'll try your downstairs one, I think."

"Ha," laughed George. "Good luck! You might meet Captain Scott on the way!" he added mysteriously.

I followed Bea past the surgery door and through another one at the end of the corridor. "The kitchen's just down there. I didn't have time to take you in there when you came for your interview." Bea pointed down a short passage to the right. "It's a bit old fashioned, I'm afraid. And that door is down to the cellar ... but we go through here." Bea led me into a small room, which was in virtual darkness. It seemed to be a laundry or scullery. I could just make out the shape of a mangle and a stone sink.

"It's out here," said Bea with a flourish as she pulled open a sturdier door – it was the back door of the house to the Artic outside. A cold wind burst its way in impatiently. It swirled around us and attacked our clothes and hair, making them flap in response.

"It's down there, at the bottom of the steps. You turn left and then down another lot. It might be frozen up though. Just check. Could be embarrassing." I shook my head and helped Bea push the door closed.

"I think I might try your other one, Bea!" I said with some feeling.

When I returned to the dining room George was by himself, with a twinkle in his eye, "Discretion the better part of valour, eh, Eric? Bea's just gone to see how the food's coming on and to get you some water. We've got time to look through the lists."

I sat and pulled the chair closer. "Are there any visits tonight, George?"

"No, thank goodness. I'll give you tomorrow's visiting list tonight so you can prepare yourself. You can ask me or Bea where the various houses are – I've got a map as well – when you come at eight tomorrow. If you wouldn't mind going in to the newsagents in Clayton at around half past ten with some prescriptions, I'd be grateful. Pretty well all the visits I've given you are round there and at this end of the village." I was very grateful to George. He was looking after me.

"I'll write the prescriptions tonight after supper. There might be some messages, requests for home visits and things at the newsagents. Anything really. Lots of our patients don't have telephones and this is their way of getting in touch. You'll get to meet Fred. Nice chap – he runs the shop. He knows the patients and sometimes tells me things I might need to know about my patients - trouble at home. Things like that."

"Would you like me to go there every day?"

"If you wouldn't mind. I go around ten thirty every day except Sundays. Clayton is quite close to your house."

"That won't be a problem, George," I smiled.

"Oh, SPLENDID. I can see we'll work together well, Eric."

"Have you other 'calling-places'?"

"I haven't but Tom has one. It's Bradshaw Post Office. He pops in most afternoons. Bit of a trek for him."

"Are there any problems I should know about with the calls?

"Nothing much really. I've put a star by them if they are repeat visits. They're all pretty straightforward but I'm concerned about this one. It's a new visit." George pushed a piece of paper towards me with names, addresses and reasons for the visit written in George's rough copperplate. "Here," he pointed. "Emily Barrett. She's a tough old biddy, eighty-two this year. It won't be just anything. She says she's getting breathless easily. Needs looking at. You'll like Emily though."

Leaving the Blunts to their meal, I returned to the surgery to peruse the list whilst waiting for any latecomers. None appeared. I decided that I would adopt my previous system with visiting lists: written in two books rather than sheets of paper, both books identical. In Margaret's I wrote any telephone numbers of any of the patients with a telephone as well as the approximate time of the visit, so that she would have some idea where I was. I would take the other on my rounds. If a late call came in, she could telephone anyone on the list to pass on a message. The book became a permanent and useful record of my visits over the year. I resolved to try and write the list up every evening before bed.

I turned up at Craig-na-Hullie the following day just before eight. The clouds had cleared overnight and the air, under a fragile blue dome of a sky, almost cracked with crisp coldness. I decided to walk round to the back door of the house. Once again, I left the car parked on the roadside and walked down the short, gravelled drive that followed a curved wall. As the drive went through empty gateposts into a cobbled yard, I stopped. There was an overgrown path falling away from the drive, down a steep hill. I remembered the view from our interview visit to the house in the previous summer. It was magnificent again today, seen more clearly as the trees to the left, behind the garage, were bare of leaves. It reached into, and refreshed, my soul.

I walked through the yard, past the stone-built garage to my right. It seemed to have a stable at the far end with a stable door, which was closed. There were bleak, cold steps leading up to a black door. This was the door, I recognised, which Bea had opened the previous night. I looked around and could see the steps she had told me about that descended into the downstairs toilet. I wondered, as I ascended to the entrance to the house, if I would ever use the outside 'facilities'! They were formidable!

After banging the door, I glanced round as I waited for it to be opened. The garage was quite a large building in its own right. There was a strange door near the top of the front wall. I could just see over the moveable, wooden fence into the back garden. Margaret would love to tackle that when we moved in, her own garden at last. My mind just wouldn't stop wondering how we would change the place when we moved in.

"Oh, hello, Eric," Bea beamed as she opened the door. "You didn't need to knock. Just come in. We're in the kitchen. George is just filling the range."

I followed Bea through the scullery. I was right. There was the sink and the mangle. The latter was ancient with its worn wooden rollers and large cast-iron handle. The kitchen was warm, at least. The overall impression was of a geriatric space struggling to maintain its life. A Belfast sink, with chipped edges and enormous dull brass taps, was standing in front of the window between two well-scrubbed bare timber draining boards. Various random cupboards and deal tables lined the room. At the far end was a wooden panelled wall, painted in the wood-grain effect that was ubiquitous to all the house's woodwork. Set in the wall were two doors, shabby now after forty-nine years without any redecoration, and a bell board between them. The maids had left years before, summoned by more interesting lives, but the board remained.

George stood up. He had been shovelling coal into the living monster of a range. Its leaded blackness dominated the room. He wiped his hands on a cloth and shook mine with a vigorous welcome. "Hello, hello, Eric. Welcome to your second day and I don't think you'll be seeing Mrs Bartholomew again – well, just yet. Any problems with the list?" He swept his hair back from his forehead.

"No, thank you, George. I'm grateful for the map and I'll be able to ask if I get lost. I'll set off straight away in case I have problems. Have you got the prescriptions for Clayton?"

"Yes, they're in the surgery. I'll pop and get them."

Whilst George was out, Bea indicated the room with a sweep of her hand, "I'm afraid it's all rather old fashioned, Eric. We had hoped to do things, but we never seemed to get round to it. Then George had his two heart attacks. I expect that Margaret would like to change it a little."

I followed Bea's hand with my eyes. "How right you are, Bea," I thought, but just nodded agreement.

The morning's visits went without any problems and I enjoyed making first contact with my patients and introducing myself. Most were very warm and friendly. Some were wary about young, new blood coming into the practice but most welcomed it. If I had accepted every cup of tea I was offered, I would have sloshed my way round Clayton rather than just driven.

It was just after half past ten when I pulled up outside Benson's Newsagents. I had seen this little shop on my rounds earlier that morning. It was built in the universal smoke-soiled sandstone with stone tiles on the roof. To exercise some sort of uniqueness the stone window surround had been painted white and the legend, "BENSON'S NEWSAGENT" sign-written on the top surface. A bell above the door tinkled a welcome as I entered. Newspapers and magazines were displayed on shelves round the customer area with one or two items of stationery on a separate stand. A wooden counter, with a trapdoor inserted, cut the shop in half and behind it a man was standing with both hands firmly pressed down on the counter top. This was, no doubt, Fred Benson.

"'Ello there, 'ello. Ah don't think we've seen yer in these parts afore. Can ah help yer?" The man was quite thin but had a well-rounded tummy that pressed into the counter top. His face was a picture of jollity. Eyes smiled above a rather large and red nose. Grey hair receded from a wrinkled brow. I was sure all these were smile lines. His frame was wrapped in a dun-coloured coat. Behind him, proudly displayed in rows of glass jars with black screw tops, was the stuff of children's dreams and memories. Sweets that could be exchanged for precious pocket money advertised themselves through the glass. I remembered many of the varieties from my own childhood and still relished the ritual of the choosing, the jar unscrewing, the sour, sweet odour escaping and the weighing out in the large brass bowl on the scales before being tipped into a white paper bag that would then be sealed by being flicked with a swift somersault that twisted the corners to seal the top.

"I'm afraid I'm not buying today, although the sweets do look tempting... I'm Dr Hainsworth. I'm the new doctor with Dr Blunt..."

"Ah, pleased ter see yer, doctor. I'm Fred. Yes, Dr Blunt leaves prescriptions here an' ah pass on messages from patients. It's grand ter see you. Ah can tell by yer voice that yer from round 'ere an' all." Fred Benson spread smiles and bonhomie with abandon.

"Oh, yes," I replied. "I was brought up in Halifax. Call me Eric, by the way. Here are the prescriptions." I handed three slips of paper over. "Are there any messages?"

"Jus' t'one today, Eric. It's from Mrs Robinson." Fred passed me an old envelope that had been folded over at the top. "Dr Blunt knows her."

I looked around again, tempting temptation. "Oh, go on then, Fred. I'll take a packet of Spangles for my rounds." Fred smiled.

My last visit before lunch was going to be Emily Barrett. She lived near an ancient coaching inn, 'The Old Dolphin', that was situated between Bradford and Queensbury. I had noticed this blackened building, misshapen with age, on my adolescent journeys. I was later to find that it was already called by that name in 1647 when it was used as a billet by some of Cromwell's troops. This was, of course, before stagecoaches existed. I was intrigued by the place and, over my years in the practice I gradually got to know it well.

Emily had the end house in a terrace built in the 1930s across the road from the inn. They were fine houses with ample gardens at the front. Emily's was larger, being on the end of the terrace. As I opened the well-maintained gate I saw, out of the corner of my eye, a face looking at me from the base of the hedge. This was unnerving enough to make me stop and bend down for a better examination. Indeed, it was a face but very crudely carved in stone made dark and green by the years. Its features were stylized but distinct: two almond eyes, a stub nose and slightly protruding lips. I looked at it further and felt that it was very old. I hadn't seen the like before and I wondered how it had ended up in Emily's hedge. I determined to find out.

I knocked on the front door, immaculate in its black shiny paint. I waited for a while but no one opened the door. I was just about to knock again when it was slowly opened from within. An old lady stood before me, carefully turned out in a floral dress, rather at odds with the season. She had a presence despite her small stature and smiled through her round rimmed spectacles. She had a walking stick in her free hand. She stood and waited. I responded in like manner, rather tongue-tied. Eventually I said the first thing that came into my head, "Oh, hello. Erm, I was just examining your bust …"

The lady looked aghast. I wanted to ingratiate myself to her so hurriedly continued, "Well, it's just magnificent!"

Emily's whole demeanour changed and she raised her stick in a determined grasp. I thought she might use it as a weapon for some reason.

I hurried to explain and pointed out into the garden, "Your stone head, out there at the bottom of your hedge. It's just wonderful."

I turned to see Emily's countenance alter once again as her body melted into laughter. Chuckles competed with her shortness of breath. I suddenly realised I hadn't introduced myself, "Oh, I'm Dr Hainsworth. I'm the new doctor and I'm working alongside Dr Blunt." For some reason this statement set of another round of Emily's chuckles.

Emily's shortness of breath came to my rescue and I stepped forward when I could see her getting distressed. "Come in, come in, doctor," she wheezed, almost soundlessly. I helped her along the short hallway and into a back room that initially may have been a dining room, but was now a sewing room. Despite the colour of the woodwork, brown and green as used for camouflage in the war, and the age spotted wallpaper, the impression the house made on my quick glance around was of care and neatness. I assisted Emily onto a dining chair and waited whilst she battled to draw air into her lungs. Her face had gone pale.

"I can see what the matter is, Miss Barrett..."

"Mrs!" Emily breathed and pointed with her stick to the fireplace. The surround, covered in swirly green tiles, supported a variety of sepia and black and white photographs in old frames on the mantelpiece. In the centre, proud in its place, was a larger picture of a handsome man in Great War uniform. He was staring into the room with self-confidence. "My Edward," Emily whispered.

Gradually Emily's breathing became less laboured. I said, "Mrs Barrett, your breathlessness could be caused by a number of things but I'll need to listen to your chest. Could you lower the top part of your dress, please?"

Emily nodded and started to undo the buttons down her front. I opened my bag and extracted the stethoscope. I hoped that my initial hunch would not be proved correct. After Emily had pulled her arms out of the dress sleeves, I listened to the secret sounds of the rhythm of life struggling in her chest. The breathing sounds were fainter than normal and I heard a faint crackle. I spent time listening, and thinking through the messages that these noises were communicating.

"Thank you, Mrs Barrett. You can get dressed again. I think I know the problem." I tried to be cheerful as I pulled up another dining chair to sit opposite Emily.

"Well, what is it, doctor? Is it bad? I thought I might be getting bronchitis." Emily looked at me with the slightly haunted expression that was becoming very familiar to me as patients waited for the verdict that would decide their future lives.

"No, Mrs Barrett, it isn't bronchitis. I am pretty sure it's something called emphysema. This is when the little air sacks in your lungs get too large and harden. We've got fluid filled spaces round our lungs called interstitial spaces. Doctors think that air can get into these spaces when you have emphysema," I explained gently but with a heavy heart, knowing what the next question would be.

"Can it be cured then, doctor?"

"I'm afraid not…at the moment. You haven't got it too badly and if you are careful, you should be able to get on with a lot of things. You don't smoke do you?"

Emily looked horrified, "Not on your life, doctor. Thank you for telling me straight. I prefer it that way." Emily stared at me and her face cleared of its clouds as she chuckled once again. "Well, doctor. What do you think of my bust now? Edward used to think it rather magnificent!" Chuckles turned to laughter, and I joined her.

On leaving Emily's I drove home for lunch. I related all the morning's events to Margaret. She also laughed when I told her about Emily. "Oh Eric! You have made a memorable impression here and you haven't been working for a whole day yet. I think I have lost you to the ladies of Queensbury already."

Chapter 6

George looked at me and smiled. "I knew it wouldn't take you long to settle down and fit in, Eric." We had assumed a comfortable routine of working together; without any serious discussion the structure of our days had just emerged. After that initial introduction into practice life, we met in Craig-na-Hullie's kitchen, following morning surgery rather than the more formal dining room – a sign of my growing acceptance. It was a homely place and was also where I waited, every evening, before taking over from George. It was about a month after that first, memorable surgery and George and I were sitting facing each other across the scrubbed deal table in the middle of the room surrounded by aged muddle and our morning coffee.

We hadn't got much to discuss that morning. Suddenly, George's eyes creased and twinkled over his coffee, "They're all talking about you, you know. They seem to like you. Every patient this morning wanted me to get to the bottom of their problem! Even after these few weeks they still say it and laugh."

I groaned. "Oh, no. They're not saying it to you as well. It's been a month since it happened after all and they're still saying the same to me…"

"Best thing you did, Eric. They don't like Mrs Bartholomew really and the silly woman has told virtually everyone who will listen about that first surgery. They all want to come to yours now. They call you 't'young doctor', you know!" He knew I was unconvinced though so added, "Honestly, you'll see. I know these folk."

"If you haven't anything better to talk about, George, move your body. I need the table," Bea interrupted.

"We don't need to get going just yet, Eric. Why don't I show you round the rest of our domain? You haven't seen it all yet, have you?" I shook my head. Margaret and I only had a cursory look upstairs on our first visit during the interview. Since then, I had got to know the kitchen and dining room well. Those rooms, and the upstairs toilet, were now familiar. The very jaded state they were in was probably replicated everywhere. The place evoked memories of nearly fifty years of doctoring, and I was excited to explore those other closed doors and meet more of the past. I agreed to George's invitation eagerly.

Bea turned from the sink and said, "Why don't you take Eric up the maids' stairs and into the attic. That'll be a good place to start."

"Good idea, Bea." We got up and George indicated a door in the painted wood-effect panelling at the end of the kitchen. "They, that's the maids, didn't use the main stairs. They came down here." He opened the door and went through. There was a small window to the left, the panes clouded with dust and redundant spiders' webs. Its faded light revealed a jumble of redundant objects that were stored on the bare wooden steps in front of us: pans and cake boxes. George was negotiating them as he climbed the stairs. I followed.

The door at the top opened into the short corridor that led to the familiar toilet. This was one of those mysteries answered. I now knew what was behind one of the mystery doors. George crossed over the corridor to another flight of stairs. Bea had shown them to us on our first visit and I wondered about them on my travels to the toilet. I had never seen a maid's room. Having been brought up in a small terraced house in Halifax such things were almost beyond my comprehension.

The stairs carpet was a threadbare, but the banister rail was of the same fine molding as the main staircase. There were three doors leading off the landing at the top. I reached for the nearest. "DON'T, ERIC!" George moved to intercept. "We don't go in there. It was Frank's room, our son, and he died in there…" George's voice and demeanour epitomised the still raw sadness. This was a new side to George and Bea's lives that was surprising. He had always given the impression of facing everything with jollity and having been unaffected by life's tragedies. I later learned that Frank had committed suicide, aged seventeen. As a new parent, I understood something of the grief and pain which must have resided as a hard kernel in George's and Bea's hearts.

George interrupted his own memories by flinging open one of the other doors. "And this is where some maids slept, probably two." The room was dull and drab, the window small; set up high. The slope of the roof cut into the space leaving walls three feet high. Both they and the angled ceiling were pale blue distempered. It was larger than I thought it would be – large enough for a train set, which I added to my immature plans.

We stood together looking around, George seeming to notice the place anew, my imagination pushing past the mounds of clutter: piles of old, ancient, magazines, a battered trunk and leather suitcases displaying tattered destination labels and one marked 'Luggage in Advance.
"So, the maids went in the war?" I asked.

"Yes. I think Dr Shields had three or four at the beginning – that was in 1909 when the house was built. We could only stretch to two in 1924, but when the war started there was only Ethel left. She went home when her brother was killed. We didn't replace her."

"Oh, so Dr Shields first came in 1909?"

"No, he bought the practice in 1900. He used to go round his house visits on a bicycle in those days but when he built this place, he had a horse and trap." George was leading the way back downstairs, away from the cold and the memories.

"That would mean he had someone to drive him… and to look after the horse?" I was wondering out aloud as I asked the question. "But he wouldn't sleep up there, would he …with the maids?"

"No, no, Eric. A chap lived across the road in one of those small houses. The last one was called Fred. He was my patient when I first arrived and he told me some tales. Fascinating really." George stopped half way down the main staircase to better emphasise the story. He was framed by winter light intruding through the art nouveau colours of the window that Margaret had so admired "What a palaver when Dr Shields had to go on a night call. He would ring for a maid who had to get up and get dressed. She would then go across the road for Fred who then had to also get dressed…"

"Ha," I laughed. "I bet the maids didn't like that! They'd have to get up early every day, anyway, to get the house going."

"Yes, Fred told me that one morning the Shields woke up to a cold house. There wasn't a sound anywhere. They thought the maids must have slept through so Mrs Shields donned her dressing gown and went up to the maids' rooms. No one was there. The whole lot of them had done a midnight flit. They'd cleared off with the few possessions they had."

"My, they must have been fed up. Did Fred give up?"

"Not then. But the Shields bought their first car soon after. I think it was an Arrol-Johnston, built up in Scotland, I believe. Fred was his first chauffeur. I'll show you the garage where they kept the car. He never passed a test though!"

"I bet Fred was pleased. It's hard work looking after a horse."

"You're right, but not only that, poor Fred had to stay sitting on the trap all the time Dr Shields was in the patient's house. In all weathers… and it can get a mite cold up here." I nodded; the weather was windy and biting that January and I was still getting used to it. "Sometimes he would be covered in snow by the time Dr Shields came out ready to go home. Poor chap got pneumonia twice."

"Cripes, that was serious… "

"He knew a good doctor though! I hope he got free treatment." George laughed as we resumed our descent.

As we walked past the surgery door George said, "Before we go and look in the garage we'll pop down into the cellar. It's amazing down there. You won't have seen anything like it."

The cellar door was by the kitchen. Cold stone steps led down into the dark below, a gloom hardly dissipated when George switched on a light. We turned left into a black space, eyes struggling to discern anything. "The coal used to come down here through a chute from the yard, but we've had it blocked off. Let in water. There's a kind of coke-fired heater here as well. The coachman used to keep it stoked – it was the height of modernity when the house was built." I peered into the blackness. My respect for Fred grew.

"Hot air from it went under the floorboards and out of gratings in the downstairs rooms," George continued.

"That sounds like a good idea," I said, warming to the subject.

"Well, in theory. Apparently, it blew out a fine dust as well so they stopped using it. Bit of a faff all round. And in here," we walked into the next section. "This is where we keep food cool."

There was a stone shelf along a wall and a cupboard with a mesh screen. Covered cakes and a half eaten joint jostled with rusty paint tins. A large leg of ham, minus slices, hung from a hook in a joist. George saw me admiring it. "Now that's a Christmas present from a patient. Mr Soames. He used to be a farmer but he still keeps a pig even in his retirement. He can't get used to not paying for my services and he thinks I just don't charge him. He gives me a ham every year. He won't let me refuse it. I tried it once and he looked devastated."

George noticed my look, "Oh, I'm sure that he'll do the same for you when you take over. He's knocking on a bit, though, so I can't imagine he'll be keeping pigs too much longer. Come and have a look at this though."

We went back up the steps, out of the gloom, but half way up George stopped by a small door on the left, half way up the wall. He opened it to reveal a further room with a rough floor, only around two feet high, extending under the hall floor. "There. Bet you've never seen anything like that, Eric."

"Erm, no," I muttered. "What in the world is it for?"

"I think it was to access the old underfloor heating system, to clean it. I use it for oil lamps." George peered proudly into the surprising depths oblivious to my incredulity.

"Oil lamps? Do you need to light the place?'

"No, Eric. Just for the heat. On cold nights I crawl in there and light them. Great fun. It's a bit like caving. When I first started doing it, I could really give Bea's guests a shock, I can tell you. Made some of them scream when I made groaning noises! Great fun! They've all rumbled it now, unfortunately."

"So, you crawl in there and light them?" I asked, shocked myself.

"Yes, that's right. You can just see two of them from here. The others are under the dining room and sitting room. Great fun. I think it makes a difference as well. Bit of one, anyway." It looked as if George was preparing for another caving expedition. I restrained him.

"But isn't it a bit dangerous? You know, fire."

"Oh, I light the furthest ones first so I don't knock over any that are lit. No problem. Just a bit cramped and dusty! Bea gets in a bit of a tizz about it. Can't understand why."

I glanced down at my watch. "Good grief, George, look at the time. We've got to get on. I've got a few visits before I get to Clayton Newsagents."

"My first is the Ramsbottoms," George pulled a face that matched the tone of his voice.

"Oh, problems?" I asked.

"I know I shouldn't rise to it, but they just rile me somehow. Two brothers. They live just down the road. They think that with the new NHS that they own me somehow. I'll keep seeing them 'til I go, so don't worry. You'll get to know them soon enough though. Hey ho. We'd better be off. We'll look in the garage another time. Fascinating. All part of the story."

We climbed the steps. "Bye, Bea," I called. "See you before evening surgery!"

"Bye, Eric. Have a good day!" a disembodied voice called out from the kitchen. I was part of the life of the practice now, part of the Blunt's lives. Her non-appearance to acknowledge my departure reflected my growing familiarity.

I managed to get home for lunch every day. Margaret had long been resigned to its timing being dependent on the length of the morning visits. She gave Charles his lunch at the same time every day, but ate her own with me. We were both eager to catch up with news especially when everything was so novel. Angus had rented a small semi-detached house on an estate of identical houses and we had taken it on when we joined the practice. For us though, after our Hull flat, it was palatial. There was room for our odd assortment of furniture, garnered over our years of marriage. They ranged from some rather lovely dark oak items, totally out of fashion at the time, given to us from our place in Bowness, to Margaret's electrical appliances, all of which she could now use. And there was an outside!

We knew that we would be in the house for about two and a half years so Margaret planned our life there, especially doing the garden. For her this was a delightful luxury after our years of temporary turmoil in various abodes. There was a patch of lawn at the front but a larger area at the back, behind and to the side of the cramped garage. Every living plant, to survive the winter, had hunkered down to a dull green stasis when we moved in, but this respite enabled plans to be made at leisure and refined.

During the course of our residency there, any delay in my arrival for lunch was mainly due to the vagaries of patients. There were occasions though when other factors intervened. One time, just before we moved to Craig-na-Hullie, the children had discovered the delight of blowing bubbles. On my way home for lunch, one day, I was met at the top of the hill, where our road started, by a host of the things bunched together and bouncing in the breeze, held by some sort of meteorological anomaly at ground level. Ruth and Charles, aided and abetted by their mother, had discovered that Stergene, a washing liquid, made good, strong bubbles. My family had made an unplanned welcoming committee.

The road, which was lined by the identical semi-detached houses like our own, was a rough and crumbling concrete affair when we arrived. The local authority eventually came round to resurfacing it with tarmacadam. It was an exciting time for our children as a steam-roller was employed alongside a team of men. It was an 'exciting' time for Margaret and me as it was, unintentionally, Ruth's first venture away from the garden without her mother.

I had to leave the car in a parallel road to ours and complete my homeward journey on foot. I assumed that the children would be well on with their lunch, but couldn't hear any of the usual noise that children seem so adept at producing, as I entered through the back door. Margaret was in the kitchen stirring something on the gas cooker. "Hello, darling. Nice to see you!"

"Hello, love. Where are the children? I thought they'd be here eating by now." I put my bag down and took off my coat in preparation for my ritual hand washing.

"No, we thought we'd wait today. They wanted to watch the men in the road. They should be by the gate. Didn't you see them?"

"No, they weren't there…" We both looked at each other, silently communicating fear in our symmetrical expressions. I grabbed my coat again. "You look around the house first, then the garden. You never know. I'll go into the road. I'm sure they won't be far."

I hadn't passed the children on my way from the car so, attempting to reduce my pace to calmness, I turned right towards the clanking monster of a machine, puffing in exhaustion. Almost immediately I saw them: two small spectators standing at the side of the road, wrapped in familiar clothes. Ruth was standing on a mound, I presumed to get a better view. Relief at the sight overwhelmed my thoughts of the 'telling off' that I planned. "Hello, you two," I shouted cheerily and waved.

They turned, waved back innocently and ran towards me, shouting greetings. I scooped Ruth up and carried her home whilst Charles started a garbled description of the morning's entertainment. We met Margaret as she was leaving the front door.

"Oh, thank goodness. Where did you find them?"

I was just about to reply when Margaret continued, "Eric, what have you done with Ruth's wellies?"

I looked down to make sure that the miscreant wellingtons hadn't landed at my feet there. No, not a boot in sight. "We'll just retrace our steps. They must have fallen off on the way home! At least the children are all right!"

We found them, stuck firm at the top of the tarmacadam viewing mound that Ruth had found so convenient.

Over lunch, Margaret and I would exchange our news. Hers gradually moved away from plans for the house and people met, to developmental 'firsts' in our children's lives. A memorable, if unconventional, stage was reached by Charles a few days later.

We were eating our lunch together when the telephone rang. "I'll get it, Eric," Margaret said as she pushed her chair back. Margaret was my unofficial receptionist and took all calls. She went through to the sitting room where the telephone was stationed. Her normal speaking voice, muffled by the wall and doors, was replaced by laughter.

She was still laughing when she returned. "Who was that?" I asked, intrigued.

"Oh, it wasn't a call," she said as she sat down. "It was Mrs Jennings, next door…" more laugher erupted, disrupting Margaret's report. She looked at Charles, "Have you been playing out with Brenda this morning?"

Charles looked up from his food. "Yes, mummy." He was starting to blush, a sure sign that the story might not involve total innocence.

Brenda was the Jennings only child and was always dressed like a princess even for 'playing out'. Margaret laughed again. "What's the matter? What's happened?" I asked.

"Well, apparently Brenda arrived home for lunch with wet knickers. It has taken her some time to get Brenda to tell her why. Apparently, Charles has been trying to teach her to wee like a boy..."

Charles, now bright red, said in self-defence, "She wanted me to. Behind the garage. It wasn't my fault. She wouldn't do all the things I told her..." Margaret and I burst out laughing leaving Charles wondering about the strange things which grown-ups thought funny, and why weeing for girls was so difficult whilst standing up against a wall.

It was during one of these lunchtime conversations when I told Margaret about my exploration of Craig-na-Hullie. Like me, Margaret was horrified at the thought of oil lamps being lit under the ground floors of a property which one day would be ours. As well as the risk to the house there was the extreme danger to George. "I don't think you'll change him," I said as Margaret finished her initial tirade. "He seems to relish going down there. We'll just have to make sure that we buy the place in summer so there won't be any last-minute hitches or fires, and hope for the best before then."

The telephone rang. I heard Margaret speak as she answered it, "Oh, it's you George. Eric was just telling me that you'd shown him round the house a bit more this morning. He found it fascinating…. Yes, yes, I'll just get him."

I started to get out of my seat. It was a Thursday, George's half-day. It was an agreement that on our half-days we would take calls until mid-day and make the visit that day if one was needed, even if this eroded our time off considerably. After twelve o'clock calls were telephoned to the doctors left on-duty. I thought I wouldn't hear from George again today so this was puzzling. I met Margaret at the door. "That was George," she said.

"Yes, I heard."

"Still alive then!" Margaret's eyes twinkled as she smiled.

"Hello, George. Any problems?" I spoke into the receiver.

"No, no, Eric. I don't think so, at least. Got a call just before twelve. Would have done it myself but thought you might like it after our chat this morning. Chap called Bill Barnes. He used to work in a quarry and he remembers Craig-na-Hullie being built. He's got loads of stories. Has terrible osteoarthritis and now has lung cancer. Used to smoke like a chimney. He's in a lot of discomfort. I'll still go, if you want, Eric."

It took a moment to decide, "No, George, I'll do it. Should be interesting and my list is light this afternoon. Where does he live?"

"At the top of the High Street round the back of the chippie there." He gave me the street and number.

"I know, opposite the Granby."

"That's right. Thanks, Eric. Tell me how you got on when we chat tomorrow."

Fortunately, the few visits I had that afternoon were routine: all return visits and no new ones. The return visits were arranged at the end of a previous home appointment. They were used to monitor the general health of patients with a chronic illness or monitor courses of treatment. Generally, diagnoses and decisions had already been made so some of these calls were very brief, often the main benefit being of emotional support, especially for old people. Sometimes I arranged to meet the District Nurse or Health Visitor at patients' houses, but I had no such meetings this afternoon.

It was another crisp winter day. We had been very blessed with fine weather so far and Bea was overjoyed at the expansiveness and clarity of the views from Craig-na-Hullie kitchen windows. George was just grateful for the lack of digging out, whilst I was being lulled into a sense that this was normal, not having experienced anything the high Pennines could inflict in winter yet. So, it was with lightness in my heart that I drove back from my penultimate house call of the afternoon past 'The Old Raggalds Inn" on the Denholme road. Sight of this inn announced the closeness of the village, and the road then went over the hill at Mountain before descending to the crossroads by the mill.

I felt a oneness with the place now. It hadn't taken long to find my way around and relate my new knowledge to the vague memories of my adolescent bus journeys. I could get around without too many stops for enquiries and the frosty reception of that first surgery just a few weeks ago was thawing nicely. I was commonly referred to as 'T'young doctor' or 'T'new doctor', but patients wanted to see me now.

I turned right at the mill and headed up the High Street. The village was not, in any way, picturesque, but I was starting to understand the sentiment of the place. It certainly wasn't in any beauty. It was deeper, embedded in the gritty community. The buildings were Victorian, in the main, and utilitarian. The mill, not only at the middle of the village geographically, was the centre of its being, economically and emotionally.

Radiating from it, roads reached out to distant towns and from these main roads, streets of terraced houses, many of them 'two up and two down', were built at right-angles to the main thoroughfare. Cobbles were laid at the entrance of each street. but only for a few feet. From then on, the roadways of these side-roads were compacted earth, which eroded away over time to expose rocks and stones. The street names reflected their Victorian ancestry: Great Street, Northern Street, Railway Street, Raglan Street, Cardigan Street, Campbell Street. The latter three I recognised as names of commanders in the Crimean War. Those houses must have been built at that time, I thought. Across each street were strung permanent washing lines, mostly adorned on Mondays. There was a fierce pride in each mean dwelling. The steps that led straight from the house door onto the pavements, were scrubbed and their edges then finished with a white or pale-yellow marking block whilst they were still wet.

Bill Barnes lived in one such street. His house was in the middle of a terrace so I parked on the main road, not daring to risk the car on the uneven surface leading to his front door. Children were playing in the street despite the cold, having been shooed out from their cramped houses. I stood waiting, after my initial knock on the smart, dark blue door. I always wondered if I should knock and then march straight in, rather than wait for shuffling footsteps to open the door from within. I had got into a habit of observing the state of the building, whilst standing for those footsteps to emerge. This house was well maintained and looked after. The brasswork on the door gleamed.

The door opened with a flourish. I gasped. I was expecting a shambling old man, but the beaming smile belonged to a woman, probably in her late forties. Her body was trim and muscular, and tall. It was encased in a neat overall. Clear brown eyes were set in a strong face, her age mainly betrayed by the grey, almost white hair, cut into an out-of-fashion bob.

"Oh, I'm sorry," I muttered. "I must have got the wrong house. I'm looking for Mr Barnes. Bill Barnes. Can you tell me where he lives?"

"Nay, you've got t'right 'ouse. Ah'm 'is daughter, Edith. You must be t'new doctor. Dr Blunt said you'd be comin'." I nodded, still slightly taken aback. "Well, come in then."

I stepped straight into the sitting room. Once again, I was struck by the clean neatness of the tiny space. A clock ticked magisterially on a crushed velvet cloth, which covered a small side-table.

A man, silent apart from the wheeze of laboured breath, sat upright in the only armchair. His clothes seemed to hang like shrouds on his skeletal frame, which must have been large at one time. Grizzled white hair was cut short and, despite the careworn, pain-wracked skin, gave him a dignified handsomeness. His eyes, though, were pulled back into the shadow under his tangle of eyebrows by deep pain. They looked at me. "Well, come in young man. Teck a seat." His immense hands, distorted and twisted by arthritis rose from their place on his knees and indicated two dining chairs.

Edith closed the door and pulled a velvet curtain across it to exclude any draft that might try and intrude. "DAD," her voice was strong but not quite a shout. "IT'S T'NEW DOCTOR, DR 'AINSWORTH, THAT'S COME TER SEE YER."

"Right, right…" wheezed Bill.

Edith turned to me as she patted her father's hand. "Ah look after me dad now. Ah live just across by t'Granby an' it's just me an' me 'usband now so ah come 'ere a lot. Dad loved us an' did for us when we were younger so it's ma turn now, IN'T IT, DAD?"

"You certainly look after the place," I said.

"Well, 'e an' mum kept it spankin' like. Ah just do what they did. Would yer like a cup o'tea?"

"Erm, no thanks," but then I reconsidered. I hoped to be here a little longer than usual if Bill was up to it. "Actually, Edith, can I have a cup of hot water?"

"'Ot water! Yer mean wi' nout in it?"

I nodded. Edith looked aghast, she had probably never met anyone who didn't drink tea before, but went through to the miniscule kitchen without further comment. I was becoming aware that tea lubricated Queensbury and kept it going.

I turned to my patient, "Well, Bill, how are things?"

Bill looked at me, "What's tha', doctor?"

"HOW ARE THINGS?" I raised my voice to Edith's volume.

"Nay, lad. Can't complain," Bill said firmly.

"OH DAD!' a disembodied voice emerged from the kitchen. "YOU TELL 'IM. THAT'S WHY 'E'S 'ERE." Then added for my benefit, "T'pain's gettin' right bad, doctor. In 'is chest."

"SO, YOU HAVE A PAIN IN YOUR CHEST, BILL?"

"Aye, lad. Can't sleep fer it. It's in 'ere," Bill raised his right hand again. The paper-thin white skin, covered in aged liver spots, was shrunken around the gnarled bones and bulbous knuckles. He indicated his lower left thorax with a swirling motion.

"I'M GOING TO HAVE TO EXAMINE YOU, BILL," I said.

Edith returned with two cups and saucers. "I'll help, doctor." She put the cups down by the clock and we pulled up Bill's shirt to reveal a hollowed chest, seemingly bereft of any flesh under that thin, pale skin, hidden in a slightly grey vest. I listened to secret noises and took Bill's blood pressure. Life was tenacious but obviously ebbing away. I could help Bill face the process of its passing by relieving the pain.

"I THINK MORPHINE WOULD HELP YOU A LOT, BILL. I'LL LET NURSE SULLIVAN KNOW AS SOON AS I LEAVE. SHE MIGHT POP IN THIS EVENING OR TOMORROW. SHE GIVES IT BY INJECTION, BILL. DO YOU KNOW HER?"

"Aye, lad. Grand lass that. Been in t'village fer seven year now. Ah helped build that there bungalow she lives in. 1925 it were."

I had only met June Sullivan once, and then only briefly. However, I knew her by her formidable reputation. She lived just by Innisfree so was very much part of the village in many ways. She was the District Nurse. The village had another nurse, Mercy Brookes, who had set up as a private nurse in 1916 and was still around. I hoped get to know June very well and develop a good working relationship with her.

"SO, YOU BUILT HOUSES, DID YOU BILL?" I almost shouted as I sipped my water. I was trying to steer Bill onto a story about Craig-na-Hullie.

"Well, not build 'em. Ah just helped…"

"OH DAD, YER DID MORE THAN THAT," Edith interrupted. She turned to me, "Dad, was a giant of a man. Could lift anything. They were allus sayin' 'GET BILLY BARNES!' WEREN'T THEY, DAD? 'E was worth two other men!" Edith looked at her father with pride in her eyes and stroked his arm.

"DID YOU HELP WITH CRAIG-NA-HULLIE? YOU KNOW, THE DOCTOR'S HOUSE ON SANDBEDS. DR SHIELDS HAD IT BUILT," I asked.

"Ah remember it well, lad. It were a few year afore t'war, T'fust un." Bill stopped to wheeze his breath back. "Ah didn't help build that'un. Ah was workin' at t'quarry darn Catherine Slack way, on t'way t'Alifax." Wheezes intervened again. "Cut most o' t'stone fer it though. Lovely stone, it is. Dust tha' know the name-stone in t'wall?"

I nodded. I had seen the carved stone embedded in the front wall by the main gate. It was large and proclaimed the name of the house in clear art nouveaux lettering. "YES, BILL. IT'S STILL THERE!"

"Well, young man. Ah lifted that. Put it into a barrer and pushed it all t'way to Sandbeds from t'quarry." Bill smiled at the memory and the pain in his eyes cleared. "Ran most o' t'way, an all!" Bill's whole body tensed and shook as he went into a coughing spasm. It took some time to abate. It was painful to watch, but he gradually calmed and caught his wheezing breath.

I gasped at what Bill had just told me. I couldn't believe this feat – pushing a loaded wheelbarrow for miles, often up steep gradients. Every time I looked at the name-stone now I would see it with different eyes.

Bill was now ready to continue, "That were jus' a few year afore t'war an' ah left t'quarry ter do ma bit." Wheezes. "When ah got back ah worked at t'mill…"

Edith stroked her father's arm again, "YES, DAD. BUT YER STILL DID JOBS FER PEOPLE. 'ELPING THEM MOVE, LIKE."

"Ah did that! I could lift this 'ere armchair and carry it down t'village. Ah helped everyone move. It were that grand. 'Get Billy Barnes', they'd say," Edith beamed at her father. "Ah didn't want no brass fer it, but they gave me stuff." Bill looked around. "See that clock there?" I nodded. "Well, it were one of them Fosters, t'mill people, what gave me that after ah helped 'em darn Littlemoor Castle."

"AND WHEN ME AN ANNIE WERE LITTLE 'E CARRIED US BOTH ON 'IS SHOULDERS AT T'SAME TIME. ONE ON EACH. DO YOU REMEMBER THAT, DAD?' Edith added. "Dad were a right gentle giant, yer know, doctor. Everyone liked 'im, would 'elp anyone."

"Aye. But then ah got this arthritis job. Fair did fer me," Bill nodded to himself as he remembered. "But it's smoking that's buggered me. Does tha' think smokin' does cause cancer, doctor?"

"Yes, Bill. YES, I DO. IT HASN'T BEEN PROVED YET AND THERE ARE LOTS OF DOCTORS

THAT WILL TELL YOU OTHERWISE, BUT THE EVIDENCE IS GETTING STRONGER."

"Started in t'war. We all smoked then, just ter get through, like. Ha, twasn't the Boche that got me, but t'war 'as!" Bill subsided into wheezes and a deep cough again.

"WELL, BILL. IT'S BEEN GOOD TO TALK WITH YOU. I'M A NEW DOCTOR HERE SO I'LL BE SEEING MORE OF YOU. Thank you, Edith, for the water. I must be going now. It's Dr Blunt's half day and I'm doing the whole surgery."

Bill suddenly leaned forward and grabbed my hand in both his. "Thank you, doctor. It's been grand ter see yer. It's been t'best afternoon. You've made me better already! Ah'll be seeing yer!"

I never did though. Two weeks later George telephoned me at home, "Just thought you would like to know, Eric, Billy Barnes died in his sleep last night. Peacefully. Edith has told me that he never stopped smiling after your visit, Eric. Whatever did you give him?"

Chapter 7

I had discovered the magical properties of Smarties and I employed them now as little John Braithwaite sat on his mother's knee with nervous eyes staring into mine. He was totally unaware that he was a special patient. He was the first infant to be brought along to my Antenatal Clinic on Wednesday afternoons for an inoculation. He was clearly worried about the situation in this strange place... until I reached into the depths of my desk and extracted my Smartie tub and put it down by my elbow.

I had started the clinic over a year before, making good on the resolution that I had made during Charles' birth, three years before I joined the practice. The decision to have a clinic was made over coffee in the Craig-na-Hullie kitchen. I had determined to use this as the first innovation I would introduce into the practice, and to make a real success of it. I knew that it was a bit of a test case and would tell me how receptive the two partners were to new ideas. I had got to know George and felt that he would welcome any developments in what we offered as long as they didn't have any impact on him. I was not sure about Tom. He seemed to like things just as they were. I would have to talk to them both. I started with George.

"Now that's an interesting idea, Eric. Why do you think it is better than the system at the moment?" George leaned back in his chair and challenged me to a reasoned response. Underneath his bonhomie he had an astute ability to dissect a way through arguments.

I had prepared for this question. "Well, at the moment our system does work. Florence is a good midwife and is well respected. I wouldn't want to replace anything that she does but to add to it. If you feel that we can give this clinic a try I will telephone her to talk it through with her and see how we can work together. I have skills and knowledge that would benefit her and vice versa. I would bring along my knowledge of the general health of the mothers-to-be as well. I also hope to do postnatal examinations. Together we can provide a really good service."

"Mmm, yes, Eric," George mused. "I can see that working well but Tom will need some convincing. However, he doesn't really like obstetrics, so might be glad to hand them over to you. How do you see it working?"

"Yes, I've thought about Tom. I'll go and chat it through with him, of course. I think the best time to hold the clinic would be after lunch, say at two o'clock, and on a Wednesday. That's Tom's half day so he wouldn't have to be involved. I could use the surgery here…" George nodded and took a swig of coffee. Bea had left us, aware that we needed to be on our own. I knew that secretly she supported my idea and would be cheering me on from the sitting room.

"It is also the day when I do the whole afternoon surgery and you just do the calls. You wouldn't be involved either. It would be just me," I continued. "I can't imagine that I would have too many takers, at the start at least. It may not meet a need anyway. We'll just have to see."

George was now nodding his head with his eyes closed. No doubt he was imagining the effect on the practice as a whole. I waited. Eventually he said, "Splendid. Yes, splendid, Eric. SPLENDID!" as he built to a crescendo.

I decided to consult Tom next before mentioning the idea to Florence. I tried to meet up with Tom face-to-face once a week at Innisfree after his morning surgery and I chose the next such meeting to broach the subject. On these occasions, we either chatted in the kitchen or the front room, where he had interviewed me. I was getting to know Tom and Chrissey through these times together. They had three boys, but as the older two had started school I hadn't met them yet. However, I was familiar with their smiling black and white faces which gazed at me from photo frames around the sitting room. Their youngest son, Douglas, was Charles' age. He even resembled him a little with his blond, almost white, hair and freckles. He was always pleased to see me and I knew he and Charles would become good friends as soon as they started getting together. He was playing in the sitting room as Tom and I entered.

"Hello, Douglas" I said cheerily.

"Hello, Dr Hainsworth," Douglas looked at me and smiled. "We're going to have a new baby!"

I glanced across to Tom. "Erm, yes, Eric. Just heard yesterday but haven't told anyone yet…" he said.

"Well, congratulations Tom. Do you want a little brother or a little sister, Douglas?" I bent down to get closer to him.

"I want one like yours," Douglas said. On the one occasion that Douglas had met Ruth he seemed enchanted by her and her tiny hands. He hadn't stopped stroking her head.

When Douglas, usually shortened to Doug, had been sent to play elsewhere, and Chrissey had brought us cups of coffee, Tom lit a cigarette. The first few minutes together were for relaxing and chatting about our families. "So, another child, Tom?"

Tom leaned his head back and blew smoke up to the ceiling. "Yep, Eric. Our last one…unless it's a boy and then I think Chrissey will be tempted for another. Due in late August… just hope it's a girl!"

I decided to use this as an introduction for my idea for the clinic. "Tom, I've been having some thoughts about having an antenatal clinic in the practice…"

"Won't do, Eric. Got too much on as it is. Couldn't fit it in. Leave it to Florence Micklethwaite." Tom, predictably, had squashed the idea. "I do the surgery in Shelf every day as well as the ones here. Couldn't possibly take on another thing. Sorry, Eric."

I had heard about the Shelf surgeries from George, but hadn't taken one yet as the only time I would be required would be when Tom was on holiday. They were needed as we had a good number of patients in Shelf. However, the practice could not afford much in terms of consultation space so had to rent two rooms in a small terraced house for an hour every day. It was not ideal though and I knew George was concerned about it.

I outlined my proposal anyway and laboured the fact that the clinic would be on Tom's half day, so he would never be involved. This helped and after one or two deep inhalations of smoke, Tom looked at me and said, "Ok, Eric. If George likes the idea, give it a go. Don't think there will be the demand though. Wouldn't want you to get your hopes up. They don't like change here," Tom paused and smiled. "Although I don't think Mrs Bartholomew will be one of your customers!"

After a very enthusiastic and encouraging discussion with Florence, who could see the possibilities and advantages of such a scheme, I wrote to all our patients. There were two at the first clinic.

After that initial, slightly disappointing, start, I became more convinced about the advantages. I could spend longer talking with the young mothers-to-be and, especially with the first-timers, could reassure them about what to expect. They also appreciated not having to wait with ill patients during the normal surgeries. During that first year I saw ten maternity cases. George was overjoyed. "SPLENDID, Eric. SPLENDID! We're taking the practice forwards. And you say Florence likes it?" I nodded. Florence really enjoyed working closer with the practice and now felt part of a team.

Through that first year a number of my new mothers asked me about inoculations for immunisation against some awful diseases that had ravaged childhoods in the past. The BCG vaccine, introduced in 1949 against tuberculosis, was administered through Local Authority clinics but I wanted to offer vaccines against smallpox, tetanus, polio and diphtheria in the clinic rather than the general surgeries. Smallpox was all but eradicated from this country by the late 1950s but the other three were still around, although in much smaller numbers, and produced harrowing symptoms in their victims. And they were deadly.

Now I had the perfect venue for administering the vaccines – my clinic. John Braithwaite was my first patient. His eyes were now on the Smartie jar and he had relaxed. I wondered what it had been like for Edward Jenner when he had first vaccinated James Phipps, the eight-year-old son of his gardener in May 1796.

Jenner was a hero of mine and through his work must have saved millions of lives. Smallpox was a killer back then, and many victims who survived were scarred for life especially on their faces. There was a vaccine against the disease but it was dangerous. Pus from a smallpox blister was introduced into the body through small cuts or scratches in the skin. This produced a milder form of the disease and immunity. However, people could still die from the disease caused by the vaccination and it could be passed on to others from those who had been inoculated. Jenner had been so vaccinated as a child and this affected his health for the rest of his life.

Jenner noticed that milkmaids rarely contracted smallpox but observed that they often suffered from a related disease, cowpox, which they had contracted from the cows they milked. Jenner surmised that this illness, which was much less severe than smallpox, gave immunity against this, more deadly, disease. He tried out his idea on James Phipps, who must have sat opposite Jenner much as John did now with me. It must have been very scary for all concerned. Jenner introduced cowpox through scratches, made by a knife, in both arms.

A few days later James developed a fever. Was this cowpox or something else? The fever went and no more symptoms developed. Later, Jenner tested James to see if he was immune from smallpox by deliberately introducing the disease through more scratches. Nothing happened. Jenner did it again and still nothing. James was indeed immune. Every time I recollected this story, I wondered if I would allow Charles to go through that first trial. I wouldn't, I was sure.

There was no fear in Mrs Braithwaite's eyes as she held John's arm for me to swab and then introduce a small needle into the muscle. John started to cry but immediately stopped as I reached for the jar and produced a Smartie. He held his hand out as his mother said, "Say thank you to Dr Hainsworth."

"Thank you," was said as John took the sweet and immediately burrowed his face in his mother's shoulder. The gratitude should really have been directed at Jenner and others like him. We take for granted the good health that we enjoy and do not give a thought to the pioneering work by many in the battle against disease. Smarties had this magical effect on children though. I often used them when examining children's throats. All I had to do was to give the child a Smartie and then wait until it had been consumed.

"Can I see where your Smartie has gone?" I would say. Often, without the Smartie, I had discovered that it needed quite a bit of cajoling to get a child to open its mouth wide enough to see to the back of the throat. Sometimes a particularly stubborn infant would clamp its mouth shut and would have to leave without the examination, much to its mother's chagrin. However, all children seemed to want to show me where the Smartie had gone. Extra encouragement might be needed. "I just can't see it. Are you sure it's down there?" I then asked. This invariably led to a mouth being opened to maximum extent. I employed Smarties from then on and adults would even request them at times. They seemed too embarrassed to call them by their name but would ask me for 'one of them there pills. Them coloured 'uns.'

The antenatal clinic became popular and George was very pleased, splendidly so. He even started to tidy up the consulting room a bit after the Wednesday morning surgery. Bea talked about it a great deal whilst I was waiting in the kitchen to relieve George at the evening surgeries. She seemed to have the ear of most of our female patients. "And I'll tell you something else, Eric," she said as we chatted over a cup of hot water and semi-pealed potatoes. "They really appreciate you attending at their deliveries. It really reassures them."

"Oh, I'm glad you told me, Bea. I was wondering how it is being received. They don't really tell me much, the mums."

"No, they wouldn't. They take life and all its ups and downs with a quiet stoicism. But I was at the Mothers' Union last night and the younger ones were all talking about it. They think it's 'right modern'. I think George is quite envious about it really, but he won't let on."

I was being recognised around the village now and I received the odd cheery wave as I drove around. I had got to know the character of the place, but there was one thing that increasingly perplexed me. I had noticed, quite early on, that people walked around the streets with a towel over an arm and, sometimes, a small bag. It seemed to be women, sometimes with small children, in the mornings and men in the evenings. A few days after administering the magic Smartie to John Braithwaite I was driving down the village towards the crossroads. I was trying to squeeze in one or two calls before I met with George after his morning surgery. It had been raining all morning so far, but now was easing. The car's windscreen wipers were relieved at the respite and celebrated by speeding up. They were perverse indeed. They even stopped when I accelerated hard.

There were one or two hardy souls out shopping and then I noticed two familiar figures hurrying along: a mother dragging along a small reluctant boy. It was Mrs Braithwaite and John. Mrs Braithwaite was carrying a bag that couldn't quite completely contain some towels, on her umbrella arm. I pulled up alongside them. I leaned across the passenger seat and, after a struggle, managed to wind down the window. "HELLO MRS BRAITHWAITE!" I bellowed. She looked round and saw me. She smiled as she approached the car, avoiding the puddles on the pavement. John smiled as well but brought up his free hand to protect his arm from another assault. "Can I give you a lift somewhere? It's a mucky day."

"Oh, thank you doctor," Jill Braithwaite's gratitude was evident in her voice. "We were jus' goin' along to t'Victoria Hall."

"Right you are, Mrs Braithwaite. Jump in. It's not far but it'll keep the rain off for a bit." She opened the door and pushed John and the bag in before joining them.

"Ah'm that glad, doctor. It seems to teck twice as long wi' John!"

"Oh, how is he after his injection? Sometimes they make you feel off colour."

"Oh, 'e's alright. 'E wants to come aggen. Jus' fer a Smartie though!"

"Can I ask what you are going to the Victoria Hall for?" The wipers slowed as I pulled away. The Hall was the other side of the crossroads on the way to Sandbeds. Margaret and I had noticed the cupola on the way to Tom's for our interview and I had passed it often now. It was an imposing building especially for such an unpretentious place. The Fosters, who owned the mill, had built it in its Victorian splendour for the inhabitants, using the local sandstone. It was built in 1887, to celebrate the Jubilee of Queen Victoria, in Queen Ann style with decorative panels on the gables depicting Science, Art and the Arms of the Fosters. It housed a large public concert hall, a reading room, a library and a science lecture theatre. The Victorians obviously reflected their high ideals in their public buildings and had high aspirations for education and entertainment.

"We're goin' for us baths, doctor."

"Baths? I know there is a swimming pool there but they have ordinary baths as well?"

"Yes, doctor. We've allus used 'em. We don't 'ave one at 'ome an' it's easier than usin' tin 'un in front o' t'fire. My Fred goes fer one on Thursday evenin' after work. You can have a grand natter in 'em, yer'll see," Jill Braithwaite was enthusiastic.

"Oh, we've got one in our house so I don't think we'll use them. They sound to be good social events though."

"Oh, come in and see. Yer'll like 'em"

We parked and, as it was still raining, we ran into the 'slipper baths', which shared an entrance with the swimming pool. I knew Mrs Jagger, who was on the door and was taking the money for both. Normally no men were allowed in at that time but Mrs Jagger reassured me. "But yer just t'doctor! They won't mind at all!" She also made sure that my sensitivities wouldn't be embarrassed by poking her head around the door to make sure that there were no sights which might disconcert me. Jill Braithewaite, and John, then ushered me into a large, hot, steamy room with a concrete floor and white tiles, the Victorian originals, on the walls. My spectacles steamed up immediately. When I replaced them, I could see that light came through skylights in the sloping roof that went up to an apex. A terrace of wooden cubicles, painted a pale cream, lined one wall. The chatter of female voices engaged in a variety of conversations echoed and two women, down at the far end, were singing a duet across the partitions. These were raised slightly off the floor and reached up to about eight feet, preserving modesty.

"This is ours, today." Jill opened the wooden door to reveal the bath, on legs, with its large taps worn through to dull brass by years of use, and accompanied by a pine chair and small table. A row of hooks adorned the wall opposite the bath. A duckboard kept wet feet off the concrete floor. "What do yer think, doctor?"

A conversation stopped. "Oh, I think it's grand Mrs Braithewaite. Just the job!" I answered.

A voice called out, "Doctor? Is that you, Dr Hainsworth?" All other chatter ceased.

"Yes, yes, ladies. I've just come to see the baths. They're super. I'm just going, though."

Another voice shouted without a hint of embarrassment, "Oh, don't go, doctor. Ah thought you'd come to give us an examination. Yer know, get t'bottom of t'problem!"

Cackles of laugher exploded and bounced round the room.

"Aye, an you've jus' missed Enid Bartholomew an' all!" another disembodied voice added cheerfully. "She'll be that vexed when ah tell 'er!"

It was a relief to escape after wishing everyone 'a good bath'. Would they ever let me forget that first surgery?

It was still raining a bit and the condensation on the Craig-na-Hullie kitchen windows seemed to add to the watery greyness by forming drops that dribbled in random pathways through the mist on the glass. George and Bea enjoyed the story as I related it to them over our morning coffee. George thought, he might go along and give the ladies a surprise one day but Bea slapped his shoulder with the back of her hand. "OH NO, YOU WON'T, GEORGE BLUNT!" George smiled at me conspiratorially.

We continued to talk about the housing stock of the village and the lack of homely comforts. "They must have been the height of luxury when they were constructed," George explained. "They were built well and are solid. People like the back-to-back terraces because they are kept warm by houses attached on three sides and are cheap to run. You sometimes get extended families living in two or three houses in the same street!"

"But they're not very big and they don't have bathrooms."

"No, that's true, Eric. I haven't heard any complaints but it must be tough having to go for a bath at The Victoria Hall…"

"Oh, I don't know. They all seemed to be enjoying it this morning. Most of the houses don't have toilets either, though, do they?"

"One or two are starting to put a cubicle in one bedroom for one but most use the things that the Victorians had. There are one or two earth closets in some gardens even now, but the Fosters put in water closets when they built houses. They're not inside the houses though, they're in small stone cubicles built in rows at the bottom of the streets."

Having exhausted the sanitary arrangements of the village, Bea left us to talk about patients and their ailments. I brought new ideas to the situations whilst George brought a wisdom forged over years of general practice and a deep knowledge of human behaviour exhibited in the many facets of our patients.

"I'd like you to visit old Tommy Duckworth up at Railway Cottages this afternoon. He's one of my chronic sick, but he's just come through a bout of pneumonia. He thought that was the end. To be honest, I did as well, but a course of Penicillin sorted him out. I still can't get over what these antibiotics do, Eric. Truly amazing." George and I had often talked about the almost miraculous transformations that these drugs had produced. I hadn't practiced medicine without them but George remembered a time when bacterial diseases were rife and killed, especially children.

"He's got a multitude of things wrong with him, but it's his chest that I'm keeping an eye on. I've got a lot on today and I'm feeling a bit jaded," George continued. I looked at him anxiously. Now he had mentioned it, he did look a bit drawn. I was always willing to shoulder more work. I wanted George to have a good retirement but he still had a year to go.

"No problem, George. I haven't been up to Railway Cottages yet…"

"Ha, you haven't missed much. They were built as temporary houses for the navvies, who built the railway in the 1870s. They should have been knocked down afterwards but nobody got round to it, and they're still occupied. You'll see what they're like."

George stopped and thought. "Eric, would you like to come with me to Joe Warren's? He's my first visit – just across the road so I walk. He used to be my 'doctor's man'. He collected money owed to the practice by the patients before the NHS came along. He had a mild stroke some months ago but is doing nicely. He likes a good chat though!"

"Yes, George. It would be good to meet him anyway. Can I leave the car in the yard?"

"Yes, Eric. Good idea. I'll just put my bag in the Rover as we go past the garage, then I won't need to come back inside."

I helped George slide back one of the two heavy, wooden garage doors. The familiar dark green car gleamed inside, waiting. The rounded shape was sensuous and George stroked it as he went passed. "Beautiful car, Eric. Rover P4, 75 model. This was built in 1953. Runs perfectly." George opened a back door to reveal green leather seats and a spotless interior. It put my Ford Anglia to shame. I knew where George's priorities lay in terms of spending money. He threw the bag onto the deep bench seat that was divided in the middle by a leather armrest, to separate the driver from the passenger, and closed the door with a deep and mature bang.

"Before the war I got a Rolls - a Wraith. They said that I could have anything on it, within reason, so got an altimeter. That was fun. Bea loved it. We're just over a thousand feet above sea level here, you know. I also got a tow bar fitted for the caravan. Ha! Got it home and the thing wouldn't fit in the garage. I had to get a hole knocked in the wall just there." He pointed to a little alcove in the back wall of the garage. "The tow bar went there but it was a squeeze. The bumper just touched the wall." It must have been a monster of a car.

'That's the pit." George pointed to a row of oily planks set into the stone flagged floor. "Dr Shields had that put in when he got his first car. In those days engineers used to come here to service it and look after it." A metal-worker's bench, shrouded in dusty, redundant spiders' webs was under a window. Panes were made opaque by years of dust, algae and empty carapaces of flies.

"When the house was first built this end was where he kept the trap. And at this end," George walked into the darker end of the garage. "This is where the pony was. We've kept the stable door. We used to keep the caravan at this end. We had these doors put in the gable end for it – we'd push the caravan onto the lawn through the doors…"

"Yes, Bea told us when we came for the interview."

"I bet she told you that I wouldn't let her back into the house even if she'd forgotten something." George's eyes twinkled mischievously.

"Well, yes, she did…"

"Couldn't be having that. We were on holiday. If she'd gone back in, she'd have been tempted to stay. I know Bea! We had fun though Eric. We always knew we'd have a nice view!"

I noticed a strange ladder attached to the wall. It was made of two planks set a few inches away from the wall and side-by-side. Hand and foot holds were made by large semi-circular holes in the planks. Looking up I saw a triangular platform, one point of which came to the ladder. "Oh, that's the hay loft," George said. "I've never been up there. Looks a bit dangerous to me. Anyway, we'd better be going. Time and tide - and patients, Eric!"

Joe lived in a terrace just up the hill from Craig-na-Hullie on the opposite side of the road. The houses were slightly larger than those closer to the village centre and had bay windows. George banged on the black door and walked straight in. This was the method of entry that I was also adopting now. It saved a great deal of time and patients preferred it. It saved them getting out of chairs or stopping what they were doing. Joe emerged from the sitting room. He was older than George, probably in his late sixties or early seventies. He seemed to keep himself immaculate with carefully cut and brushed white hair and clean shaving that left a neat moustache. He walked well but betrayed his condition by carrying a walking stick.

"Oh, hello, doctor. And who's this young man then?" he asked in a jovial voice.

I was introduced. "Oh aye, yer t'young doctor! Millie, MILDRED." Joe called out in a voice that filled the house. "Ah must be bad. We've got two of 'em doctors today!" Joe saw my face and broke out into cheery laughter.

We went into the front room with the bay window. It had a deep, slightly dusty, sense of not being disturbed often. Like many families in the village, Joe and Mildred would use the back room to live in and keep the front as 'best' for when 'comp'ny' came. Antimacassars, cloths draped over the backs of chairs and sofas to protect the fabric from hair-oil and dirt, were on each chair. A small mahogany cabinet held glassware inside and a multitude of photograph frames on top.

George asked Joe a few questions and took his blood pressure. He was evidently on track for a good recovery. "Joe, I've brought Dr Hainsworth along today to meet you. He joined the practice over a year ago now, you might remember I wrote to all the patients about him and the revised surgery times." Joe nodded. "Well, he'll be taking over from me in a year's time and he's interested in what you did as my doctor's man."

Joe smiled. It seemed that all the older patients loved talking about the 'olden days' and what they used to do. I was genuinely interested, but it also gave them pleasure and dignity. He invited George and me to 'mek yerselves comfie', which we did, but declined Millie's offer of coffee. I was aware, however interesting the story, that other patients were waiting for me.

"Them were t'days, doctor. Ah used ter work darn at t'station. We were Dr Blunt's patients an' 'e offered me t'job o'doctor's man. Ah were lookin' fer a change, any road. T'railway were losin' money especially after t'buses were brought in in 1930. People didn't like walkin' all that way ter t'station, 'bout a mile an' 'alf. We 'adn't got over t'slump either so ah knew it were no good. You offered me t'job in 1938…"

"No, Joe," George interrupted. "It was the summer of 1937…"

"Ah, yer right there, doctor. It were. Ah'm glad yer did. Look at t'railway now. They were nationalised in '48, same as when t' National Health started. They put wrong engines on then an' it got wuss. They 'ad an A4 Pacific on once. Fancy, a main-line express engine on our little line!

What a nonsense. They stopped the passenger trains in '55 an' there isn't much freight now."

I was really interested in Joe's story but the tick of the clock in the back room, loud enough to penetrate into our gathering, reminded me of the time slipping away. I had to get on. "What did you have to do as a doctor's man, Joe?" I asked.

"Oh, ah 'ad to collect t'money fer t'doctors – t'other un was Dr Glenn, then." George nodded. "Ah went round all t'patients' 'ouses. Ah got ter know when ter go. Some ah went in mornin's when t' misses were at 'ome. They were t'ones that were given all 'usband's wages to look after. But then ah went t'others on Fridays. That were pay day at t'mill. Ah went in t'meal time. Ah 'ad ter go then afore t'money 'ad gone, payin' off last week's tabs or drink."

"Yes," George added. "Some patients just paid sixpence ($2\frac{1}{2}$p) a week, that was the price of a pint and a half of beer, as a kind of club. Even then, we knew who couldn't even pay that much, so we let them off."

"Aye, we 'ad some beggars though, doctor. 'Usbands who said they couldn't pay an' then went off t' pub, mostly it were T' Stag, leavin' their families wi' nout!" Joe looked at me and smiled. "But then ah got a job at t'Stag, just part time, like. That fettled 'em. Ah knew they could pay then. They could put beer away like a fish."

"How much were you paid for being the doctor's man, Joe?" I asked. I wanted to go but this question fascinated me.

"Oh, it all depended on 'ow much ah collected. Ah think it were thre'pence fer every pound ah collected." Joe looked at George, who nodded his confirmation. "That were why ah 'ad ter get job at T' Stag. It were grand when t' monthly bills went out though. That made up fer it."

Millie came back in wiping her red hands on her pinny, her hair wrapped in a cloth for her housework. "Those were good days, weren't they Joe. You were allus good to us, doctor. An' now Joe's nearly better."

I got up, "I really must be going. I need to get on with my visits. It's been lovely to meet you and you can tell me more when I next come."

Joe pushed himself up and grabbed my hand. "Ah've wanted ter meet t' young doctor an' it's been grand. Thank you."

There was a sort of symmetry to that day. My first visit was to Joe, who had worked on the railway, and my last was Tommy Duckworth who lived in the houses built for the railway navvies. It was close to half past three when I drew up in the main road by the 'Navvy Houses'. They were in part of the village called Mountain. At one time it had been a separate hamlet on the Denholme road going out of the village. Unsurprisingly it was on a hill, the highest point of the village.

Other names in the village were equally descriptive, if uninspiring. Ford and Swamp were areas just the other side of the church, on the way to Halifax. Beggarington was even further along. Farms around the village were equally bluntly named: Causeway End, Hill Top, Green Field, Brown Field and Windy Bank. As a family, in years to come, we often wondered how others received their appellation and made up strange stories for each: Blackmires, Hunger Hill, Folly Hall and Mutton Pits.

The terraced rows of the 'Navvy Houses' were so close together there was no road, just a wide and rough pathway, between them. The houses themselves were made of stone, no doubt from the quarry that was just down the road from them, but were showing real signs of their temporary nature now. The multitude of waiting repairs to roofs, gutters and windows was overwhelming. Even if these were remedied, it wouldn't have raised the houses above hovel status. In fact, they had been condemned in 1957, just after I had arrived in the practice. They still hadn't been cleared though. They were on George's patch and I hadn't had to visit any yet. It would be an education for me. Tommy Duckworth lived in one toward the end of one of the terraces, Northern Street.

Fortunately, it had stopped raining by the time I climbed out of the car and made my way, assiduously avoiding the puddles, some of which were large and deep. The clouds were oppressive with a cloying greyness and dripping moisture. I found the door. It had probably been painted when the navvies' had moved in, but didn't look as though it had been touched since. I had adopted George's mode of entry into patient's houses and was just about to bang loudly on the door when something caught my eye. It was the 'sneck' that held the door closed. It was obviously old but had been well made out of brass, probably in the heyday of the industrial revolution. It was shining proudly.

I banged the door, pushed the sneck down and crashed into the door, expecting it to open. It didn't. A loud yapping and barking from a number of dogs inside the dwelling erupted though. I looked round to make sure that my painful collision hadn't been observed. It would have become yet another story doing the rounds. I banged the door again and this time waited.

I heard a shuffling sound and then a wheezy voice called weakly, "Oo is it?"

"It's the doctor, Tommy," I called back.

"Yer don't sound like 'im!"

"I'm the new doctor. Dr Hainsworth."

There was a considerable pause during which I envisaged a strange consultation happening across the barrier of the door.

"Ho'd on, lad. Ho'd on!" Tommy wheezed.

The high-pitched yapping gradually subsided and, finally, a deadbolt was scraped back and the sneck lifted. The door opened gradually and a gnarled hand grabbed the edge of it. Even before going in, I was aware of the odour of dogs and damp decay. The door led straight into a dingy room. I entered, almost overcome by the smell. The stone flags were dirty and worn, only slightly relieved by two small and very dirty rag-rugs. Meager heat emerged from the rusting range that, in more energetic days, had been black-leaded. In the centre of the room, standing forlornly with two mismatching wooden chairs in attendance, was a crude pine table, now grey with age and dirt. Tommy's one, sagging armchair had to be helped in its decrepitude with a pile of cushions, whilst the arms were black, like the table with age and dirt. However, they had also been buffed into a gloss by years of use.

Beneath the one small window, which deigned to let in a diffuse light through its encrusted panes, there was what resembled an old and battered sideboard. The old man stood by it. He was hollow-chested and bent backed. White hair straggled over the creased dome of his head and bristled in tufts from his carelessly shaved chin. His face was wan. He was wearing a blue and white collarless shirt. It was undone at the top and revealed a grey vest. But Tommy's eyes shone with no sign of defeat. He had produced a well-used handkerchief and dabbed his purpling, bulbous nose with a single wipe.

"'Ello, lad. So, you're t'new doctor. It's grand ter see yer."

"Yes, I'm helping Dr Blunt and will take over from him when he retires next year," I explained. "And how are you feeling today? I hear you've had a bout of pneumonia."

"Ah did that, lad. Ah did that. It near did fer me. But them pills t'doctor gave me were reight good."

"And how are you feeling now, Tommy?"

"Oh, nobbut middlin'. Ah can't complain," Tommy wheezed.

"Well, I'll give you an examination to make sure everything is alright with your lungs."

I dropped my bag on top of the sideboard. Yapping and scuffling noises exploded from within. I looked down to inspect it properly. The central section of the front had been replaced with plain plywood and the panels in the doors at either end had been substituted with stair rods to make a rudimentary cage. There were a number of whippets churning around.

"Oh, do you like ma dogs, doctor? Them's me friends. They keep me goin', t'little fellas. They keep me young!"

I helped Tommy in his struggle to pull out his shabby shirt and tatty thick vest from his waistline that was defined by an old necktie, now enjoying a second life as a belt. I listened through the distinct form of his emaciated rib cage with my stethoscope. His lungs sounded anything but young. However, the wheezes, reminiscent of those emerging from a poor pair of bellows, didn't indicate more treatment at the moment.

As I helped Tommy pull down his shirt and vest again, I said, "Those dogs of yours seem to have done the trick, Tommy. I'll just pop in this time next week just to make sure though. Still, you shouldn't be playing football just yet!" I smiled. The puzzled look on Tommy's face changed into a beaming grin at the realisation I had pulled his leg.

I hardly spoke to George when I took over the evening surgery from him so I asked Bea, when it had finished, if I could see him.

"Yes, Eric. He'd love to have a chat. He's upstairs in the bedroom."

I entered the Blunts' bedroom to find George in bed, reading. He was in pyjamas and a nightcap finished off his ensemble. He was obviously feeling under the weather. However, his face when he lifted it on my entry broke into a welcoming smile. "Hello, Eric. Hope you don't mind if I don't get up! I go to bed early some days. Anyway, how did you get on at Tommy Duckworth's?"

I told George what had happened and when I related what Tommy had said, he threw his head back and laughed. "Ha! I'll tell Bea we're just going to have to get some whippets! HA! KEEPS HIM YOUNG!"

PHOTOGRAPHS OF CRAIG-NA-HULLIE

Craig-na-Hullie c 1920, just before George Blunt took it over. The surgery porch is on the left.

The surgery in 1957. The doctor's desk is on the left with a muddle of papers and paraphernalia on the top. The door is the exit for the patients and leads to the surgery door. The trolley has patients' records on the top, in cardboard boxes, and implements on a shelf below.

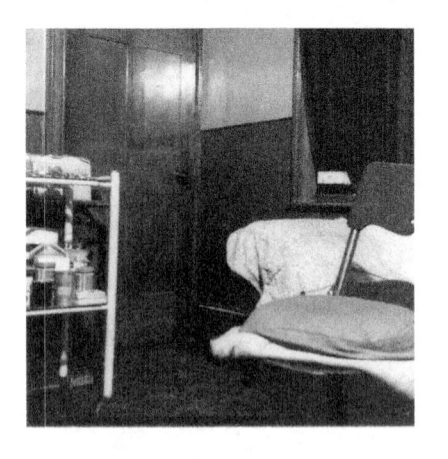

The surgery 1957. The trolley is on the left. This doorway leads from the waiting room. The window, to the right, is heavily curtained so that patients wouldn't see Mrs Blunt in the garden.

The chaise-longue examination couch is in front of the window.

The surgery 1957. The window is on the left. The curtained arch leads to the dispensary. The shelf over the fireplace holds some of the oil lamps that were placed under the floorboards in winter.

Chapter 8

"Well, George, you've made it – and without the aid of whippets to keep you going!" I said as I grasped George's hand. Margaret looked at me as if I was going slightly insane. We had joined Tom and Chrissey at Craig-na-Hullie for a final dinner together with Bea and George before they headed off to their retirement, and well-deserved rest, on the South Coast. We had chosen a Sunday evening as the time we were all least busy, although I was officially on duty. Mrs Scott, our babysitter, would telephone through any emergency calls.

It was the last Sunday of May and we were blessed with a fine, almost balmy evening. It was still quite warm when we assembled on the back lawn for preprandial drinks. Such evenings in May, at the altitude we enjoyed in Queensbury, were rare and we all wanted to take advantage of this one. It was an emotional occasion for all. I had grown close to George over the past two and a half years. I would miss our morning chats when he often revealed his wisdom and understanding of human nature. I had learned a great deal from him.

George had regaled us with stories of the caravanning exploits on the back lawn. It was then that he felt brave enough to let Bea know, for the first time since the incident, of their first such trip. "I'd pushed back the wooden fence there, ready for our adventure," George indicated the fence on stands.

"Oh, I'd wondered what that was for," Chrissey said. Apparently, this was the first time, in all the ten years that Tom had been part of the practice, that she had been on the lawn or even really admired the view.

"Yes. After that I opened the new doors there. We had those specially put in, Chrissey, for the caravan. Unfortunately, I hadn't got the brake system quite worked out, bit of a crude affair with a lever and wire to each wheel. So, when I was at the tow-bar to pull and guide the caravan and Bea was at the back pushing, the breaks were still half on…"

"GEORGE, YOU RASCAL!" Bea burst out.

"We worked up quite a sweat, I can tell you. Bea was positively glowing. Red all over."

"George, I was half DEAD. You just kept shouting 'Push harder, Bea'. It was just like being in labour again! Honestly George. You never told me. And then you said you'd have to start pulling more and suddenly the caravan shot forward. I bet that was …"

"Yes, Bea. Ha! It was then that I discovered the brake was half-on and released it. Never told you." George ducked as Bea pretended to hit him. "I'm sorry, Bea…ha!" They both laughed.

We wandered off the hard paved area and onto the lawn strip at the top of the rockery. "It's quite some view you've got here, George," Tom said gazing north up into the Dales. "Chrissey, they can see Ingleborough from here but I don't think you can see it this evening." Chrissey stood, revelling in the view, which was gloriously rural despite the proximity of Bradford.

"No, it's a bit too hazy. It's still lovely though, isn't it?" Bea said. "Down there is the station. It isn't used now but freight trains still go through. Yew's Green is just beyond. One of our favourite walks is down that path and through Yew's Green." Bea pointed to the right. We could see an overgrown path, dark green and sprinkled with the colours of spring flowers, heading straight down from the other side of the garage, between two parallel dry-stone walls that bounded fields on either side, to an unsealed road. We followed her finger down the road to the station. "We'll miss this," she added wistfully. "And the people, of course."

"You are going a long way away, though," Margaret added leaving the question 'why so far away?' unsaid.

"Yes, down to the South Coast. We'll be nearer our daughter and she tells me it hardly ever snows there! That'll be a relief," George explained.

"And it might make you relax more, George. Keep you going for a bit longer," Bea said.

"And keep me out of your hair, Eric. You wouldn't want me looking over your shoulder all the time. The patients are so used to having me around I just need to be well away. Best for all really."

I looked into George's eyes. He turned and met mine. He glanced away but I had detected a greater moisture in them. "And it's been some time… how long exactly have you been here?" I asked.

"Thirty-five years, Eric. Thirty-five. I can hardly believe it…"

"Good grief, George, I hadn't realised it was that long," Tom exclaimed. "I bet the patients have been saying their goodbyes."

"Ha! Nearly every consultation for the past month has ended with a 'do you remember when …'. It's strange though. It's the younger ones who aren't bothered. Now they don't have to pay they just seem to regard me more as a commodity," George mused. "It's mainly the older ones. It seems that the ones who had to pay for me and my services, back before '48, really appreciated me. We had some tough struggles, as well. It's terrible seeing children suffer with Diphtheria… awful. And I don't want to see another child dying despite my best efforts. Thank God for these antibiotics. The sulphonamides were good but antibiotics have really changed things. Have I told you …"

"Come on inside. It's getting chilly," Bea interrupted. "Once George gets going, we'll never stop him!"

We trailed back through the yard and up the steps. Tom and Chrissey chatted with George and Bea; Margaret and I were silent. Both of us knew that we were each thinking about the same thing: the steps we were climbing to the back door would soon be ours. We followed the others into the dining room with its brown, sun-faded velvet curtains and strange inglenook fireplace. It was looking even more forlorn now that the pictures and ornaments had been removed.

Bea and George excused themselves and left; they soon returned. Bea was carrying a huge slab of sizzling beef on a tray. George followed her, tugging on a white, chef's coat. We had seen it before – George and Bea had invited us to a Christmas meal just before I started working in the practice, when we were living over in Kirkburton. He had appeared in this outfit to carve a turkey and then had removed it solemnly to eat the meal. Margaret and I had looked at each other on that occasion, but both of us had been too polite to comment on George's sanity. He was, after all, my new employer.

George exclaimed, "I can see you remember my carving jacket! You didn't comment then. Ha! What do you think?"

"Oh, George, you tease. I'll say it," Bea exclaimed. "You're quite mad!"

"It was fun though. I could see you glancing at each other then. I bet you wondered what sort of place you had come to!" George started to strop the carving knife on the steel, extravagantly.

"Well, erm, now that you ask, erm, yes, George, we did. But we've got to know you …"

Bea intervened, "And now you KNOW he's mad."

George roared with laughter. He then began to attack the meat with gusto. The valedictory meal was under way.

The meal continued with much conviviality. Tom and I, and even Bea, allowed George to lose himself in reminiscences. He was particularly voluble about the infectious diseases that were still rife when he had bought the practice. "There were just the sulphonamides so we still made use of the old Fever Hospital on Long Lane. Have you seen it, Eric?"

"Yes, it's a private house now. What was it like?"

"Well, there were two wards, one at each end – twenty beds in all. The ends were for different diseases.

Had to keep people separate. The matron lived in the block in the middle."

"I heard that you had to deal with smallpox, George," Tom said.

"Yes, it was still around in Queensbury and the patients had to go to the Fever Hospital but we had an epidemic in '26, or was it '27, Bea?"

"1927," Bea answered. "The October. I remember it clearly. It really shook George up. But he didn't lose one patient."

"Fifty-eight got it that year. Then we had a few more virtually every year until 1931. Haven't had any more since, thank God." George rambled on through pudding. "I still can't get over the changes that the Health Service has brought, though…"

I was interested in his views and decided to encourage his volubility, "Do you think it's a good idea, over all?"

"Tough question to answer right now, Eric. People still remember the days of paying for the doctor and appreciate it, but the next generation will just take it for granted. You'll see. Demand will go up. William Beveridge was a fool to think that demand would go down when the nation's health had been improved overall by the NHS and better diets…"

Tom was stung. He admired the architect of the scheme. "Oh, do you think so? I think it's a brilliant concept – free at point of delivery. No one worries about their health and paying for treatment any more. We really show the world how to do it. They'll all copy us."

"I'll grant you the benefits, Tom. But when people don't know the cost, they don't know how to value it. They just want more. I'm the same – human nature."

Tom was determined to defend the scheme, "I'll bet you, er, how about fifty quid, George, that Beveridge was right?"

George laughed, "Oh, I won't be around when you have to pay me! Just remember my words though, Tom."

George stood up, "Nearly forgot. I've just got to go out. Please excuse me."

Bea brought in a tray of coffee. It was reminiscent of the times when George and I had used this room to discuss the organisation of the practice, and my role in it, over two years previously. We carried on talking to Bea about their plans for retirement.

Suddenly, there was a strange scuffling sound coming from below us and then a ghastly 'Whoaaah!' emerged from the grating in the skirting board. We stopped talking and Bea whispered, "Shhh!" She stood and walked silently towards the grating.

Another 'Whoaaah!' emerged again.

Bea knelt and shouted, "GEORGE, BEHAVE YOURSELF!"

There was a loud thump, then "Oh, BUGGER!" followed by more muffled exclamations.

Bea left us to chuckle amongst ourselves. Chrissey said, "Life isn't going to be the same, is it?"

Soon George and Bea reappeared. George was brushing dust and cobwebs out of his hair. "Just had to do it. One last time underneath the floorboards. Ah well."

Margaret and I visited the Blunts one more time the next day, to bring the children to the house so we could prepare them for the move. They liked the bedrooms that we had chosen for them, but we were a little alarmed that the main thing that Charles liked about his room was the enormous bed. As in all the rooms, the wallpaper was going brown and was peeling in the corners. The remains of a floral pattern could just be discerned. However, Charles seemed oblivious to this and jumped on the bed. This was a monster of a thing and was crowned with a shapeless feather mattress of vast proportions. Charles landed in a cloud of dust and sank beneath the waves of bedclothes into it. He was smitten and despite our rebukes for having jumped on someone else's furniture, talked of little else afterwards. He clearly thought the bed went with the room.

Both children couldn't believe the size of the house. They started planning games of 'tag' and 'hide and seek' as they discovered new rooms and especially the various staircases. Margaret said her goodbyes as we left the Blunts to their boxes and packing. Craig-na-Hullie was entering a kind of stasis, waiting for the new arrivals.

The following Friday, when I would collect the keys, soon arrived. Tom had kindly offered to do all the work on that day as well, which was a tremendous help. I went alone – Margaret looked after the children. The removal lorry was pulling away from the kerb outside Craig-na-Hullie, as I arrived. I went in through the open front door. "Oh, hello, Eric," Bea said. "We're just saying goodbye to the house." I could tell that they wanted to do this alone.

"That's fine. Just take as long as you want. I'm in no rush," I said. George and Bea walked around the echoing house, hand in hand, for the last time. From the hallway I saw them climb the main staircase, then the stairs to the maids' attic rooms. I heard the door open to the middle room, the one Gorge had forbidden me to enter. When they returned, some twenty minutes later, it was obvious that they had both been crying. They had laid ghosts to rest.

"Well, that's that then," George muttered. "Here are the keys, Eric. There's a luggage label on each one." He looked round again at the empty carapace of their lives. "It's been good, hasn't it, Bea? Hard at times but good, and I think I've been a real help to the people here in Queensbury." Bea nodded, unable to speak. "It's over to you now, Eric. We'll keep in contact of course. I'm sure you'll …" George faltered and stopped.

I led them through the back scullery, devoid of muddle and life, to the top of the stone steps above the back yard. I grabbed George's hand. Suddenly, I wanted to express the enormity of my thanks for all that he had done for me and taught me. I hoped I would be able to fill his shoes. "Thank you, George. Thank you," was all I could say. My limited vocabulary, inadequate as it was, was even more restricted by the emotion of the moment.

George looked into my eyes for seconds. I could tell he understood. Eventually, he said, "Well, all the best, Eric. I was right about you. You'll do." And with that George and Bea were gone. There was an emptiness inside me as I turned to lock the back door, my back door: the back door to the doctor's house.

I walked back through the hollow hallway. I had intended to inspect my - my family's - new domain after George and Bea had left, but I couldn't. Their memories still resounded here and I would leave the house to them for a little longer. I locked the front door behind me.

Margaret and I had thought and talked of little else other than our new abode for the past three or four months.

Initially it had been the seemingly insurmountable problem of how we would finance not just the purchase, but also the necessary alterations that had to be done before our arrival with our two small children. Fortunately, the local bank manager had come to our rescue. He was a patient of ours, and we had been in discussion with a building firm, also owned by a patient. He had been very helpful and knew how difficult it would be for us to finance all the building work at once. It was his suggestion that we paid for it over time, whenever we could.

I had discussed the problems with Tom on one of our regular chats over coffee during the previous winter, as well as the changes which would have to happen with the practice organisation, when George had gone. Initially, I had wanted to try and have a central surgery for the practice and to be guided by principles laid out by the College of General Practitioners. It was a difficult subject as it involved change and Tom, who would soon be the senior partner, was happy with things as they were. He knew that the cost of a central surgery would be almost prohibitive. We elected to meet in the family sitting room rather than being surrounded by the drying washed clothes of a young family, in the Innisfree kitchen. Chrissey had cleared the house of school children. A full cigarette box and lighter was ready to aid thought.

As she struggled Ann, the latest addition to the Holdroyd household, into a coat, Chrissey announced, "I'm just popping down the village for some shopping Tom. Do you need anything?" Tom shook his head. "I'll take Ann so you'll have peace and quiet. I have quite a bit to do so you'll probably be gone, Eric, by the time I get back. Not long now until George goes?"

"No, he goes in June. I can't believe how quickly it has come. We've got to sort out so much in the next few months," I said.

"Well, if we can do anything to help you must let us know," Chrissey hadn't lost her soft Scottish burr. "Give my love to Margaret. Come on Ann!"

As the door closed, I looked across at Tom and said, "Good grief, Tom. I can't believe how Ann is growing. She seems taller every week."

Tom was reaching for the cigarette box, "I know. And thank goodness she was a girl, our last. The washing keeps growing as well, I can tell you. The boys can make clothes dirty in seconds." Tom paused as he tapped the cigarette end. "So, Eric, have you started planning yet?"

"Well, yes, Tom. There are so many things to consider though. I was wondering if you could help me think things through today?" Tom nodded as he lit his cigarette. "George wants us to pay more for the house than it's worth, about twenty percent more, in fact."

Tom leant back and stared at me hard, "Yes, I can understand the problem. I'm sure that it's because he had to buy the practice when he came in 1924 and, now with the NHS, you don't need to buy into the practice. He must have thought, when he started here, that he would be able to sell the house with the practice and get his money back when he retired. Poor George. Then there were the changes with the pensions…"

"Oh, I know. When I accepted the job, I knew I'd have to buy Craig-na-Hullie. It's going to be tight financially as it is. I'm going to see the bank manager about it all. You know Frank Dobson. One of George's patients. It has helped knowing that I will be an equal share partner in five years' time. Even so, Margaret and I will only be able to tackle two rooms, the surgery and the kitchen."

Tom smiled, "Yes, rather archaic aren't they?"

"Yes, and the rest of the house is much the same. But the thing is, Tom, I've been thinking about the surgery. The College of GPs is recommending central surgeries so that all the doctors and clinics are under the same roof. We'd only need one receptionist…"

I could see Tom stiffen and his cigarette halt before his lips. "Oh, I don't think we can run to that, Eric. I know it would be a good time to change, but think of the expense! No, Eric. And then you're thinking of a receptionist, which we don't have now. Could you see us running to all that? Really?"

I reddened. I had jumped in without preparing the ground. "It's just that I need to know before doing up the rooms at Craig-na-Hullie. I could put in the money I would be using to …"

"But it means buying or renting another place and we've already got the surgery in Shelf. And then there's the receptionist. Can't be done, Eric, I'm afraid. Chrissey is my receptionist and Margaret is yours, sort of comes with being married to a GP." He smiled. "Chrissey chats in bed every night about the practice. You wouldn't be able to do that with just anyone, Eric!" We both smiled at the thought, but my face was probably in more of a grimace.

Each doctor had to devise his own methods of receiving requests for home visits and organising the surgeries. Very often, wives were utilised as informal receptionists without payment. Bea was one and it sounded as if Chrissey was another. Margaret also took calls at the moment, but I hoped to be able to pay her something after we had moved, to go towards a small pension for her. It tied her to the house, and the telephone, though. We had come up with the idea of having a cleaner once a week. Mrs Scott was one of my patients. She lived round the corner from our little semi-detached house. Despite her name, she was as Yorkshire as they come. Underneath her dour, almost gruff, exterior she had a kind heart. She loved the children and they responded well to her. On the odd occasions when we could have an evening out together, she was a willing babysitter. And she was excellent at taking calls. There were even times when a chat with Mrs Scott was all that was needed for patients to feel better. The times when she came to clean were when Margaret could escape the house to shop. She had fulfilled this role in our small semi and was eager to continue when we were at Craig-na-Hullie.

"Well, I'd like to try and make my consulting rooms as modern as possible. I think that the patients will like them…possibly not Mrs Bartholomew. I mean they seem to really like the antenatal clinic, don't they?"

"Yes, Eric. I'll give you that. The thing is that didn't cost anything. We just used what we had." I noticed that Tom had used the plural pronoun. He hadn't done anything in the formation or running of the clinic. I decided that I would just have to show him.

"I've got an idea for a filing system for the patients' records as well…"

"New cardboard boxes?" Tom teased as he tilted his head back to blow smoke at the ceiling.

I smiled. Tom was easy to get on with as long as I didn't require much from him. However, I had one last item before we started to discuss the practicalities of the day.

"No. It's a sort of large trolley with two trays to hold all the records. I can push it out of the way when I don't need it. I'll have to have it made specially." I paused. "There is something else though. I don't know if you've started making plans for your summer holiday yet but I'd like to take mine between the Blunts going and us moving in." Each partner had three weeks holiday a year, but normally we only took two at any one time so the burden was not as great on the others. This time there was only Tom to hold the fort. He'd be run off his feet.

Tom looked at me with a thoughtful look and paused. I held my breath. "Ok, Eric. That's fine. I'll do it."

I smiled my thanks, but there was something else. "Actually Tom, could it be the three weeks before I move in? I was just wondering…"

"Eric, you old rascal. Nabbed me that time. Of course, I'll do it, though. Chrissey would kill me if I said no. You must promise you'll pass on any of those cardboard boxes George used for filing though. I may want to modernise!"

"There is only one thing to say really, Tom, in George's words: splendid! SPLENDID!"

Our three weeks holiday became a montage of builders, rubble, dust, noise and endless discussions about things I had no real idea about, but were happening, rather frantically, in the house to make it fit for our family and surgeries. I was delegated to a sort of project-manager, a role I smiled about as I struggle with anything to do with building. I have, after all, been known to hammer in screws rather than screw them in. On these occasions, Margaret always ended up saying, "Oh, give it here, Eric!" However, nodding at seemingly appropriate times in a conversation helped. I always came away with reports for Margaret that things were going well and would be finished on time, our main worry. Charles was at school but Ruth wasn't, and we had decided that the safest thing was to keep her well away in our small semi-detached house, although Margaret increasingly found this frustrating as time went on. She wanted to be at Craig-na-Hullie as much as possible.

There were three areas that were being tackled and I would inspect each one with Bert. He was the 'main man' and every morning appeared in a spotlessly clean white boiler suit, and a sharp pencil stuck behind his ear. He wasn't particularly tall but his burly physique mixed with a strong personality turned him into a giant. His lack of even a wisp of hair on his shiny pate was over compensated for by greying tangles of sideburns and eyebrows that seemed as untamed as bramble patches. After his 'Mornin' Dr 'Ainsworth!' his words were rare, unless he was describing the building work, when he revealed his passion in his fluency.

I would quiz him about the day's plans and he would stand, silently listening, with his hands clasped over his shrouded tummy, his entwined fingers looking like rows of hairy sausages. Usually, we would start outside in the yard.

"There's t' outside toilet. Yer'd never know it 'ad been there." He stroked the new stonework that filled in the doorway lovingly. "Same wi' t' coal 'ole. By the way what do yer want me ter do wi' t'old toilet bowl?"

"Erm, yes, yes. The stonework is lovely, Bert. It blends in well," I added quickly to show my sham knowledge but equal passion. "The toilet bowl? Oh, just leave it at the back of the garage for the moment." We both stood back, stroking and patting the new work with our eyes.

"It's all coming on a treat, Bert," I said as we climbed the stone steps. The door at the top was open. The scullery was now a blank space. A man, this time in a blue boiler suit, was drawing a door shape on the wall opposite.

"We'll be knocking through that terday," Bert pointed with a massive finger. "Then we'll brick up t'arch - t'old way into t'surgery." The old dispensary would then become the downstairs toilet. "An' through 'ere," Bert led the way into the kitchen through swirling motes of dust in the air. "T'lads are knocking down t'partition wall and stairs at t'far end…" A crash confirmed his statement.

The whole room seemed to be filled with broken wood and rubble. I exclaimed, "It looks a bit of a mess…"

"Oh, it's nout, doctor. We'll soon clear it, then we'll put a new floor over." He pointed to the hole in the ceiling where the maids' stairs had emerged through into the floor above. "An' then we'll get t'cooker put in. T'missus'll like that, no doubt!"

We met Brian, the carpenter – 't'chippy' – in the waiting room. The passageway, that ran from the hallway to the surgery door and used by the maids of old, was no more. The entrance had been bricked up and was waiting for its new plaster. The wall dividing it from the surgery had been removed and the mess of rubble and dust of yesterday was gone. This extra space, made from the passage, would house the new examination couch. Brian had just finished the new benches around the edge of the waiting room and

Bert spent some enraptured time wandering and stroking the new woodwork. "Grand job, Brian. Grand job," he muttered.

I emulated Bert's praise. "You've done a, erm, grand job there. Lovely." There was now only one door into, and out of, the waiting room. It was much more satisfactory. The new bench seating would mean that the patients would not need to stand up to change seats when someone went into the surgery, they would just slide along.

"Well, doctor, ah'll leave yer wi' Brian an' yer can chat about t'trolley yer want done. Ah'll be upstairs. We've done so well, doctor, that we can put in that stud wall round t'top stairs." Bert's expansive chest swelled further as he smiled, "All fer t'same price an' all."

"Oh, Bert. Thank you. It will make a big difference keeping this place heated in winter."

Bert was embarrassed with pleasure and muttered, "Well ah'd best be getting' on wi' it." Brian and I were left to discuss the final details of the trolley that would have two slanting trays to contain the patients' records. Swiveling wheels would enable it to be moved around the surgery. It would be a massive improvement on the cardboard boxes. It might even achieve a Mrs Bartholomew accolade.

Three days later, a somber Bert met me at the corner of the drive as I arrived for my morning visit. It was obvious that he was agitated and wanted to see me as soon as possible. He waved both arms as I drove across the road and pulled up alongside him. I wound down the window. "Hello, Bert. Is everything all right?"

"Mornin', doctor. There is sommat, but you'd best come an' see."

We walked down the curve of the drive into the yard. Bert broke his usual reticence and said, "Ah've got sommat ter tell yer, doctor. There's some good news an' …"

"Oh, tell me the good news first, Bert," I tried to be jovial.

"Well, doctor, we got the cooker in…"

"That IS good news, Bert. Does it look good?" We had got to the bottom of the stone steps.

"It's a mite tricky to see actually," Bert muttered. "T'problem is, doctor, it's in t' cellar…."

"The cellar? Why did you put it there?" I was aghast. Poor Margaret. The cooker was her pride, her dream. And she didn't want it there!

Bert stopped at the top of the steps and faced me. He was forlorn. He wrenched the words out of himself, "We didn't put it there, it kind o' went there by issen! It fell through t'floor!"

"Through the floor. So, there's NO floor in the kitchen?" I gasped.

"Well, there is … but there's a big hole an' all." I pushed past Bert into the kitchen corridor.

"Nay, doctor, don't go right in. We've got ter mek t'floor safe," Bert almost shouted as he grabbed my arm. "If yer want ter see it go into t'cellar." I went down the cellar steps. The darkness at the bottom was gone and a murky light filtered through a jagged hole in the ceiling. On the floor, directly under the hole, Margaret's cooker rested, solid but at an angle, on a pile of crunched wooden flooring. Its enamel was made grey and lacklustre by a thick layer of dust

I looked at it carefully from all sides. Bert said, "Aye, we've also looked at it an'all. It seems fine. Nout wrong! We'll just have to see when we teck it apart to teck it back into t'kitchen."

"This'll put things back, Bert. We won't get in on time, will we?" I was starting to panic. We had immovably fixed deadlines.

Bert sounded a bit more optimistic as he explained that it wouldn't take long to repair the floor and move the cooker, as long as it hadn't suffered in the fall. He was pleased that we had found the weakness in the floor now rather than later. They would work through the night if needed. "There might be one or two painting jobs that we can't finish, that's all. Can you or t'missus paint?'

I thought for a moment. I knew Margaret was good with a paintbrush, but I was also taken by the idea of adding my own mark on the house renovation. It couldn't be that difficult, could it? "Margaret likes painting, could you make sure you leave the surgery door, Bert? The one into the hall. I'd like to do that one!"

"Right you are, doctor. If yer sure." Bert looked at me with a rather strange expression.

I decided to change the subject. "Well, Bert, now you've told me the good news, what's the bad?"

Bert's whole being seemed to erupt into an almighty guffaw and more dust was dislodged from around the hole. "BAD NEWS, HA, HA! That's a good un, doctor. Yer're a one!"

Bert was as good as his word. The next day I could inspect the kitchen floor, with its clean, white rectangle of floorboards surrounded by a sea of dirty, old ones, and a polished cooker, unharmed and in place. It gleamed as if nothing had happened. Bert and Brian had indeed worked through the night.

Soon the 'lino' floor covering was hiding any trace of this upset and the kitchen units, an unusual novelty in those days, were installed. The surgery was painted up, apart from its hall door. The bedrooms were ready to receive our furniture and all mess cleaned to Margaret's standards. There was still much to do, as and when money and time allowed, but we could move in.

We actually managed to move a day earlier than expected, on a Thursday. We had decided to leave all the last-minute packing and removals to a company so we could take the children away from the situation. We spent the day with Margaret's mother in her house just the other side of Huddersfield and returned in the afternoon, for the last time, to our small 'semi' that had been our home for two and a half years. We met Arthur Prichard, the owner of our building firm renovating Craig-na-Hullie. He was also our present landlord.

"Well, thank you for leaving this place in such good condition. I hope it helped you as you got started in the practice," Arthur said after looking around. "It's a bit small, but cosy! You'll find that small houses sometimes have their advantages when you move to Craig-na-Hullie." He smiled. "I hope the men have been good up there?"

"Yes, they've been excellent. Please thank all of them. And thank you, Arthur. You've been very helpful and we're grateful." I shook his hand and had a sudden realisation that we would become good friends. I handed over the keys. "We must be going now, though. I want to catch up with the removal men before they finish."

The lorry, the rear doors open revealing an emptied space, was still at the kerbside when we arrived at our new home. I reversed down the drive and parked in the yard. There was no Bert waiting, just the stone steps leading up to our house. We went in and the removal men were just taking the last bed upstairs. I said, "Margaret, why don't you take the children outside for a play on the lawn? I'll just have a word with the men and then we can look around together when they've gone."

Margaret looked a little downcast but said, "Oh well, what's a few extra minutes after all this time. Come on you two." Margaret grabbed the children before they could wander off and dragged them to the garden. I found them there, five minutes later, sitting on the edge of the lawn at the top of the rockery. They were all gazing into the valley below. Margaret pointed, "Look, Eric, there's a train down there."

There were three tracks coming from different directions. The one coming towards us from the North curved its way through a cutting, and then over a viaduct, to meet the other two in a triangle of lines. An old station that looked decrepit and unused even at this distance was arranged around this triangle with a platform on each side. It looked very complex and I could see that the two lines going off to our left and right were both going into tunnels. It was fascinating. So that was where Joe Warren had worked before becoming George's 'Doctor's Man'. The family were all watching a goods train emerging round through the cutting, from Keighley to the north.

"Look, daddy, it's making smoke signals," Charles exclaimed. We could not hear anything at this distance but the puffs of white smoke were distinct.

"What do you think it's saying to us?" Margaret said.

"Hello," suggested Ruth.

"Come and see me as soon as you can," was Charles' more adventurous idea.

"Well, I think it's saying 'welcome, you'll like it here!'" I concluded.

Margaret mused, "I think we will. It's a lovely spot and you two can do lots of exploring when you play out. Come on though." She scrambled up and said, "I can't wait to see what they've done in the kitchen!" I cast a final look at the train. It had now reached the station and was heading towards the right-hand tunnel, on the way to Bradford.

We rushed up the stone steps and ceremonially opened the back door. There was the new door through to the new toilet. Brian had also constructed a large cupboard in the old scullery for cleaning stuff and my tool box, but we hardly gave it a glance. Margaret was in the kitchen. It did look good and the cooker glistened proudly in its fresh enamel. It hadn't suffered in its adventures. Margaret was silent. She sniffed as tears welled up. She walked around, touching the cupboards, the work surface and then stopped at the cooker. "It's wonderful, Eric!"

"Oh, no!" Charles was almost shouting. "The Blunts have taken the stairs with them!"

"No, Charles. It was the builders. We don't have any maids and it gives mummy more space…" I started to explain.

"But we're going to use them for hide and seek!"

"Why don't you and Ruth go and have a look at your bedrooms. There should be your boxes of toys in them," I suggested.

Margaret and I were left alone. She came across and we wrapped each other in our arms. "Thank you, darling," Margaret whispered. "I think we will love it here." Her brimful eyes looked up into mine. She smiled.

"OH, NO!" we heard Charles shout from the landing. We walked through to the hallway. "The builders have taken the bed from my room AS WELL!"

I smiled, "No, that was the Blunt's. It was their bed. They need it…"

"Well, it was a jolly good bed and it was in my room…"

"Why don't I show you the play rooms, Charles?" I asked. In truth, virtually the whole house could be described as such. Our meager furniture hardly made any impression on the space. Charles began to see the potential for the place and was satisfied.

I went back to Margaret who was opening cupboard doors in the kitchen. "Erm, there are one or two bits of paintwork to finish off, Margaret. I was wondering…"

"Yes, I noticed the surgery door," Margaret's voice emerged from a cupboard.

"Oh, that. I'm going to do that. Probably over the weekend."

Margaret's face appeared shocked, "Are you sure, Eric?" Honestly, she was sounding just like Bert.

"Yes, yes," I said defensively. "It's not that difficult, you know!"

A gentle tap, tapping on the back door prevented me from giving a further vindication of my decorating skills. Margaret and I went through to the door together. We weren't expecting visitors, but it was quite an occasion to open the back door for our first one. A little old lady stood on the top step, beaming behind her National Health spectacles and holding an upside-down old toffee tin carefully in front of her. Goodness knows what her true height would have been had it not been for the rickets she obviously had had as an adolescent. There were still people in the village bearing the curved bones that resulted from this illness when they were growing up. They had started work in the mill and the lack of sunlight on their skin due to their working hours had caused a deficiency of vitamin D. I recognised Mrs Bristow. She lived just down the road on a side street and had been one of George's patients. However, I had seen her once or twice. Her ailments could all be attributed to old age, and she bore them with fortitude. Mrs Bristow's legs were so bent that they almost seemed to make a circle between them

"Hello, Mrs Bristow. Welcome. You're our first visitor, you know. What can I do for you? Do you want to come in?'

"Nay, doctor. Ah won't bother yer. Ah thought ah'd welcome yer in wi' a cake," she said in a chirpy voice. She held the tin out and Margaret took it.

"Oh, thank you Mrs Bristow," Margaret said. I was very pleased. George and I had eaten slices of Mrs Bristow's cakes on a number of occasions with our morning coffee. She only seemed to do one sort, a delicious sponge with a delicate, but slightly crunchy, skin. Her gift indicated that she would be continuing the tradition with me.

"Thank you, Mrs Bristow. That's very kind of you. I think you kept Dr Blunt going with your cakes..." I started.

"Oh, yer are a one, doctor. Get away wi' yer!" She turned to Margaret. "An' it's lovely ter see Mrs

'Ainsworth, an' all." Charles had appeared and had squeezed between Margaret and me. "An' who's this then?"

"Oh, this is Charles, our eldest. Ruth is upstairs somewhere," I explained.

"It's grand ter see children 'ere aggen. It's a grand 'ouse, it is, but it needs children. Well, ah'll be leavin' t'cake. Keep t'tin for t'moment."

"Oh, thank you. I'm sure Eric, er, the doctor, will bring it to you soon."

"Ah made one fer Dr Blunt when they came 'ere back in 1924, tha knows. I were only thirty-four then but ah was known fer my cakes even then." Mrs Bristow stopped and smiled. "Ah remember when Dr Blunt fust came. 'E was a one. 'E allus had a nice car. Ah remember jus' after 'e came, we 'ad a new bobby. Geoffrey was 'is name, 'e didn't know Dr Blunt's car."

Mrs Bristow started chuckling. "Well, t'young doctor was out on 'is visits an' that Geoffrey didn't like the way 'e'd parked, even though in them days yer could park jus' anywhere. Dr Blunt would jus' stop in t'middle o' t'road an' get out without pulling in or turning t'engine off." I could tell that Margaret was desperate to get on inside the house and was squirming beside me. But Mrs Bristow was in full flow. She had an audience and she had paid them to listen with a cake.

"Geoffrey didn't know the car an' 'e just waited fer Dr Blunt to come back. Then 'e started ter tell 'im. I was there! It were jus' outside t'Co-op. Dr Blunt jus' held up 'is hand an' said, 'Yer've got yer fust aid exam termorrer, aven't yer?' Geoffrey just nodded an' Dr Blunt, 'e were a one, said, 'Well, yer've failed!' Just like that. But then 'e patted Geoffrey's hand an' smiled. From then on, they were t' best o'pals." Mrs Bristow's chuckles involved her whole body.

"Well ah'd best be off. Welcome, doctor. Yer'll like it 'ere!"

Chapter 9

The next morning was the last of our 'holiday' that year and I hoped that we might manage a bit of a 'lie-in', bought for us by the hard work of Bert and his workmates by finishing their work a day early. I knew that I would have to spend the weekend sorting out the surgery and waiting room; my first surgery was due to take place on Monday morning. I had outlined my idea of painting the surgery door again to Margaret before going to bed; and for some reason she had just smiled. Since talking with Bert in the cellar, I had secretly fantasised about this job and it had grown in importance in my mind. I would be making my mark on the surgery as well as the house. In my imagination I had performed the task many times from opening the tin to stroking my loaded brush over the door. It appeared easy. What was all the fuss about?

    I hadn't set the alarm and in my semi-comatose state was luxuriating in the soft warmth of the bed, with only a vague awareness of the soft, rhythmical breathing of Margaret next to me. I was drifting away again when the bedroom door burst open. I was awake instantly, senses propelled into action.

"There are MEN outside!" It was Charles. I relaxed a little but was perplexed by his comment.

"Men, Charles?" I asked. He seemed either agitated or excited and climbed over the bumps of my legs to get closer.

"Yes, and they're making a funny noise," Charles whispered in my ear so that he wouldn't disturb his mother, an action rendered useless by the volume of whisper and the wriggling onto the bed.

"What are the men doing, Charles?"

"They're just walking, Daddy. They're all going into the village."

I glanced at our alarm clock. It was only twenty minutes to seven. "I'd better come and have a look. Come on." Charles pulled me out of bed. We had managed to rig up curtains in all the bedrooms the evening before by hooking them over the brass curtain rails left by the Blunts. They wouldn't pull back so Charles and I pushed our way behind them.

He was right. Small groups of men, in twos and threes were walking along, some had pipes or cigarettes but all were wearing flat caps. Some were chatting but most were just walking along together in a sleepy silence in the still morning air. It was this action that was producing the noise, a sort of metallic scraping sound. We watched.

"Did you see that, daddy?" Charles said, excited.

"What was it?"

"That man," Charles pointed. "He made a spark!"

I kept my eyes on the culprit. There it was! I could see what was happening. All the men were shod in the same fashion. Their shoes all seemed over large and I thought I could see that the soles were made of wood. The scraping sound and odd spark were made as the shoes scraped the ground.

"Oh, they're wearing clogs, Charles. I've seen them in the village before. No one anywhere else wears clogs quite like these. They say they are really comfortable. They have rubber bits underneath and metal bits at the ends. The metal bits make a spark on the road. There! There's another one. Did you see it?" Charles nodded. "Well, now you're up you can play with your toys a bit. Mummy and I want to have a bit longer in bed."

I had just got back into bed and had pulled the sheet over my head when there was a dreadful wailing sound. Both Margaret and I sat bolt upright, sleep expelled. "What in the world is that, Eric?" Margaret said.

"Oh, I think I know what it is…" the door suddenly burst open again. I was expecting Charles to come and announce this next strange occurrence. He had.

"Can you hear THAT?" he said to a background cacophony that rose and fell in pitch. Suddenly, it stopped. "What was it, daddy?"

I looked at the clock again. That confirmed it. I hadn't heard the siren before, but George had warned me about it. "It's the mill hooter. It goes off ten minutes before seven every day to let the workers know they have only got ten minutes to get inside the gates before they are locked…"

"What happens if they don't?" Charles asked.

"They can't work that day," I explained.

"That's good, isn't it?" Charles was obviously enchanted with the idea of not having to work.

"Well, they don't get paid either and then they won't be able to buy things. Not only that but if they're late too many times they lose their jobs. I was talking to a patient the other day and there are two sets of gates, one in the High Street and the others down the road from the crossroads. If they are just too late for first gates the men all run round the corner and try and beat the man who locks the gates. They all try and get there just on time."

Ruth appeared at the doorway. "What was that horrid noise, mummy?"

Margaret sighed loudly and swung her legs out of bed. "It was just the mill making a noise, Ruth. It's nothing to worry about, but now we are all wide awake we might as well get up."

Breakfast was contrived amongst the removal boxes left in the kitchen. It was made memorable, at least for the children, by the addition of a slice of Mrs Bristow's cake. It was a little like camping, but inside, and on a much larger scale. During it, Margaret announced, "Daddy is going to do some painting today so we need to be out of the way. You two can come shopping with me. We'll find out what the village is like … "

"Oh, I don't think you need to go, do you?" I said, trying to keep the tinge of panic out of my voice. I had hoped that Margaret would be around in case I needed advice or assistance.

"Well, darling, we haven't got any food in the house and you wouldn't want the children to get in your way. Why, do you think you'll need my help? You could wait…" Margaret was looking at me with a rather strange expression on her face.

"Oh, no, no. It can't be that difficult. I just thought the children might like to explore round here?" I tried to keep any sound of desperation out of my voice.

"We won't be long. It'll give you time to do the door and they can play when we get back."

Eventually the family went out and I was left. I would approach it like a surgical operation, methodically. I would lay out everything needed carefully on the bare floorboards by the surgery door and get myself dressed in suitable clothing, like 'scrubs' for an operation; Margaret had found my 'dirty jobs' clothes in one of our bags. The paint and brushes had been left in the cellar, on the stone slab, by the workmen when they had left. Everything was ready. With some trepidation I approached the paint tin with my screwdriver and discovered that having gloves on my hands to keep any paint off was not such a good idea; I couldn't grip the screwdriver well enough, and would probably have difficulties with the brush.

Having levered off the lid I discovered that the tin was nearly full of some creamy coloured oil. It didn't look like paint in the slightest. I looked at the label: White, gloss. I was sure that was what I wanted. I carefully put the tip of the bristles of my brush into the stuff and started painting with the loving strokes that I had imagined in my fantasies. It made the door look wet and shiny but certainly not white, and, to make matter worse, it dribbled down the door. I stopped and decided to start again. On reading the small writing on the tin, I discovered that I didn't really understand much of it, but I knew 'stir well'. This I did with the screwdriver. The paint was transformed – much better.

There were now two other problems. I had started with a brush that was clearly far too small. It would take me the whole weekend to paint the one door. There was another, larger one in the cellar. I also had to clean off the oily stuff from the door. The only piece of cloth I could think of using, that wasn't packed, was the tea towel we had used to dry the breakfast things. I went to get it and wiped as much of the oily paint as I could. I then left the small brush to clean, floating in water, in our brand new, stainless-steel kitchen sink. The cloth did the job with the oil, though.

I quite enjoyed painting that door. I found I could get quite a lot of paint on the brush by pushing all parts of the bristles, down to the metal bit round the handle, into the tin. It was lovely seeing the glistening white covering the brown. Well, not quite. The brown kept reappearing through the white in ugly streaks, often where the thicker bristles had been. I put more paint on to hide the brown. There was something strange that I hadn't encountered in my fantasies. It seemed as though the paint on the door wanted to move downwards and I kept having to push it back upwards with the loaded brush. However, it was all very satisfying, and in its own way, relaxing. Maybe I could paint more doors – Margaret would be pleased. We would need more paint though; this was nearly all gone. I was sure that she would be amazed at my prowess on her return.

I had almost finished when I heard the children clamouring outside the back door. I stood with arms opened wide to protect my work when they came in. Margaret, preceded by a tumbling Charles and Ruth, pushed her way in clutching bags. I said firmly, "DON"T go near the surgery door! I've nearly finished it."

"Oh, darling. Well done. It wasn't too difficult, was it? Can I see?" Margaret stepped forward and I stood back to one side.

The stunned silence, not just from Margaret but also both children, was not quite the reaction I expected. I turned round to see what had caused the looks of bemusement (children) and horror (Margaret). The surface of the door seemed to be moving gradually downwards. In fact, it looked as though it was melting in slow motion. A white puddle was forming on the floorboards.

"Do you think I've put a bit too much paint on?"

"That's one way of putting it. How much did you use, Eric?" Margaret was struggling with her words.

"Well, erm, just the one tin…"

"A WHOLE tin! On one door?" Margaret was amazed. I stood helpless. "Oh, give it here, Eric. I'll sort it out."

It was then that she discovered the tea towel, and the use to which I had put it. And then she discovered the brush in the sink.

I spent the rest of the day in the surgery getting that ready, trying to obliterate Margaret's loud clatterings, mutterings and grumblings in the kitchen and hall as she rectified my mistakes before they hardened into permanence, and kept well out of her way. I have not painted anything since, or done any sort of decorating. Margaret soon calmed down and eventually we laughed about it between ourselves, then with friends and eventually the whole village. I haven't known Margaret get so cross, though, except for the time I cleaned out the drains in the yard with her soup ladle.

The consulting room and waiting area were very well prepared, and exceedingly tidy, for the Monday morning surgery, needless to say, as I spent rather a long time in there over the weekend. Margaret had managed to clean off all my painting attempts by scraping the door downwards so that gravity was aided in its assault on my paint. The gloss topcoat was collected in reams of newspaper, of which we had a fortunate abundance in the packing cases, and an undercoat, apparently that was what one applied first, painted on carefully. I was too busy tidying the surgery to watch, so missed this opportunity to further my education, but the children found it absolutely fascinating.

It was with some excitement, mixed with trepidation, that I opened the inner and outer surgery doors that Monday morning. Tom had telephoned me on the previous evening. He briefly told me how the three weeks had been but we arranged to meet at 'Innisfree' after the morning surgery to go into details and talk about the future. Tom's good wishes were still resounding in my memory as I slid the bolts back at 8 o'clock precisely. This was earlier than I would normally open them but I wanted to make a good impression on my first day. I looked round with some pride at the newly painted walls, shiny in pale grey-green gloss paint. Everything was ready. I had bought a new chair on wheels for myself and sat on this behind the roll top desk that George had kindly sold me. He had taken his great brass dome of a bell as a memento of his years of doctoring, but I had replaced it with an electric buzzer. This was linked to a sign in the waiting room that lit up with 'Next please.' It was the height of modernity indeed.

I pushed back on my chair and its ability to move with ease shocked me as I shot backwards and collided with my new wooden trolley, now replete with patients' record cards. Ah well, it was better to find out now rather than with a patient present. I stroked its varnished surface. I wondered if my first 'customer' would be Mrs Bartholomew. It'd be just like her to come along with a spurious ailment just to find out if any changes had taken place and to express her opinion.

I ate a Smartie and got up. I straightened the things on my glass-doored cabinet. And everything inside. It was amazing that they needed tidying again after a day when they hadn't been disturbed. I picked up the Elliot forceps, which George had left for me and gave them a polish. I presumed that he had wanted to give me something and had chosen these because of my interest in obstetrics. These were old, probably from George's early days and were long. Long forceps are hardly used now. They are for attaching round a baby's head that is high up in the birth canal. I knew I wouldn't use them but they reminded me of the extensive history of medicine that my own story would now become a part of.

I heard a sound. It was the outer surgery door being opened. Heavy footsteps announced my first patient. Soon others followed.

It seemed that each new entrant into the waiting room was greeted with a deep female voice booming out, "'ELLO THERE!" I couldn't recognise the patient by the disembodied voice. Each person's name was added to this welcome so I gained some idea of my patients before even seeing them. The level of conversation rose in crescendo, peppered with contributions at full volume from the mysterious female. I suddenly needed to use the toilet. I was grateful for our decision to convert the old dispensary into a cloakroom and that Bert and his crew had managed to finish it.

Eventually, the hands on my watch had crept round to half past eight. I leant forward and pressed the buzzer button. The conversation stopped briefly but then resumed at a lower volume but no one appeared. I pressed the button again. This time the interlude in the babble of banter was longer and the female voice boomed, "DID YER 'EAR THAT THERE NOISE, DORIS? WHAT'S GOIN' ON? THERE'S BEEN NO BELL AN' IT'S GONE 'ALF PAST! IT'S THAT NEW DOCTOR, AH'LL BE BOUND!"

I decided that I would go into the waiting room and welcome my patients to my first surgery. I would then be able to ascertain why they hadn't responded to the buzzer and sign. There were quite a few waiting when I entered, sitting in order on the new bench. After all the greetings which I had heard I felt I could name nearly everyone.

"Good morning, I'm Doctor Hainsworth. I can recognise most of your faces but one or two of you I haven't met yet. I hope you all like the things we have done to make the waiting room and surgery a bit more comfortable and efficient." There was a murmur as people glanced round, as if they hadn't noticed anything when they had come in, and acknowledged the changes. There were one or two exclamations of, "Oh, 'ello, doctor."

"By the way," I went on. "Dr Blunt took his bell with him so I have got a buzzer instead. That sign will also light up. Did it work just now?" I looked at the rather stern lady who was sitting nearest the door. From her place in the room, I guessed that she would be the first in the queue. She wore a dress that daringly showed her ankles and some of her calf, but hid everything else effectively inside a cloth that looked as though it had been sprinkled in small flowers. She had retained her stern expression and I predicted that she also had the strident voice.

"WHAT WAS THAT?" she boomed. I was right, it was her. "YER'LL 'AVE TER SPEAK UP THA' KNOWS. AH CAN'T BE DOIN' WI' MUTTERIN'"

"I'M SORRY, MRS, erm. DID YOU SEE THE SIGN LIGHT UP?" I pointed to it on the wall by the door.

"THAT IT DID, YOUNG DOCTOR. BUT IT SAID 'NEX' PLEASE.'"

"YOU'RE RIGHT, MRS… erm."

"FISH. MRS FISH. BUT AH COULDN' GO IN, COULD I? THERE WASN' A FUST. AH COULDN' BE NEXT AFTER NO ONE. YER NEED A SIGN THAT SAYS 'FUST PLEASE.' THEN ALL T'OTHERS CAN BE NEXT."

"Oh, I see what you mean. Very good Mrs Fish." I had to acknowledge the logic of this. I was beginning to lose my enthusiasm for my modernisations.

"EY, SPEAK UP, YOUNG DOCTOR. YOU'RE MUTTERIN' AGGEN!"

"YOU'RE RIGHT, MRS FISH. BUT YOU CAN COME IN NOW. WHEN THE BUZZER… when the buzzer goes again, please could the next one just come in from now on." I led the way into the consulting room.

Mrs Fish looked round and sniffed at the smell of new paint. A faint smile flickered across her features. I took this as a sign of her approval. "Please sit down." I indicated the chair by the desk.

"Now what can…" I could see Mrs Fish preparing to tell me to speak up. "WHAT CAN I DO FOR YOU, MRS FISH?"

Mrs Fish nodded. "WELL, IT'S ME BOTTOM!"

I sat back aghast. It couldn't be. My very first patient. Was Mrs Fish somehow in collusion with Mrs

Bartholomew? Was she somehow sent to set me up for more ribald remarks? I would go carefully with my questioning.

"ERM, YOUR erm bottom?" I said the last word quietly. I knew that Mrs Fish's loud voice could be heard in the waiting room and mine would be as well. In fact, I was sure that the volume of chatter had decreased in there so I acted out this last word by tapping my own buttock.

"AYE, DOCTOR. ME BOTTOM. THEY'VE DROPPED AGGEN... ME PILES."

I couldn't believe it. Was it a total coincidence that my first patient under our new regime had this complaint? I nearly asked if she knew Mrs Bartholomew, but then she might be reminded of that very first surgery. I studied the notes that George had written in her records. She indeed had haemorrhoids in the past, a few times, and I could see what he had prescribed.

"THEY'RE LIKE A BUNCH O' GRAPES, DOCTOR. DANGLIN'. IT'S 'APPENED AFORE. THEY'RE RIGHT PAINFUL, LIKE."

I couldn't hear any conversation in the waiting room now. I pulled my chair closer to Mrs Fish so that I could reduce my voice level. "Well. Mrs Fish. They'll probably disappear by themselves again."

"WHAT WAS THAT, DOCTOR?'

"THEY''LL GO BY THEMSELVES. YOU COULD TRY SITTING IN A WARM BATH FOR TEN MINUTES EVERY DAY. DON'T USE SOAP WHEN YOU WASH YOUR BOTTOM. I'LL GIVE YOU SOME CREAM TO RUB ON THEM AND THAT WILL MAKE YOU MORE COMFORTABLE. IF IT'S REALLY PAINFUL FOR YOU TO SIT, TWIST A TOWEL INTO A

RING AND SIT ON THAT. TRY TO DRINK MORE AND don't strain on the toilet…"

"WHAT WAS THAT?"

I came even closer. "DON'T STRAIN WHEN YOU ARE GOING TO THE TOILET."

"OH, AYE. WELL, THANK YOU, YOUNG DOCTOR. YER CAN PRESS THE BUZZER NOW. THERE IS A NEX'!"

I could hear Mrs Fish going out of the surgery door, but she didn't quite close it for a moment or two. I heard her bellowing out to someone on the surgery path, "NOW THEN, YOU MUS' BE MRS 'AINSWORTH. AH'VE JUS' BEEN TER SEE T'YOUNG DOCTOR ABOUT ME PILES…" The door was slammed shut. I buzzed and thankfully someone came in after a timorous knock on the door. It was another old lady, Doris Tyler. She was Mrs Fish's opposite though. She was small and thin, and she was smiling, almost smirking. I had no doubt at all that she had heard everything of my previous consultation.

Mrs Tyler stood at the door looking around the room carefully. I said, "Oh, come in. Sit down, won't you?' I said cheerfully.

"I like what you've done here, doctor. It's very posh, isn't it? We've all been saying it's nice to have a young doctor."

"Thank you, Mrs Tyler. We have worked hard. I'm sorry you've had to wait so long this morning." I was pleased with her reaction.

"Oh, don't worry about that, doctor. We're always glad to see Mrs Fish in the waiting room. We always hear every word she says. It's quite entertaining really!"

The surgery progressed smoothly and it was with some satisfaction that I closed the surgery doors when the last patient had left, and went through to the kitchen. During the surgery I had heard Margaret answering the telephone, which was sitting on a small table by the door in the hallway and I needed to catch up with her about any late visits before I went to see Tom. I had also heard Ruth making a noise in the hall during the surgery and I knew that she, and Charles when he was at home, would have to play somewhere else. They would also have to be very quiet during surgery times.

Margaret was in the kitchen sorting out her cupboards. Discarded newspaper littered the floor amongst piles of crockery and pans. I cleared a space to pull out one of our kitchen chairs and sat down.

"Hello, darling. How did your surgery go?" she asked.

"Really well. I think the patients like the changes. By the way, you met a Mrs Fish? Talks loudly. Quite deaf…"

"I certainly did. I was just outside in the front garden, planning what I am going to do out there, when she came out of the surgery. She nabbed me for over a half an hour. She has told me, in no uncertain terms, what I have to do with the garden."

"Poor you. I'll tell you later what she came for. You'll never believe it, and on my first surgery! I bet Tom'll laugh. Anyway, I must be getting along to see him."

"Oh, she told me! Won't you have a coffee first?" Margaret asked.

"No, I'll have one there. Tom will have a lot to tell me. Did any late calls come in? I heard you on the 'phone."

"Yes, I've put them by your visiting book. What shall I do with others when you're out, though?"

I remembered a conversation with George after I had noticed a newspaper leaning up against his dining room window back when I had joined the practice. Bea placed it there when she took a late call. If George passed in his car, he would look at the window and, if the newspaper was there, he stopped and collected the details, probably parking somewhere in the middle of the road outside. I told Margaret about the newspaper and she decided it was a great idea. She also had the duplicate visiting book so she knew roughly where I was during the day. I had put in the patients' telephone numbers, if they had a 'phone, so she could leave a message for me at patients' houses if necessary.

Over coffee, I related to Tom about my consultation with Mrs Fish. As I expected, he roared with laughter, which dissolved into a coughing fit. He told me about the past three weeks. I was extremely grateful to him. "It's been tough, Eric, I can tell you. It wouldn't have been so bad, but it was those trips to the 'calling places' in Bradshaw and Clayton that did it for me. I think we are going to have to do something about them."

I had been wondering how to broach the subject of my daily visit to Clayton that even a packet of Spangles couldn't make better. I had thought that Tom would be reluctant to make any changes, but he was suggesting them himself now. "Yes, I've been wondering about that during this last three weeks. There seems to be a greater demand everywhere, especially in Queensbury, and it would be good to ask people in those two outlying places to look for a doctor closer to them. Anyway, more people have their own telephones now, they don't need those calling places to leave messages for us." I had rehearsed my reasoning in my head for some time. "I'll talk through the idea with Fred Benson this morning when I call in. See what he says."

Tom smiled at me. "Oh, I think he'll like the idea. I've spoken to him already. He finds it a bit annoying as well."

Before setting out for Clayton, I thanked Tom once more for holding the fort during the previous three weeks. It was good of him. He was looking forward to examining our changes when he next came to Craig-na-Hullie for the next 'practice' meeting.

Fred Benson was just finishing looking through a range of birthday cards with a 'rep' as I entered his shop with a ping. He looked up at the sound. "Hello, Eric. I'll be with you in a moment. I'm considering branching out a bit. Cards and the like. What do you think?" He folded his hands over his tummy seemingly to aid his thinking.

"I think it's a good idea, Fred. Always keep developing your ideas." The 'rep' packed his bags and left with an initial order.

I told Fred what Tom and I had discussed. Fred said, "Well, I won't be sad, Eric, if you want my opinion. It's been a pleasure to help Dr Blunt and you but we've always got to keep developing our ideas as you say. It's got to be a bit of a bind, if you don't mind me telling you."

"No, Fred. Dr Akroyd and I have been talking. He's done all the work in the practice this last three weeks and we both realise that it covers too large an area. The demands and needs of the patients are changing and we are having to adapt to the new situation. It seems a good time now that Dr Akroyd has just become senior partner, and we're making other changes as well." I looked round at this friendly shop. I had got to know it over the past two and a half years. The shelves and glass bottles, redolent of many childhoods, were still the same but I could tell that Fred had introduced new ideas. A shiny new cabinet held Corona bottles of 'fizzy pop'. I leant forward to see the range.

"Oh, I see you've got Dandelion and Burdock. We used to have that when I was growing up and it's one of my favourites. I'll take a bottle. Maybe Charles and Ruth will like it as well." I put the bottle on the counter.

Fred slid a tube of Spangles alongside it. "For old times' sake, Doctor," he said. He held his hand up as I produced my wallet. "No, this is on the house. It's been good working with you and Dr Blunt. I hope I'll be seeing you around."

"I have no doubt, Fred," I smiled. "I've got to bring the bottle back!"

The morning went well and I was feeling pleased with my first day as I pulled up at the kerb by our house. I was getting adept at reversing round the curved wall into the yard by steering with my right hand as I twisted my body round to look over my left shoulder through the back window.

Over lunch I related the events of the morning to Margaret. She looked somewhat stony when I mentioned Mrs Fish again. "Huh! That woman!" she exclaimed.

"So, what did she say was her reason for coming to the surgery?' I asked.

"Mention it! The whole of Sandbeds probably heard her as well. She went into graphic detail, Eric. She kept rubbing her bottom all through our conversation. She was very graphic!" Margaret giggled at the thought

The afternoon also went well and, although I passed the house a few times on my rounds, the newspaper was never displayed in the dining room window. So, it was with a sense of satisfaction that I approached the evening surgery at half past five.

I could hear a babble of conversation emerging from the waiting room as I entered the consulting room. I quickly checked that everything was straight, and that the trolley containing the records was in place just behind my chair, before going through to the waiting room to invite the first patient in. I wasn't going to be caught out again with perverse logic regarding my electronic sign. The waiting room was nearly full when I entered. The conversation stopped and everyone's heads turned to me. There were a number of hearty greetings: 'Evenin', doctor'.

"Welcome," I said. I started to explain about the 'Next Please' sign but was interrupted.

"Yer've no reason ter tell us. We'd a come in." A man in the corner explained. I recognised him, Tom Hardacre. He had been one of George's patients but I had seen him once or twice.

"It's just that I had problems…"

"Oh, we know, doctor. We were havin' a right laff about it. Don't worry about us, lad."

I looked around again. Everyone was nodding and smiling. The waiting room was nearly full and more would arrive during the surgery. I knew that I wouldn't be finished at seven and it might even go on until eight o'clock. With a slight feeling of despair, I went to press the buzzer. My mood wasn't lightened when, about twenty minutes into the surgery, I heard a new voice in the waiting room. It was Mrs Bartholomew. I just knew that she wouldn't be able to resist coming on my first day without George to inspect any changes I had made. However, all the patients responded to the 'Next Please' sign with no problems. At ten to eight I was sure that I hadn't heard that voice for some time. Maybe she had gone away. She should really have come into the consulting room some time ago. I pressed the buzzer one more time to make sure that the waiting room was empty.

I stopped breathing when I heard distinct footsteps in the waiting room. My body froze as they approached, doom laden, towards the surgery door. There was a knock and the familiar yet undesirable voice boomed, "Are yer there, doctor?"

I was tempted to remain absolutely silent and still, in the hope that Mrs Bartholomew might yet depart, but the Hyppocratic Oath forbade me. After all, I argued with myself, this time it might be different. I might win Mrs Bartholomew around. The words from the Oath, remembered from my training, popped into my memory: '…may I long experience the joy of healing those who seek my help.' I forced myself to respond, "Yes, Mrs Bartholomew. Please come in!"

Mrs Bartholomew was wearing her summer outfit, which was exactly the same as her winter one but without the coat. She still wore the felt hat and her moustache held my reluctant gaze even more with its addition of biscuit crumbs.

"Come in, come in. I hope you haven't been waiting long. There have been a lot in tonight…"

"About two hour, young doctor," Mrs Bartholomew said. I didn't hear any resentment in her voice though.

"Oh, you should've been seen ages ago. What went wrong?"

"Well, ah let 'em all go in front o' me. Ah've 'ad a grand natter an' ah wanted to see what yer've done. Yer've done away wi' t'bell, then?"

"Yes, Dr Blunt took that with him when he left. I've got a new buzzer and sign now …"

"Umpph!"

I was determined to bring Mrs Bartholomew to a more positive frame of mind. I said, "Seeing as you have waited all this time, perhaps I can show you my alterations in here?"

Mrs Bartholomew followed me around observing the differences wrought in the consulting room. Her only comments, expressed at odd intervals, were grunts and more 'umpphs. Eventually she stood in the middle of the room and I could see her struggling with something nice to say. I waited. It was obviously costing some effort.

"Well…" she started then waned. "Ah'm glad..." I smiled. I knew that even Mrs Bartholomew could not fail to be impressed.

"…Ah'm glad that yer've put yer pictures up straight! But what have tha done wi' t'Bronco boxes?"

I took a moment of stunned silence to recover before I muttered, "Please sit down, Mrs Bartholomew. Tell me how I can help you." I sat opposite her on my new swivel chair.

"Well, doctor. It's, er, um," Mrs Bartholomew touched her nose.

I had a flashback to that very first surgery. She had touched her nose then so I rushed in to cover her embarrassment, "Oh, you've got problems with your bottom again?"

Mrs Bartholomew jerked upwards as if electrified. "Ma BOTTOM! Nay, young doctor. It's nout ter do wi'it. It's ma nose. Ah've 'ad this cold fer a week now an' ah want 'em new-fangled pills. Emily 'ad 'em an' they cured her." Mrs Bartholomew sat staring, challenging me to refuse her.

"Oh, antibiotics. I can't give you them for a cold." I heard the shrill ringing of the telephone bell outside in the hall being answered by Margaret. I longed to be with her, out of here.

"Why ever not, young man? Aren't ah good enough? Ah pay me taxes, tha knows," Mrs Bartholomew's voice had a hard edge.

"It's nothing like that. Antibiotics kill bacteria but colds are caused by viruses…"

"Well, they're all germs aren't they?"

"They are, but they're different. However, if you go to the chemist, they can give you a few things to help with the symptoms…"

"Give?' Mrs Bartholomew looked interested.

"Well, NOT give. You have to buy them."

"But do they work?" Mrs Bartholomew continued.

I chuckled, "I always say that if you don't treat a cold it lasts for a fortnight but if you do, it lasts for two weeks."

"Why didn't yer say that at beginnin'. Ah'll get it fust thing." Mrs Bartholomew jumped up. "Thank you, doctor. Dr Blunt would never do anything fer ma colds an' ah'm a martyr to 'em. TWO WEEKS. That means ah've only got another un ter go!" And with that she stomped out. Happy.

I tidied the surgery, and put Mrs Bartholomew's growing records back into the trolley. I turned off the lights in the waiting room and locked both surgery doors and wearily walked through to the kitchen.

"Eight o'clock, Eric. That was a long one!" Margaret looked at me sympathetically. I went across to the kitchen sink to wash my hands.

"Yes, and Mrs Bartholomew came right at the end. I think she went away happy though…"

"Eric, tell me over supper, but you've got an emergency call you'll have to do first. It's only just come in. Mrs Baker in Chapel Street. Her baby's got croup."

Chapter 10

When my family and I climbed the worn stone steps of Craig-na-Hullie, and went through the back door, we entered not only our new home, but also joined a community. I had met, and ministered to many of that close-knit group of people over the previous two and a half years, but now we lived amongst them, we were part of them. The Hyppocratic Oath emphasises the importance of this and I had repeated the oath in my training as a doctor: "I will remember that I remain a member of society, with special obligations to all my fellow human beings, those of sound mind and body as well as the infirm." When we moved to the doctor's house I determined to get as involved in village life as possible.

Queensbury is a long, thin village that straggles over the hill between Bradford and Halifax. As the road ascends the hill out of Bradford, it enters Queensbury through an area called Scarlet Heights. That was where Craig-na-Hullie was situated. Ambler Thorn is the last part of the village at the Halifax end. The remoteness of the place, together with its relative inaccessibility and lack of anything that would attract a casual visit, had produced a separate development of language during Victorian times. Queensbury had its own dialect. This had gradually died out during the first half of the twentieth century. However, for two of my elderly patients this was their natural tongue. They both rejoiced in wonderful names: Zylpha Tempest and Zuba Wood. In fact, so extended was the village that, in the past, the dialect had slight variations along its length.

The Hipperholme to Denholme road, along which Margaret and I had travelled to the interview, cut across the main road to form a crossroads. This seemed to be the heart of the place and was untroubled by many cars in the late '50s. The oldest buildings in the area were farms and inns, reflecting the loneliness of the district before the main habitation was created in Victorian times. One such farm just by the crossroads had been called Black Dyke Farm and its land had been sold for the erection of a mill that manufactured worsted cloth. It was this mill that not only provided employment but also was the source of a great deal of local pride.

A few months after I started working alongside George and Tom, one or two of my patients, at the end of a consultation, enquired whether I thought that 'we' would win. Thinking that they were asking for reassurance that the treatment would work, I replied in the affirmative with confidence and a heartening smile. I often got the rejoinder, "Well, ah think yer raight there, doctor."

I mentioned this strange suffix to consultations that I hadn't come across in previous practices to George, over the kitchen table. "Oh, they'll be talking about the local band," he chuckled. "Have you heard of the Black Dyke Mills Band? It's probably the most famous in the world actually." I nodded. Somewhere in the forgotten recesses of my memory I now vaguely recollected my father mentioning the band. His prize possession was a collection of a number of shellac disc records (78 rpm) that contained the whole of Handel's Messiah. It was by the Huddersfield Choral Society and I was sure the brass band accompanying them was the Black Dyke.

George continued, "Well, the whole village supports them whether they like brass band music or not. They're going in for the British Open Championship at the moment and we're all waiting to see if they'll win. They entered the Northern Championship last year and only came sixth, but I know they have been working hard to improve. They have a good conductor in George Willcocks and he knows what to do."

"That's amazing! How come such a small place like Queensbury can produce a world class anything?"

Bea had come into the kitchen carrying a bag of groceries and added to the conversation, "Yes, and most of the band members live in Queensbury. A lot work at the mill as well. You'll get to know some of the bandsmen as they're our patients, aren't they George?"

George nodded then continued, "Quite a few, anyway. How they manage to be the best though is a good question and lots of other bands, no doubt, would like to know the secret…"

"What do you think?" I asked.

"Well, when I talk to band members, they all seem to think it's because of the band room where they practise. It has strange acoustics apparently and they reckon that if they can make a good sound in there it is brilliant anywhere else," George explained.

"Yes. They won't let anyone even entertain the idea of getting a new practice room," Bea added. "It's been the same one since they started and it doesn't look much. The roof is bowed. By all accounts it is worse inside but they daren't do anything to it!"

I asked, "Where is it? I don't think I've seen it yet, have I? I'll look out for it when I pass, if I know where to look."

"Oh, you will have passed it a number of times but you wouldn't have known unless you knew it was there," George said. "You know the Albert Memorial at the cross roads?" I nodded. "Well, the house across the Brighouse Road from there is Prospect House facing 'The Stag'. Prospect House was where John Foster lived. He built the mill and got that going."

"Not very grand for a mill owner though," I mused. It was a rather austere place, built in the local sandstone, which had darkened and streaked like all the older buildings in the village due to the smoke-laden air of the past century.

"You're right, Eric," George agreed. "He must have put all his money into the mill. Part of the building is an old warehouse as well, his first. Just this side of Prospect House is a smaller cottage-like building." I nodded again. I had seen it. Some of Gorge's patients lived in the rather large terraced houses opposite, on the other side of the main road. They had fine, well-proportioned rooms. In front of them, imposing gardens held paths going up to the front doors. They must have been built for the more senior workers at the mill and looked much more hospitable than Prospect House.

"If you look just behind there you can see another building with arched windows. That's the band room."

"Oh, it's there!" I exclaimed. I determined to have a better look as soon as I could. "What happens if they win the British Open then?"

"We all cheer, Eric. In public! When the band comes back, I expect their coach will stop outside the church, or somewhere along there. The band forms up in the road and they process back to the band room playing all the time. Virtually the whole village lines the High Street and cheers. SPLENDID occasion."

Bea said, "It is that, George. And don't they look good in their black uniforms with red lapels? The band kind of brings us together and makes us feel proud."

"I'd like to go to one of their concerts to listen to them properly though, if they are that good. Do they do any in the village?" I asked.

"Yes," George nodded. "They do one every year in the church. I think that's for church funds and then they do occasional ones in The Victoria Hall. Worth going to."

On the next day the early rain had passed leaving the air clean and the stone flagged pavements gleaming as I went up the village to start my rounds. I pulled across the High Street and parked outside the Post Office to post the practice letters. Normally, I would jump out and return to the car without turning off the engine but I looked across at the mill behind its ornate, black cast iron railings and remembered our conversation of the previous day. I persuaded myself that I had time enough to do some exploring. I walked back down the High Street, past Lee's greengrocers shop on the crossroads corner. There I went across diagonally to Prospect House.

This was more spartan on closer examination than I had thought. It was well built but lacked any softening details apart from a strange box-like square arch, housing the front gate, set into the front boundary railings. Behind this a glazed passageway led to the front door. I walked past the open gates to the left of the dwelling. The yard behind the house was cobbled.

I proceeded to the next building. George had mentioned this. It appeared to be a stone-built cottage, with stone tiles on the roof, but on closer inspection it looked as though it was used by the mill for some purpose. To the right of it was a paved area and I wandered down this. Immediately, I saw the practice room. It was actually a two-storey building. Nothing proclaimed its superior function except those arched windows. "So, this is it," I said aloud to myself.

I ambled back past Prospect House and glanced up at the severe windows with their net curtains forbidding any signs of comfort from escaping. I wondered at the stories of strife and hard work that those walls could tell. We had only just heard, in the previous week, that my father's mill, up in Cumberland, was in difficulties. They were desperate times for him and I am sure that John Foster went through equally nerve-racking episodes.

I could see the old mill buildings down the side of the Brighouse Road as I crossed to the Albert Memorial and up the High Street. For the first time, I examined the buildings with care. I stood peering through the iron railings at the nearest building. The sandstone, and its colourings, was very familiar now but I was unprepared for the detailing that turned an ordinary structure, with a very down-to-earth function, into something that added refinement to the High Street. The windows could have been built as strict rectangles, which would have sufficed, but these had a gentle curve on their tops. Between the windows, flat pilasters relieved the stark elevation of the building. I carried on up to the iron mill gates, closed now for the day.

I had been entranced, possibly because of my family's deep connection with woollen manufacturing. I resolved to have a look round inside sometime.

The opportunity never seemed to arise despite my patients who worked there. They were voluble in their invitation to 'come t'mill, doctor'. They were obviously proud of the place and of their skills that the mill utilised.

Later that September, the village had turned out for the parade. Black Dyke Mills Band had won the British Open. They were at the top again.

Now, two years later, George had gone and I still hadn't visited the mill. Autumn had arrived. Tom and I had discovered a good working relationship, based on genuine friendship. We discussed ideas to improve the practice openly, although I was always aware that words came easily whilst actions were hard and rare. We also helped each other with difficult diagnoses. I had settled into a routine that the patients found functioned well for them. Mrs Bartholomew's particular ailments had been thankfully forgotten. However, my knowledge of the mill and its interior and indeed, its very workings, was to deepen suddenly.

The evening surgery was under way and the light had nearly departed from the sky, turning the garden into a deep shadow outside the surgery window. I heard the telephone ring on its small table just outside the hall door. A patient had just left so I paused before pressing the 'Next Please' buzzer to listen to Margaret's part of the conversation. It was rare for calls to come in at this hour, but those that did were often important.

"Hello, this is Doctor Hainsworth's residence. Can I help…"

A long pause caused a silence only faintly interrupted by the gentle murmur of conversation emerging from the waiting room. "Yes, yes," Margaret continued. "He's taking a surgery at…Oh, yes, I understand… Yes, I'll just see if he's available. Please hold the line for a minute." I could hear the urgency in her voice. The door was knocked rapidly and opened immediately. I jumped up as Margaret entered. She was holding a hand over the mouthpiece of the telephone receiver; its curly cable was stretched taut.

"That was Angus Dawson, the factory manager at the mill," Margaret explained in rushed hushed tones. "He sounded very disturbed and panicky. He wants to speak to you immediately, Eric. Can you talk now?"

I nodded and took the receiver from Margaret's grasp, pulling the surgery door closed behind me with my foot as I went into the hall. "Hello, hello. It's Doctor Hainsworth here. Can I help you?"

"Oh, thank goodness. It's Angus Dawson here at the mill. I've just been called back in. One of our men, a patient of yours, has trapped his arm in a carding machine, Henry Briggs…"

I interrupted, "Is the machine still going, Angus? You've got to make sure no more damage can happen."

"Yes, yes. It stopped when his arm got jammed between one of the rollers and the main drum."

"But have you turned off the power?" I was trying to restrain my gabble and prevent any panic at the other end of the line. "Could you look and see if there is much blood around as well. If there is, you must tie a tourniquet of some sort around the upper arm as soon as possible. I'll be on my way immediately. 'Phone for an ambulance as soon as you hang up. I'll see you soon."

"Oh, thank you doctor. Thank you. I'll be waiting by the main gates on the High Street." Relief underlined every word. Margaret had been listening with a white and drawn face. She went through to the waiting room. As I grabbed all that I thought I needed from the surgery, including syringes and a phial of morphine, and threw them in my bag, I heard her explaining the situation to the remaining patients there. Without saying goodbye, I slammed the back door to dash to the car, heart beating and senses awakened. My mind flooded with every possibility. As I drove up through the village everything seemed eerily normal. The mill gates were open and, lit by the streetlights, a coatless man strode towards the car as I pulled up.

He opened the passenger door and sat down, "I'm Angus Dawson, doctor. I'll show you the way. Fortunately, I was able to grab two engineers. They're there already. I have sent the rest of the night shift in the department home but Fred Robinson is helping. If we need anyone else, I can get them from elsewhere in the mill," Angus spoke in an agitated flurry of words. "Drive down here. That's right. Now turn down here. You can park anywhere." I stopped the car and quickly looked around. Dark mill buildings surrounded this yard. The lights of the night shift blazed from most of the windows. The mill was still alive. I followed Angus through an open door, clutching my bag. I was vaguely aware of a corridor: shiny cream paint and stone floor. Red fire-buckets hung on brackets that lined the walls. And then we were in a large room, full of machines but devoid of people. Cast iron pillars reached up to the high roof. Most of the floor space round the machines was filled with large wicker baskets leaving accessible pathways in between. Some baskets contained raw, but washed white, wool, others contained empty spools and others spools full of shining ribbons of white wool. The state of the place testified to a rapid evacuation.

"He's over here, doctor," Angus urged. We weaved through the wicker baskets, round one great machine in dull dark green paint, attached to wooden spools by drooping ribbons of washed wool. Baskets of raw wool were waiting everywhere. And there they were: a purposeful group surrounding a machine in silence. Two men seemed to be stripping the monster of its green carapace, wrenches and spanners working intensely.

Henry was conscious, just. He was a whippet of a man in his early thirties. His wiry body was limp and had to be held upright by someone I didn't recognise, but was probably chosen for this gruesome task for his height and strength. Henry's thinning black hair was plastered over his forehead by a sheen of cold sweat. His breathing was shallow, betraying the onset of shock. I knew this could kill so speed was of the essence. Henry looked up beseechingly. His eyes were sunken into their sockets by pain. It was then that I followed his right arm across into the hard machine itself. Where the men had taken off the various casings, I could see a large drum with smaller rollers around it. All these were covered in backward facing spikes, shining in awful menace like malevolent teeth. Between the drum and one of the rollers, partly eaten, was Henry's right arm.

"Good grief," I thought. "This is too much for me. It'll need the fire service as well." I looked at Henry and knew that there just wasn't the time to wait. Between us, we would have to manage.

"Is that you, doctor?" Henry breathed in agony.

"It is, Henry. I'm going to give you something for the pain, an injection and then we can get you out of there." I looked at him. A brief smile touched his white lips and a tear welled up as he nodded. I smiled back, trying to be reassuring.

I dug around in my bag and produced the syringe case. I quickly worked out what sort of dose of morphine to administer and drew it up the needle that I had inserted into the phial through the rubber seal at the top. I quickly injected it into Henry's left arm. He didn't flinch.

I faced Angus. "I need to assess the situation with his arm, Angus." I looked at the engineers. "If you could stop working on the machine for a moment, I'll just see what possible damage there may be and what to do about it." They stopped without a word from Angus and I went forward.

It was remarkable. There was no blood at all on the roller. Even the wool that was in the machine, in the process of being carded when it had abruptly halted, was white still. Wisps of it wafted innocently in air currents. The arm must have been punctured, without a doubt. The palm and inside forearm were facing the roller. The machine must also have instantly stopped just as the arm was pulled in, before those fearsome teeth could gobble it. Amazingly, it must also have put just the right amount of pressure on the main blood vessels, so preventing bleeding. It was totally incredible. If this hadn't happened, Henry's arm would surely have been shredded to bits and bleeding would have been profuse. In those circumstances I doubt that we could have saved him.

I looked at the men standing over the machine in their white overalls, spanners in hands. "Are you taking the machine apart?" They nodded. "That's the right thing to do. We need to get the roller off but with Henry's arm still attached to it. He needs to get flat on the ground so he can get down with it, to reduce the shock, but the spikes might have done quite a bit of damage to his forearm. I don't want the spikes to be removed here so we'll hold the arm in place on the drum. Angus, you'll have to help me there, as the roller is lifted off. First though I'll just tighten this tourniquet to make sure that there is no blood pumping in the arteries especially when we take the pressure off with the roller."

I got a screwdriver, not daring to mention that I was normally useless at wielding one, and inserted it under the cloth that someone had tied around Henry's arm. I twisted the cloth around the screwdriver until I was satisfied that no blood could get through to Henry's lower arm.

"Right then, Angus, if you could squeeze in here and push on Henry's hand whilst the roller is pulled away, I'll hold his elbow." I glanced at the two men disassembling the machine. "Right, we're ready. If you can lift the roller then bring it this way. You'll have to carry it across the machine." I addressed the man on the far side of the drum. "Then you can prop it on this edge of the machine. While you come to this side, I'll wrap some cloth round Henry's arm and the roller to hold them in place. We'll all move together. NOW."

Gradually, carefully we inched backwards from the recumbent machine. I had not known such intense concentration even in the most delicate of surgical operations. Henry's arm was wrapped and he was laid on the floor, the roller lying perpendicular to his body like a dreadful appendage. The morphine had worked by this stage and Henry was still conscious but slightly euphoric. He explained haltingly that the machine had stopped twice. Each time he had switched it off and then on again and it had started. On the third occasion he looked inside the casing and thought he could see something in the wool. He reached inside to clear it, thinking he had turned the power off from the machine. He hadn't. For some reason the drum started and immediately stopped again. That brief moment was enough for the machine to gobble Henry's arm but not to shred it. Incredible!

By the time the ambulance came Henry was drinking a cup of hot, sweet tea. He could walk into the ambulance but the roller was taken in on a stretcher, with Henry still strapped to it by the bandage. I marvelled at this strange and probably unique, use of a stretcher. Eventually, Fred, Angus and I watched the ambulance disappear round the corner of the next mill building and into the night with its strange cargo.

"Right then, Mr Dawson, ah'll best be off," Fred said, as if the whole episode was just part of life.

"Oh, yes. Fred, thank you. You were a real help in there. We needed you. I hope you can get a good night's rest. And take tomorrow off as well. You've earned it." Angus held his hand out and the two men shook hands.

I stayed for a while chatting with Angus in pools of light thrown from the mill windows by the night shift. He was about my height and build, but I found it difficult to judge his age. His wavy hair hadn't receded and I couldn't detect any flecks of grey in its dark-blond colour. Lines were deep on his brow though, and in the corner of his eyes.

Rather than age, they gave the impression of maturity and competence, something of which I had witnessed in his handling of the situation that evening. It could easily have resulted in panic and Fred had shown his respect in his handshake.

"That was a rum job in there, Angus. I still can't understand how the machine stopped. I would imagine that normally Henry's arm would have been shredded," I said.

"Yes, unbelievable really. I'll have a chat with the engineers in the morning. I can only think that the fault that caused the machine to stop earlier on, stopped it again immediately his arm got jammed," Angus mused and then went on. "And thank you for coming out so quickly, Eric. I have to admit that I didn't know what to do. The ambulance people said that it might take some time to get up from Bradford and I knew that every second counted."

I wanted to reassure him, "You did all the right things. Fortunately, Henry wasn't bleeding but it's the shock that can kill. Henry will be all right now, I'm sure."

"You were in the middle of a surgery your receptionist said?"

"Margaret, my wife. She takes the calls. Yes, I think that all the remaining patients will have gone home. They'll be back tomorrow. This story will go round the village in no time. It'll be the main topic of conversation in the waiting room for days." I glanced at my watch and exclaimed, "Good grief, do you realise all that took just over an hour! It felt as though time had completely stopped!"

We chatted a little longer and finally Angus said, "By the way, Eric, have you been round the mill yet?"

I shook my head. "I've always wanted to have a look since coming to Queensbury. Quite a few of my patients work here and they keep inviting me…"

"Well, any time you can make it, Eric, just phone the office. I'll show you round myself."

I arrived home soon after to meet a rather concerned wife as she opened the back door for me. Relief washed over her features when she saw me and my smile. As I stood by the kitchen sink washing my hands, I quickly told her how events of the evening had progressed and the successful and absolutely incredible outcome.

Suddenly, Margaret interrupted, "Oh, I'm sorry Eric. I think you might have two people in the waiting room still. The others all went home when I told them about the situation but these two stayed. And…" I could see that she was reluctant to finish. "Well, one of them is Mrs Bartholomew."

"How does that woman do it? She has a nose for news. I'll see her but I won't tell her anything!" I went through to finish the surgery.

I telephoned the Bradford Royal Infirmary the next day and got a report about Henry's arm. He was a very lucky man indeed. Three days later he walked into the surgery smiling and telling the waiting patients about his remarkable escape. He had suffered no broken bones, mangled blood vessels, shredded muscle or lacerated nerves. Although it was still covered in bandages, and held across his chest in a sling, so couldn't be seen, he explained that his arm had just had some small puncture wounds and torn skin, as well as deep bruising. And he certainly looked better without that great big appendage that had needed the stretcher.

His thanks were profuse and left me feeling rather embarrassed but also grateful that my training had overcome my natural inclination to take time thinking through important decisions. The outcome of the whole episode had been enormously successful and I was deeply pleased for Henry. Not only that, but now I had an invitation to go round the mill.

I was looking forward to taking Angus up on his offer. The John Foster and Son mill was much larger than my father's and I was naturally inquisitive about how a modern textile factory produced such lovely cloth. Fosters worsted was justifiably renowned, but also, I felt that it would give me a deeper connection with my patients who worked there. However much I wanted to visit, the opportunity didn't arise for a number of weeks. It was a Tuesday, my half day. It was a crisp autumn day and, unusually, the sky was deep blue with a hint of cold crispness that seemed to revitalise me. Almost uniquely I had a very short list of home visits so I telephoned the mill office as soon as the morning surgery had finished. I asked to speak to Angus Dawson.

After about two minutes I heard faint footsteps and then Angus' familiar voice, "Eric, I'm glad you called. It's good to hear you. I take it you'd like a look round."

"Yes, if it is at all possible." I explained how the opportunity had arisen.

"Well, you're in luck, Eric. I don't have any appointments until four this afternoon. The factory is chuntering along nicely. I was going to go round each department for a kind of inspection and have a chat with the managers, but showing you round will be much more enjoyable. Can you make it for eleven? We can have a coffee then look around. We could even have lunch together if you like. I go to the work's canteen. I think it's shepherd's pie today."

"That sounds good, Angus. Hold on, I'll just ask Margaret." After a quick chat and Margaret's nod everything was arranged.

After coffee and introductions in the relative quiet of the mill office Angus and I stood at a window overlooking the site. "What you see today hasn't really changed since about 1890. Apart from the stone becoming more stained with the smoke, of course," Angus smiled. "We are planning to fill in the reservoirs and create a new office block by knocking down the oldest part of the mill. That was erected in 1835. We'll begin at the beginning and I'll take you through the different processes. We'll miss out the wool washing and sorting so we'll go to the carding shed. You'll recognise someone there!"

I followed Angus down the steps and across the cobbled yard and round a corner. I identified the carding building immediately. We stepped into the room, now filled with noise and people tending the machines. Angus picked up some raw wool from a wicker basket. "When it gets to the factory, the wool has to be washed to get the dirt and lanolin out. It also has to be sorted. We dye most at that stage but we also dye after fulling the woven cloth. Obviously dying at that stage results in a uniform colour through the cloth. This wool has had spinning oil added so the fibres can hold together through the carding, combing and spinning processes. Come on, Henry's looking forward to showing you what he does."

We walked along the avenues between the wicker baskets. Henry looked up from the reassembled machine and beamed. "It's grand to see yer, doctor. I'll show yer me arm. It's nearly healed." Henry's arm had livid red pockmarks over it and paler pink scars, but I knew that they would all fade. The yellow tinge was the only evidence of the deep bruising.

"You're a very lucky man, Henry. I thought you would have serious injuries – you could easily have lost that arm of yours, you know."

"Oh, ah know, doctor. Ah'm that grateful. The machine's doing well, an all," Henry showed me what the carding machines did. Raw wool, dyed or snow-white, was fed into it and the action of the rollers made the long fibres parallel and took out the last bits of dirt and fibres that were too short for worsted. The final stage was when the carded and combed wool was split into rovings – unspun ribbons – and wound onto the spools I had seen on the night of the accident.

Angus picked up a spool out of a basket. He pulled on the end of a roving. It separated with no force at all leaving straggling ends of wool fibres. "It's mainly held together by the spinning oil. There is no strength in it. But if you twist it…" He twisted the roving between his thumb and index finger, "it's stronger." He pulled the twirled roving and needed a good tug to separate it. "That's what spinning does. We'll go there next."

One or two people tending the machines recognised me as we went through into the cooler, quieter air of the corridor. They greeted me with a smile or wave. I would have something to talk about when I next met them in the surgery. I found a little piece of conversation helped patients relax in consultations and gave me a human face.

I found the action of the spinning machines fascinating as well as the speed at which they worked. The twisted strands were amazingly thin but strong. Angus seemed to be enraptured by the process even though it was an every-day familiarity for him. "We don't use single strands but twist two or three strands together to make the yarn. We then weave this into our cloth." I nodded, trying to absorb all the factual information as well as the distinctive sights, sounds and rich smells of the factory.

We had been able to talk, in raised voices, in the carding and spinning sheds but when we entered the weaving-shed we met a cacophony of noise that was almost a physical object that we had to push into. It now totally prohibited any conversation. I had heard that the weavers used a sort of sign language in there and I understood why immediately. But the sight was spellbinding. Most of the looms seemed old: cast iron frames with wooden parts that moved hypnotically to a strange dance around the emerging cloth stretched down the frame. Many yarns extending lengthways down the looms to form the warp. They were held in order by comb-like things on arms that raised and lowered different yarns according to the pattern required as the shuttle, aptly named 'flying', was batted at immense speed from side to side trailing its weft yarn as it went. Every time the shuttle flew, the comb arms moved the warp yarns up and down. And so, cloth was made that was taut round a roller at the front end of the machine, and wound onto a roll beneath.

People were in obeisance to the machines. They seemed to look after a number of looms each, watching the yarns intensely. The weft yarn, mounted on bobbins and held inside the shuttle, sometimes broke or ran out. The machine was stopped and new yarn was knotted to the old. When a full bobbin replaced an empty one, the weaver would suck the yarn through a hole in the shuttle before tying the yarns and restarting. The operation was dexterous and swiftly accomplished. The machine demanded it.

I watched fascinated. Many of the attendants were patients of mine and I saw flashes of recognition and welcome pass across faces before eyes were drawn back to those yarns again.

Angus tapped me on my shoulder and pointed to his watch. We needed to move on. We walked in silence to let our ears recover from their battering. "After the cloth has been woven it is washed. That's the fulling. It removes the spinning oil and the wool fibres in the cloth interlock more. Then, at the end of everything, the finished cloth is brought along here to be inspected."

Angus pushed against massive swing doors that revealed a long room made bright by windows on either side. Two immense tables with shiny, smooth tops went down each side of the room. Rolls of cloth, perfect to my eye, were unrolled on the tables and just two men were there, studying the cloth intensely. Occasionally they flicked a stylus into the cloth, sometimes they peered at its surface more severely, producing a strange magnifying glass. All was done in quick, deft movements. A flick of the hand and a white chalk mark was left on the cloth. "Why in the world are they doing that?" I asked.

"We want our cloth to be perfect so every square inch has to be inspected. Any ends from knots are pushed through now but other problems like small holes have to be dealt with in the mending room. Anything that can't be mended has to be cut out – a whole section of cloth goes. We don't like doing that but our reputation relies on it."

Angus went in and spoke with both the men who looked at him with respect as they replied to his enquiries. I stood and waited at the door. My thoughts were often with my father and, having looked around this mill, I was more aware of the weight on his shoulders. Angus strode back to me. "Come on, Eric, we'll go for lunch and we can carry on chatting in the canteen. We are a little early but we'll miss the queue."

"Don't the managers have their own section in the dining room?"

"They do, but I prefer to eat with the people from the shop floor. It keeps me connected with them. I can answer their questions and I pick up how they are feeling. You'd be amazed at how many good ideas they have passed on to me over a simple lunch."

We climbed up another flight of concrete steps and through a battered and scratched swing door, painted a pale green-colour, into a long room. There lights were hanging from metal rods stretching from one side to the other, under the inverted W of the roof. Deal tables with blue and white oilcloth coverings were laid out in regimented rows. We weaved our way through them to the service counter at the far end. "It's shepherds pie today, Eric. I can recommend it. The veg will be overcooked though, but it's good food."

I was taken back, in a comfortable willingness, to previous institutional meals I had experienced at school and in hospital, as I waited for my plate of steaming food and glass of water.

After a few quiet mouthfuls, Angus leaned back and asked, "Well, what do you think of the mill, Eric?"

"It's impressive, Angus. What an amazing operation though. My father would be astounded if he saw it…"

"Oh, why? Is he in the trade?" Angus showed real interest.

"Yes, he owns a weaving mill up in Cumberland, Workington actually. It's on the west coast." Angus nodded. "It's quite a long story but he had a mill in Mixenden, near Halifax, before the war. It was doing well and he made khaki for the army so hadn't got any problems then. However, when the Government encouraged businesses to relocate into so-called Depressed Areas after the war he went to Workington. Why, I just don't know. He's been asking himself the same thing since he went. It's been a constant slog and a worry."

"I'm not surprised, Eric. It's a long way away."

"Yes, it's a heck of a trip. He buys the spun yarn in Bradford and that's where his markets are. But he knew about those problems. We all told him but my father is rather stubborn. He hadn't really reckoned with the workforce, though. They didn't have the right skills and most had been unemployed so long they had lost the work ethic."

Angus nodded. "I know the problem. We hang on to our skilled workers as much as we can. We still run a night-shift, as you know, but it is getting more difficult with foreign cloth coming in … and the new man-made fibres. We're going to have to replace all our looms with faster American ones. Northrop – have you heard of them?"

"Yes. I think so. My brother is father's main engineer and he's mentioned these machines. They can't invest now though. When father started, he asked his brother, John, to help finance the company. About two years ago, John asked for his share, all in one go. It's been hand to mouth since then. Poor Dad. We told him to become a limited liability company ages ago, but he wouldn't listen."

"Good grief, Eric. He could lose everything!"

"I know, I know. He's an honourable man as well, and always sees everyone else is right before himself. I'm really worried, to be honest."

"Has the mill been in your family a long time?" Angus said as he pushed his empty plate back slightly on the table. More workers were entering the dining room and the noise level was increasing.

"No, my father started it just after the first war. His family had worked in a textile mill for two or three generations, on the edge of Bradford. Dad was in the navy, based at Scapa Flow, during the war and I think when he was there, he came across new ideas and he returned determined to start his own mill. It's been really hard for him from the start. The first mill he had was when he rented a loom in a small building. He lived seven miles away so he stayed in the building all week, just going home at weekends. He slept under the loom at night. The business built up from there and he managed to keep it going through The Slump."

"My goodness, Eric. He did well. And now he's struggling? It's tough."

"I know. I keep remembering one of his friends telling me when I was about twelve that in business you can make a lot of money, but you can also lose a lot. 'You are going into the professions where you won't be very rich but you won't be poor either.' He was right but I'm worried that my father is going to lose everything."

I glanced up and saw a number of people were looking our way from different tables. A number waved frantically and smiled when I looked in their direction. I recognised them as my patients. "Angus, I'm really grateful that you brought me here today. It has made me feel more part of the place." I gestured back at a particularly exuberant hand waver. I left the mill a happy man. I felt I had taken another step towards being accepted in the village. I certainly understood the lives of my patients more and their struggles better.

It was Mrs Bristow who completed my education about Black Dyke Mills sometime later. She was one of my 'repeat visit' patients and I tried to insert them in the middle of my visiting list. They often liked a bit of a chat and the forced rest was welcome to me. I banged on the door of her back-to-back terraced house down Campbell Street and shouted, "It's Doctor Hainsworth here, Mrs Bristow," as I entered. There was no one in the one downstairs room as I entered straight from the street. Her television was on though. It was the 'I Love Lucy' show, Mrs Bristow's favourite. It always seemed to be on, flickering into the gloom, but Mrs Bristow was strangely absent on this occasion.

I was just about to leave this Mary Celeste of a situation when I heard some clomping on the floorboards above followed by a shout, "Is that you, doctor? Sit yerself darn an' watch Lucy. Ah'm just enjoyin' ma new toilet." Mrs Bristow had been planning this for some time now and it had been the main topic of conversation on previous visits. She couldn't face another winter of walking down the street in all weathers to the outside closets. And, not only that, her friend Mary had had one installed. I could see that it might replace the television that her children had bought her, as her most prized possession.

I was getting a little impatient sometime later when Mrs Bristow appeared, her bowed legs negotiating the steep stairs carefully. "Oh, 'ello, doctor. Is it a good 'un today?" and looked across at the television. Without waiting for an answer, she continued, "Ah've heard yer've been in t'mill."

"Yes, Mrs Bristow. Just last week…"

"Did tha' know that ah used to work there? Ah was there all me working life, except when t' bairns were small. Ah started in 1900 when ah was just ten. Ah was still at school but ah was a 'alf-timer." Mrs Bristow walked across and turned Lucy into a small dot in the centre of the television screen. This was serious; normally Lucy stayed on, albeit minus the sound, throughout my visits.

Over the next few visits Mrs Bristow described her childhood in the mill. It was a fascinating story and I found myself looking forward to each visit. Her parents were forever short of money and as soon as Mrs Bristow was old enough she worked in the mill in the mornings and went to school in the afternoons. She didn't learn anything, though, as she was too tired. She had to get up at half past five for a rushed breakfast of a mug of tea with her bread and dripping. "Ah had ter run t'mill fer ten ter six. If ah was even a little bit late, ah had ter creep in through t'penny 'oil…"

"A penny-hole? What was that, Mrs Bristow?"

"Oh, that were a small door into t'mill, just above t'bottom gate, yer know t'one down Brighuss Road. T'gateman would be waitin' an' e'd knock off a penny from my wages."

"Can you remember how much you got, Mrs Bristow, er…Ethel?" I asked.

"Well, t'alf timers, we 'ad to put in thirty-two hours a week, and fer that we got three an' six (seventeen and a half pence after decimalisation)."

"That was quite good for half a day's work, Ethel. Wasn't it?"

Mrs Bristow broke out into chuckles, "Nay, lad. That weren't fer one day, it were fer t'ole week. An' if ah got a penny knocked off ma dad would gi'me a smack! It only 'appened twice, ah can tell yer. It weren't t'smack ah didn't like, it were the look on mam's face. She'd miss that penny."

"Do you know if that happens nowadays, Ethel? I know the men have to run down to the bottom gate if they're late, but I thought they lost a day's work and wages if they couldn't get in then."

"Oh, t'mill wouldn't send them away. They need them fer t'machines. They get wages docked, just like us. By t'way, if ah'd worked afternoons at t'mill ah'd only've got 'alf a crown (twelve and a half pence). That's why ah went in t'mornings."

Mrs Bristow had to be behind the spinning frame when the engine started at six o'clock otherwise her wages were cut again and she would have lost her job if it had happened too often. She had another breakfast, of bread and dripping, bread and jam or bread and treacle, at half past eight in the mill. Then she worked from 9 o'clock until 12.30. She had a dinner in the mill, probably on the very tables at which Angus and I had sat. It was a good hot meal such as liver and onions or a meat and potato pie – all 'home-made' in the mill kitchens.

"Ah had ter be in school fer twenty past one an then we finished that at four in t'afternoon. Ah then went 'ome ter help ma wi' t' housework. Ah can tell yer, young doctor, ah looked for'ard ter Sat'day afternoon. After me mornin' shift at t'mill ah could play out then wi' me friends. It were grand on Sat'days."

I enjoyed my visits and chats with Mrs Bristow. I tried to be strict with myself about the time taken but often the stories overtook my concerns. And there was always cake.

It was just after the first of these conversations that we had a telephone call from my father one evening that emphasised that it wasn't just the workers who found the textile industry hard and unforgiving. "Eric," I heard my father's voice say over the crackling line from Cumberland. "I've had to give up, close the mill. I thought you should know."

"Oh, Dad, I'm sorry. I knew it was bad for you. How are you financially? How's Mother?"

"Well, your mother's taken it badly. She won't let on though. We're almost bankrupt ourselves but I think we'll get through. I need to find some work and textiles is all I know. A mill in Bradford has talked about a possible job. I'll be seeing them next week."

"Oh, come and stay with us. I'll collect you from the station, unless you drive down. What about your creditors, dad? Do you still owe money?"

"No, I paid off all of them out of my own pocket but at least I don't owe a penny now. I gave the workers their redundancy money. Poor blighters, there's not much up here for them. It's bleak, Eric."

"Oh, dad. That's all you've worked for, gone. I'm dreadfully sorry."

"We'll get over it, Eric. No use crying over spilt milk. No, we'll be all right. Just you see.

I replaced the receiver slowly.

Chapter 11

"Eric, can you just…?" were Margaret's well-worn words that preceded a range of requests. These extended from passing the salt in meals to more time-consuming shopping expeditions. However, they never included any work on the house, not even wielding a humble hammer. I had discovered that the correct answer on all of these occasions was, "Yes, dear."

We always ate in the kitchen, often under washing that was drying like colourful and eerie stalactites hanging from the creel. This was a wooden frame that could be lowered on a pulley system. It was hanging close to the ceiling in front of the constantly warm cooker. I had been on time for my lunch, a rare occurrence, and it was a luxury to be able to savour it. My list for the afternoon was shorter than normal, so I didn't eat at my usual high speed which I had developed in training. We had discussed the morning's news and my latest, and often unattainable, ideas for the practice when Margaret uttered the customary words, "Eric, can you just pop down to Cyril's after lunch? I need some stewing steak for tea and I know you don't have many visits this afternoon."

I nodded before uttering my well-used and useful reply. Cyril was one of my patients and had juvenile diabetes and had been injecting insulin into his leg muscle for many years. I was concerned about the onset of cardiovascular disease and foot ulcers. His circulation was certainly not good in his lower legs, and they often felt cold and looked white. I hadn't been to Cyril's butcher's shop before but Margaret had often told me that a visit there was always entertaining. Not only that but I found it extremely helpful to be able to meet patients, not for a consultation, but on their own ground to get a sense of their lifestyle.

"Erm, I'll pop in on the way home from my rounds, before the evening surgery. Or do you need it earlier than that?" I asked.

"Oh, I need it as soon as possible. It's got to cook for quite a long time. His shop is just down the road. The walk will do you good, Eric. You're getting quite a paunch, you know! It's a lovely day. Just wrap up well and walk fast."

"I'm not sure about walking there, Margaret. I don't mind the walk but..."

"Eric! Really!" Margaret looked puzzled by my reluctance, but then a look of realisation appeared on her face. "You're not worried about Cain Ramsbottom are you? Just say yes to whatever he asks you. Or you could cross over the road before his house. And anyway, I doubt he'll be outside today. It's rather cold to be sitting out."

Nobody could really fathom the parental motives that resulted in the two Ramsbottom brothers being called Cain and Abel. If their parents had had high ideals for their boys, such as a calling to the clergy, they must surely have been sorely disabused. The brothers were in many respects very different but in one main characteristic they were very similar, because both Cain and Abel were exceedingly disagreeable.

I tried to find something about each patient that I could genuinely like. For everyone else, this was not really a problem. But, whenever I thought that either Ramsbottom was showing signs of likeableness, they quickly disproved it. It was uncanny. In fact, they seemed to go out of their way to rub me up the wrong way. However, some years later a mention of their name brought a smile to my lips.

I was on a training course run by a drug company. It was just at a time when new management techniques were being imported from America and were infiltrating the NHS. The company had taken over the dining room of a large hotel in the centre of Bradford, near one of the two railway stations there. We were assembling over weak cups of morning coffee and uninspiring biscuits. I knew many of the assembled delegates. They were colleagues of long standing and such occasions were excellent times to escape practice demands for a day, and to share amusing stories and ways of tackling common problems. The resulting camaraderie helped develop strength to persevere when we were on our own, back in practice. We all knew the heartache and frustration underlying these stories and sharing them somehow gave us all encouragement.

The loud babble of conversation, in the faded and shabby Victorian splendour of the room, was brought to an abrupt close by a bell. Our attention was brought to bear on a man in a dapper suit and pomaded black hair that looked as if it had been grafted on from a cartoon. I had met him before; he was the regional manager of the drug company.

He liked the sound of his own voice and now he had a captive audience.

"Good MORNING, doctors!" His raised voice captured the muttered tail ends of conversations. "Welcome to our training session on the history of the treatment of staphylococcal infections and modern approaches to diagnosis and therapy." He looked round on our dulling eyes. "But first, as a little ice breaker we are going to announce to each other who we are and where we are from." He had obviously learnt something on a management course and was keen to try it out on us.

The assembled mass looked around rather embarrassed; we all knew nearly everyone else in the room. This seemed a pointless and time-consuming exercise.

"HOWEVER," the man's voice rose to overcome our skeptical concerns, "I would like you all to choose a new surname for yourselves. Choose one of your patient's names. You keep your own first name, of course." He beamed around at us. A quick glance round showed me that everyone had the same puzzled expression, but seemed to have decided to humour the fellow. After all we were getting a free lunch.

"Right, now, I would like you to come forward and take your seats. Don't forget your new names!" We all moved to the chairs arranged in rows at one end of the room and sat down. No one occupied the front row; we were all cautious creatures now, wondering what we were going to do with our strange appellations. The name jumped into my mind as I sat down. I would be that old so-and-so. I would be Eric Ramsbottom. I had had to restrain myself from being somewhat rude the previous day to Abel, who always seemed to treat me like a servant.

"Thank you, doctors. I am aware that you know each other, and your names, very well. But now you have new names. It is a little like when a new patient comes into your lives. Names are important to each one of us." He paused to give a chuckle. "Whatever they are like, and I know that some of us might not like our names, they give dignity and for a patient, entering a situation where their dignity might be strained, this is important. In our company we want everyone to be excellent at remembering names." I smiled inwardly. I wouldn't forget Mrs Fish. Come to think of it my new name had stuck in my head without any problems either.

Our host continued, "When we introduce ourselves now, we will all try and remember our new name using a simple technique. Apparently, they are recommending this to business people in the States. We will all try and imagine you somehow with a picture that your name inspires. For instance, ladies and gentlemen, I am Derek Pickles." There were a few guffaws of laughter. "Oh, yes. I see you can picture me and my name." I was overcome with a ghastly picture of my new name vividly impressed on my mind. "And please, don't be tempted to change your names now. Keep the one you first thought of."

We started introducing ourselves. Some names created groans because they were difficult to visualise but others were amusing. We all laughed when Gordon Graham stood up, "I am Gordon Shears from Heaton!" and then looked around as if he had just realised what he had said – everyone smiled as they thought of garden shears.

My mouth dried as my turn came closer. A sort of panic enveloped me. Should I cheat? Suddenly, I felt a nudge and Tom, sitting next to me, was indicating it was time for me to stand. "Erm, my name is Eric, erm…Ramsbottom…" I didn't get to the 'from Queensbury' bit; the laughter was washing over me. Everyone had a very vivid picture in their minds of me with my name. Suddenly, I felt a release and I was laughing too. A boil had been lanced.

The reason the shopping expedition caused me to baulk a little was, as Margaret had ascertained, the Ramsbottoms. They lived in the end house of Campbell Street. On this side of the main road going through Sandbeds, the part of Queensbury below Scarlet Heights, the end buildings of the terraced rows were all houses. They were larger than the others in the row and had a very small garden next to the wall separating it from the main road. On the other side of that road the buildings at the end of the terraced rows were shops. This is where one of the Co-operative Stores in the village was situated. Near it was Cyril's Butchers.

The Ramsbottom brothers seemed to share the same old, grey suits but Cain was a large man. The suit strained, and groaned on his ample frame and the taut cloth shone with aged grease and dirt. However, his brother Abel's suits hung like curtains on his wiry body. His trousers were rucked up around his waist in rough pleats and then tied round with string. Both brothers sported flat caps pulled down roughly over ragged clumps of white hair, and they both grew straggling eyebrows. For a diminutive man Abel's nose was memorably huge and its red surface was covered in small blue blood vessels that resembled minor roads on a map. I always remember being fascinated by the cigarette that was always attached to his lower lip in the corner of his mouth. It was a mouth that never smiled.

Even when he was talking the cigarette clung on and bobbed up and down hypnotically.

Cain Ramsbottom was what everyone in the village described as 'soft in t'ead'. His main occupation in life seemed to be to sit in wait in his little patch of garden for passers-by. Whilst waiting he would hold a newspaper of indeterminate age. Margaret and the children had discovered him on one of their first forays up the village that summer. They had just finished crossing Campbell Street when a voice boomed out, "Dust tha know Mr 'Elliwell?" Margaret turned and saw Cain's enormous shape stand and lean across the wall. He was looking, from underneath his cap and eyebrows, directly at her. The children automatically recoiled behind her.

"Er, no. I don't think I do," Margaret replied. This was obviously the wrong answer as Cain instantly rolled up his newspaper and tried to hit her with it. Margaret and the children scrabbled past, somewhat alarmed. I later was told that his question contained the only words that Cain had been heard to utter but the name changed randomly. He had been banned from travelling on buses as his actions in such a confined space, and on people who couldn't escape, were considered dangerous.

However, on that autumn day Cain was absent from his post and I could cross the road to Cyril's unmolested.

The shop window was the only form of advertising used by most shopkeepers, but this one was wonderful. The different cuts were not just displayed, they were lovingly exhibited. The meat, laid out symmetrically, created patterns and fans, which were decorated with a filigree of thin, white paper in delicate swirls and curls.

If his window was a picture, actually purchasing in Cyril Threlfall's shop was almost theatrical, according to Margaret. I was about to experience it. However, the act of being served took some time and there was always a number of people waiting their turn. Cyril Threlfall was slightly balding and had a round tummy over which was stretched his striped apron. He had an enduring joviality and treated each customer as the most important in the world.

I stepped forward, having watched others before me take the centre stage of the drama. "Mornin', Dr 'Ainsworth. It's a sight ter see yer 'ere. It's yer first time in my shop, isn't it?" Cyril enveloped me with his welcome.

"Good morning, Cyril. Yes, it is my first visit. You keep it well, I can see. And how are you today?"

"Oh! Not s'bad, not s'bad. Fair t'middlin, like. But ah think ah'll be seein' yer aggen abart me feet. It's all this standin'." He looked down. I had already decided to mention the amount of standing that Cyril obviously did, on his next visit to the surgery. He needed to sit more often, if we were to prevent those ulcers. He continued, "What can ah do fer yer today, doctor?"

"I'd only come in for some stewing steak, Cyril, but that bit of fillet steak looks lovely. I think I'll take some of it for Margaret." I pointed into the glass case.

"Oh, Dr 'Ainsworth, ah can tell yer know what's good. That's a fine bit o' fillet." Cyril picked it up in both hands as if it was a sleeping kitten. It nestled in his large but gentle hands. "Nah then, look. Jus' t'right amount o' fat. That bit o' fillet will be grand." Cyril gently placed the rolled meat onto a slab.

"'Ow much does tha want, Dr 'Ainsworth?" He flourished a curved knife like a sword and laid it on the waiting succulent meat.

"No, I think I'll have a little less than that, Cyril." The knife moved; the fillet trembled. "That's right. That'll do, thank you."

Cyril's knife bit deep, almost rapturously, as his arm swung. Once through, he scooped up the desired joint and placed it with loving care on a square of grease-proof paper. He cupped this in both hands and came round from behind the counter and offered it for my inspection. The others in the shop all gathered around to have a look.

"Nah then, Dr 'Ainsworth, that's a right lovely bit o' meat." Cyril looked around as if waiting for applause.

Cyril bowed slightly and went back behind the counter.

Money was exchanged, more out of appreciation than payment, and deposited in a cash-till sculptured out of shiny silvery metal. A visit to the butchers, I could see, was a cultural event. Margaret, I sensed, had to struggle to appreciate her fillet gift. She told me that it had completely used up her house-keeping budget for the whole week.

It transpired that Cyril and his wife were good friends with Mr and Mrs Fish, who lived just around the corner from the shop. The Fishes had their silver wedding anniversary later that autumn. The Threlfalls wanted to arrange something special for this event and, for some reason, had booked a hall in a nearby town rather than the village. Having the event there was possible as it was on a bus route and the Fishes were also the proud owners of a car so they could get themselves there. Cars were a scarcity in the village of the late 1950s so the sight of the Fishes in theirs produced one or two glances.

However, most glances became stares at this particular vehicle, but not because of its beauty or style. In fact, it was quite dilapidated. No, the stares were for its occupants. Mr Fish, Harry, would always drive. If Mrs Fish was on board she sat in the back. The cursory glance would have seen two people on the back seat. One was the familiar outline of Mrs Fish and the other was only slightly smaller but with a strange and shaggy outline. This was, a further look would have ascertained, a dog of undecipherable pedigree, but it was certainly nearly as tall, as it sat there, and more hairy than its owner. It clearly enjoyed being chauffeured around as it sat bolt upright appreciating the route being taken. There was quite a bit of speculation as to why Mrs Fish preferred this arrangement until she confided to someone that it was because she always expected "OUR 'ARRY" to have a crash and she thought it safer in the back. Why all the windows were always open, whatever the weather, was totally due to the other passenger.

Wiff, the dog, had a sort of languorous approach to life and rarely broke out into anything resembling enthusiasm, except for his one deep passion: stuffing. How the Fishes discovered Wiff's proclivity for stuffing, the village never found out, but everyone suffered the consequences on numerous occasions. When they had first acquired the dog, the Fishes had given him the name Wilf. However, the effect of his favourite food on Wilf's digestive system soon became apparent. Wilf was banned from every shop in the village and then nearly every enclosed space. Fresh air was of some help but there was one famous occasion, at least within the village, when even this was of no real assistance.

The parish 'Garden Party and Sale of Work' was held annually in the largest garden in the village. The largest earner, by far, was the tea tent. It eclipsed the next in economic importance, which was the cake stall with its memorable brandy snaps. The tea tent, with its sides open to allow free flow of people and air, had an array of mismatched tables and chairs that appeared from some place or other every year. Mrs Fish had stridden in with her young Wilf who sat down obediently at her feet. He surveyed the scene with a look of slight distain.

Now and then, however, he glanced round with a look of puzzlement. It soon became obvious that he was intrigued about the source of the most awful and over-ripe smells that wafted lazily on the warm and sultry summer air. That afternoon there wasn't the faintest breath of wind in the tea tent, unfortunately, and the odour just hung there. Gradually the friendly chatter was replaced with a silence and then the sound of people leaving, starting with those nearest Mrs Fish. She, for her part, didn't seem to notice the pong and sat, drinking her tea, eating dainty sandwiches and cake and smiling pleasant goodbyes to the evacuating customers.

That year the cake stall knocked the teas into second place because the income generated in the latter had been reduced somewhat – the astronomic effect of a dog and its farts. And Wilf had a name change within the village culture. He was Wiff from that day on. "That dog is just a biological weapon!" Tom commented wryly when I related the story to him in our next telephone call. "Still, the Fishes are your patients, Eric." I could sense his smile coming down the telephone line.

People were coming to the Fishes' silver wedding 'do' from all over the village and beyond, once they had ascertained that Wiff would be safely left at home. It was going to be a highlight in the village social calendar and, as everyone was bringing items of favourite food, it held the promise of a 'right good nosh up'. For most of the village, including the main participants, the Fishes, the event had become the main topic of conversation for weeks. Margaret and I had been invited but it was my weekend 'on duty' and Tom and his family had a long-standing arrangement with his folks, and I felt I could not ask him to change. I heard about nothing else at the tail end of many consultations. There was definitely a buzz in the air.

However, they hadn't reckoned on the capriciousness of the main celebrants. For "our 'Arry" was a part-time fireman. Mrs Fish would proudly tell anyone who hadn't heard about this before, and quite a number who had, that "our 'Arry loves a fire." On the very afternoon of the party, Mrs Fish telephoned Cyril. One can only imagine the conversation, conducted at full blast.

"'Ello, Cyril. It's Cynthia 'ere."

"Oh, 'ello, Cynthia. Are ya lookin' for'ard…"

"'Ello, 'ello. Is anyone there? Canst tha' speak up?"

"Yes, Cythia. It's CYRIL."

"Cyril, ah'm just telephonin' ter say we won't be coming to t'do tonight."

"Ye won't be comin'. But it's your do. 'As anything 'appened, Cynthia?"

"No, no, Cyril, but 'Arry is on duty tonight an' there might be a fire. We'll just stay at 'ome."

"But, Cynthia!" Cyril by now must have been somewhat exasperated. "It's all arranged. Everyone's comin' an' it's all fer you!"

"Nay, Cyril. Don't upset thissen. You just go ahead an' we'll stay at 'ome. 'Ave a grand time.''

The party went ahead without the Fishes, who, unfortunately were not recompensed with a fire. The 'do' was 'right grand' and remained the chief topic of conversation for some time. Once again, though, the Fishes had become the centre of village gossip and jocularity and the story of their non-appearance at their own party became part of local legend.

Very soon it became apparent that my family and I were welcome additions to the rich tapestry of village life and part of this same culture. People waved at me, in my now familiar car, as I drove up the High Street and it was rare for me not to be greeted when I was out on foot. This was often just a quick "'Ello, doctor. 'Ow ist'a, then?" but, on occasions, I was asked about personal medical matters. I always totally discouraged these informal, al fresco consultations and soon patients knew that they were unacceptable. However, Isaiah Shaw just wouldn't respond to the message. Initially, as with everyone else, it was a gentle hint, but as time progressed, I had to use blunter language. Nothing worked with Isaiah Shaw.

Isaiah was a trim, sprightly man but of somewhat short stature and he inflated his own ego by being voluble. His face, carefully groomed, shone. His wire-framed spectacles with round lenses were permanently clean because part of Isaiah's conversational technique was to remove them with a flourish, clean them and then wave them in front of the face of the person he was addressing. Strands of sandy grey hair, combed into careful parallel wires, stretched from just above his left ear to his right. Unfortunately, any sense of humour seemed to have been submerged under Isaiah's sense of earnestness and conviction at 'being right'. It was Isaiah Shaw's self-appointed role in life to use this assurance for the benefit of all his fellow human beings.

In a way, I had brought the problem onto myself. It was during the week after taking up residence at Craig-na-Hullie. I had just parked the car outside the Post Office to post the practice letters, a daily task, when I saw two men standing by the door to the building. I recognised one as a patient but the other, waving his spectacles around liberally, hadn't been to see me professionally. I posted the letters and heard a greeting, "'Ello, doctor. 'Ow are things?"

I turned and replied, "Oh, hello Sam. Very well thank you. How are you?"

At that, Sam's companion stepped forward, smile shining. "Doctor? Dr Hainsworth?" I nodded. "I'm in your practice, doctor. I always attended Dr Blunt though, but I don't need to go to the surgery often…"

I recognised the signs of a potentially prolonged conversation so I quickly interrupted, "Yes, but you know where it is, Mr…Er …"

"It's Shaw, Isaiah Shaw. And how are you today, doctor?"

"Very well, thank you, Mr Shaw. How are you?" With those fateful innocent words of greeting, I seemed to have invited the ad hoc consultations that followed, at least in his eyes.

"Oh, thank you, doctor. Since you asked…" Isaiah came closer. I could smell carbolic soap as he leant forward conspiratorially. "Well, I've got this pain right here." Isaiah indicated his shoulder. "I was wondering what it could be?"

I backed away hurriedly. "It could be a number of things, Isaiah, but you need to come to the surgery for a proper consultation." I retreated rapidly to the car and drove away.

Now, after a number of ambushes on the street, I started to look around at the people milling around the shops to make sure that Isaiah Shaw was not amongst them, before getting out of the car. By this means I avoided Isaiah for some time, but I knew that it couldn't last. I was eventually trapped, as I left the bank, through lack of caution and sudden sunshine that blinded me for an instant. I had lowered my guard and stepped through the door into the bright autumn day from the gloom of the bank's interior. A figure emerged from a group walking up the High Street. He was waving his wire-framed spectacles around. "Ah, Dr Hainsworth. Just the person I want to see!" He stepped forward as I retreated back against the wall of the bank.

"I don't know what it is, doctor, but I don't seem to have seen you for some time, even at church. I hope you haven't missed me."

"Oh, it's you, Mr Shaw. Yes, I always seem rather busy these days."

He inched closer. Carbolic fumes enveloped me once again. "Well, I've got this itch down here," he whispered in conspiratorial tones and indicated his groin area. I decided that enough was enough.

"Well," I proclaimed in a loud voice that others could hear. "I think, Mr Shaw, that needs an examination. Would you just drop your trousers and underpants and lie down here." I indicated the pavement.

"Oh, doctor. Take my trousers down?" Isaiah was shocked. The shine left his face.

"You'd like a consultation, Mr Shaw, and I'm prepared to do one. I have a few minutes. But I need to do an examination to find out what the problem could be."

"But take my trousers down and right here? I couldn't do that!" Isaiah Shaw looked deflated for the first time since our initial meeting that summer. "Not here!"

"Then I can't continue our consultation. Just pop into the surgery like everyone else. Goodbye, Mr Shaw."

The parish church was also a central part of community life. The building shared its foundation with most of the public buildings in the village: they had been built with Foster money and motivated by the Foster sense of education and betterment. The church was constructed out of local sandstone, now nearly black, and was inspired in design by the popular gothic revival of the mid-nineteenth century. It seemed to shrink down into the ground but proudly exhibited a high tower with its clock face. This dominated the whole district from the top of the High Street to way past Tom and Chrissey's house, almost to Ambler Thorn. We became active members of the congregation as soon as we had taken up our residence in Queensbury.

The Reverend Maurice Slighter was the minister. On our first Sunday attendance at the church, he had grasped my hand in his much larger one, after the service. I looked up into his smiling eyes. His tall, muscular body reflected his youthful passion - he had been a rugby prop forward. His voice was melodious and commanding. His impressive nose was made even more so by the few whiskers that sprouted from its surface and nostrils. He exclaimed, "Good morning, good morning. You're new here, I take it? I'm Maurice Slighter, but just call me Maurice. Everyone does!"

"Oh hello, er, Maurice. I'm Dr Hainsworth. Eric. And this is Margaret and our children Ruth and, er, well, Charles is around here somewhere. Yes, we've just moved into Craig-na-Hullie. I think you are patients in our practice…"

"Wonderful to meet you. I have heard a little about you. We were with Dr Blunt and have had all the letters from the practice about you becoming a partner in it. We're never ill though so haven't had reason to call on you professionally. Come and meet Jean and the children. We've got three girls."

Maurice led us through the maze of the chatting, post-service congregation to his wife who was talking near the font at the back of the building. During his brief introduction to us he had managed to convey the feeling that meeting us was the best thing that had happened to him all day, if not all week. During the years we knew Maurice, I always felt like this and he became a very close friend, one with whom I could be totally honest, knowing that anything I said would not be repeated, even to Jean.

Jean was like a female version of Maurice. Her strong face and smile shone confidence and openness. She was shaking hands and asking about each person as if they were also the most important aspect of her life at that particular moment. "Ah, Jean, Jean. You must meet Dr

Hainsworth, Eric and Margaret. This is their first time at church. They've just moved into Craig-na-Hullie, you know. Isn't that wonderful, darling?"

It was during one such conversation that I was almost ambushed by Isaiah Shaw again. My guard was relaxed and down as I spoke to Maurice. During the previous week I had actually seen Maurice doing something quite strange. I had just finished a home visit and was rushing to the next. As I drove away from the curb, I observed his impressive, black clad figure pushing what seemed to be a barrel organ around the corner. I didn't stop then - I was in too much of a hurry. However, now that I had a few moments with Maurice, I determined to ask him about this rather bizarre behaviour.

I was just about to ask when Maurice said, "Oh, here's Isaiah." I looked around at the mention of that ominous name. Indeed, there was that familiar body, with its polished face, pushing its way through the small groups of chatting people towards us. His eyes, behind those familiar round lenses, were set on me. My heart sank. "I'll just head him off, Jean, so you can talk to Eric and Margaret."

I watched as Maurice enveloped Isaiah in an arm and guided him away. Whatever Isaiah's previous destination and intent, it had now been skillfully changed by the vicar.

We chatted away amicably for some time and then I said, "By the way, Jean, I think I saw Maurice out last week, pushing ... well, it looked like a barrel organ!"

"Oh that! Yes, it is a barrel organ. He's had it a few years now and when the sun's out he wheels it into a side street and starts playing. And then he starts singing hymns."

I could imagine that. His fine baritone voice led all the singing in the services. "People come out of the houses just to listen. Quite a few join in as well. The children love him."

"Goodness, Jean. Why does he do that?" Margaret asked.

"He's always done it since becoming a minister in 1950. There's so much tosh floating around in the church about how the bible isn't really true, people just aren't prepared to give up a morning to come here for that sort of stuff. But when Maurice goes out, he tells them the wonderful things God has done and wants to do for them. Just a bit, then says they can find out more in church. Look around. When we came here the congregation was falling fast and now look."

The church was full of people and chatter. Maurice had clearly managed to communicate out on the streets. We talked on for some time. Our friendship with Maurice and Jean Slighter had begun. It was to be an important friendship for all of us.

We were a little late arriving on the following Sunday and the only pews that were left were at the front. I led my family down a side aisle and occupied the one on the right, directly in front of the impressive brass lectern in the shape of an eagle. This seemed to become our pew forever, from that moment onward. I didn't mind, as I wanted to support Maurice as much as I could and, from then on, I belted out the hymns in what I considered a fine voice every Sunday, despite the amused comments from my family and those in the pew behind. We were waiting for the service to start when I noticed a slight disturbance through the corner of my eye. I turned and saw the familiar polished smile of

Isaiah Shaw. He had chosen to sit opposite me, across the aisle. He was waving to me. I waved back, unsure. Now he was pointing to me and then to himself. The smile, that I was forcing onto my face, died as I realised that he wanted a talk with me. I shook my head violently and looked straight ahead. The first hymn began.

For some weeks this became a pattern. However, I escaped any further communication, either verbal or non-verbal, with Isaiah after the services by some deft avoidance tactics and the use of other conversations with parishioners, who were often surprised at my sudden appearance. It was well into the autumn, a few weeks after Isaiah's last impromptu consultation outside the bank and I was enjoying a post-service cup of coffee and a chat with Mrs Hill about life in the village. We had just got to a break in our conversation to drink some of the cooling coffee, when I felt a pat on my shoulder.

Before I could turn, I heard the fateful voice, "Ah, Dr Hainsworth. I'm glad I've got you. I've been wanting to see you again for some time but I always miss you for some reason or another." The smile and spectacles were waving in front of my face. Mrs Hill walked away. I was alone with Isaiah Shaw.

"Erm, yes, Mr Shaw. I try and have some good chats with people when we are all together. I hadn't finished with Mrs Hill…"

"Well, I think she's finished with you, doctor. And now that you're here I've been getting these headaches…"

I tried to assume a stern countenance with a voice that would finally end these ambushes. "Headaches, Mr Shaw? I thought that you had an itch…"

"Oh, that's gone, doctor. But these headaches. I can't imagine what they can be. Do you think it's cancer?"

I was just about to sternly advise Isaiah to come along to the surgery when an imp whispered to me. I said, "Oh I think I'd better just have a look in your ear, Mr Shaw. Just come over here into the light." I led a beaming Mr Shaw across to a window.

"Now just tilt your head a bit. That's it." I looked inside Isaiah's ear carefully. "Yes, I think I can see the problem, Mr Shaw…'

"Oh, can you? I knew it was something serious," Isaiah's voice was gushing with pleasure. "That Sam said it was because I don't drink enough water. Just wait 'til I tell him. What do you think it is, doctor?"

"Woodworm!"

"Woodworm? Are you sure, doctor? Well, I'll be. I didn't know you could get that. The wonders of modern medicine, doctor!"

"Yes, there's one sort. It gets in through your ears. They sometimes fall out if you shake your head. Have you noticed them on your pillow in the mornings?"

'Well, no. I can't say that I have, doctor…"

I looked at Isaiah full in the face. "Well, Mr Shaw, the only way to really find out is to come to the surgery for a proper consultation, where I've got all the proper equipment to make sure." And with that I turned and walked away.

A few minutes later, I noticed Isaiah heading to the church door to leave. He stopped, leant his head over and banged his ear with an open hand. He then looked intensely at his palm before leaving. Margaret, the children and I left soon after.

In the car on the way home, I related the story to Margaret. She smiled but chided me, "Eric! Don't you think that's a bit cruel?"

"Well, I have had enough of Isaiah's ambushes. I have told him over and over again to come to the surgery. I knew that the only way would be to give him a ridiculous diagnosis. Maybe he'll come along to get a proper one now!"

Margaret looked at me, "I wouldn't be so sure, Eric. It'll take more than that to get him there."

The rest of my conversations round the font, whilst drinking coffee, were enjoyable and we gradually got to know more village residents through them. And they got to know us as people, rather than 'the young doctor' and his family. However, there was one person I particularly enjoyed talking with every week. Mrs Williamson was a patient. Her husband had had prostate cancer and I had seen him through the terminal stages that summer. He left a widow who now had to look after their young son, Christopher, alone. Mrs Williamson also regarded our weekly discussions with pride. They obviously were a support to her at this very raw emotional time.

Christopher would also look forward to telling me all that was going on in his young life. He was the sole focus of Mrs Williamson's love and attention and this showed in his immaculate appearance. I often wondered how she had managed this, as we could never attain the same with Charles, whatever we tried. Charles, minutes after a careful wash and hair brush, would sport smears of dirt on his face and his hair defined the word 'wayward'.

Christopher would approach me with a well-scrubbed face and his jet-black hair, cut with a flawless fringe, was brushed to a shine. "Now, Christopher," Mrs Williamson would always say with palpable pride at what she knew would follow, "Tell Dr 'Ainsworth what they've learned you at school this week."

Christopher would then delight in telling me the most exciting and memorable aspects of school life that week. I listened carefully and encouragingly. It really mattered to me that Christopher was doing so well despite the dreadful summer he had had. I always concluded with an, "I'm really pleased, Christopher. You'll do your best at school, won't you?"

He was responding well to his new teacher, Mrs Thomas, so it was with a great deal of conspiratorial pride that he told me on one of our Sunday chats that he had seen Mrs Thomas' lungs. He obviously thought that I should know, as I was a doctor.

I was very perplexed and asked, "Have you, Christopher? How did you do that?"

"Yes, ah 'ave. She leaned over when I was sitting down and I looked down here." Christopher indicated his collar and the gap between it and his neck. "An' I could see 'em. Both o' them."

"Goodness, Christopher. I hope you didn't tell her."

"I didn't, doctor. But I thought you would like to know."

Mrs Williamson blushed.

On very rare occasions, I broke my own rule and mentioned medical matters in post-service conversations. A few weeks after Isaiah Shaw's ambush, during which time I had not seen him at the surgery but neither would he look at me from across the aisle, I saw an old lady standing at the back of the church on her own. It was the first time I had seen her at church. She and her husband were patients in the other - a single man - practice in the village. Tom and I 'covered' for this practice so that Tommy Wilson, the doctor, could have some time off and I had ministered to Mr Bairstow a number of times.

"Oh, hello, Mrs Bairstow. I haven't seen you for a bit," I said cheerfully.

"Thank you, doctor. No. I don't come here often. But..." Mrs Bairstow's voice dried up.

I stepped in. "And how's George by the way? I hope he's taking it carefully now."

"Mrs Bairstow's eyes filled with tears and her voice jerked as she replied, "Haven't you heard, doctor? George died, a while back."

"Oh, I'm sorry to hear that, Mrs Bairstow. I knew his heart was bad, but it's always a shock when this happens."

"It were a shock, yer right, doctor. An' I blame meself in a way an' all. I needed some carrots for our tea an' I sent George out to dig some up in the back garden. He took longer than normal so I went out to see what he were doing. An' there he were. Out. Gone!" Mrs Bairstow sniffed into a handkerchief.

I quickly went on, "Goodness, Mrs Bairstow. I am sorry. Whatever did you do?"

"Well, doctor. I just had to open a tin of peas instead."

Chapter 12

Emily died. It was the culmination of the untreatable ravages of the disease that I had diagnosed nearly three years before; hers being the first diagnosis I had made in the practice and it had given me no joy to do so. Emphysema had made Emily's lungs ineffective in a series of increasingly incapacitating increments. She had faced each one with fortitude and good humour. She was one of my 'repeat visits', and every time I went her closing words, accompanied by a wry chuckle, were always, "And what do you think of my bust, doctor?"

Emily had been in hospital once or twice for oxygen treatment to alleviate her symptoms, but the underlying disease was untouched and she didn't want to endure hospital again. I measured her illness's progress through the stages of incapability that Emily endured without one word of complaint. She could no longer come to the door on my knock without stopping for breath; I knocked and entered anyway now, but she always wanted to greet me. She found getting out of her chair a struggle, leaving her fighting for breath. Climbing the stairs on her bottom, to bed or the bathroom, took increasingly longer on every step up. A commode was brought in but the day finally arrived when her daughter, Joan, was summoned and offered to move in to the house to look after her mother. At some time during this progression, I had stopped calling her Mrs Barrett and now called her a less formal 'Emily'.

I helped Joan bring Emily's bed downstairs into her old sewing room that now became, in effect, a hospital ward. Emily was already in her night–clothes with a crocheted shawl around her shoulders. She wanted the bed to face the fireplace so she could see the young Edward, her late husband, looking back at her past the decades. They had grown old together and Emily had nursed him through his final illness. It was now her turn, and I had increasingly been using my visits just to talk with her. She haltingly, and with encroaching weakness, talked about her life and faith in Christ. "There's no real hope at all outside Him, is there, Doctor?" she would ask rhetorically. We talked about Edward and the children, about what really mattered in life. She was looking forward to being with Edward again. Her eyes sparkled at the thought.

I looked down at her feeble frame and said, "Right, Emily. I'll lift you into bed."

"Oh, doctor!" I could just hear her whisper, "Edward used to do that!"

I picked her up gently and placed her on the bed. As I did so, before extracting my arms from underneath her, she whispered again, "You won't treat me, will you, doctor? If I get anything else." I hesitated. "Will you, doctor?"

"No, Emily. I won't. I'll look after you. I'll just give you something, if you're in pain."

"Thank you, doctor. And what do you think of my bust now?"

Maurice also visited Emily daily. She was content as she faced her death.

However, later that first Craig-na-Hullie autumn, the inevitable telephone call came through one evening from Joan. "I think Mum's got a temperature, doctor. Do you think you could come?"

"Don't worry, Joan. I'll be down in a jiffy." I hoped my compassion reached out along the telephone wire. I took my doctor's case but I knew I wouldn't be opening it.

At the familiar door, I knocked quietly and let myself in. Joan was in semi-darkness of the back room in a chair by the bed. Emily was lying flat on her back with the photograph of Edward on the next pillow. I could see that Emily's face was flushed and her normally laboured breathing was even shallower.

"Can I get you a cup of hot water, doctor? I'm just going to make myself some tea," Joan asked.

I said, "No thanks, Joan. But I'd like to just sit here with Emily, if you don't mind."

"That's all right, doctor. Do you think you can do anything for Mum?" Joan pushed her hands down her thighs to straighten her dress as she stood.

"I'm afraid not, Joan. Your mother wouldn't want me to, even if I could. I just want a few moments with her." Joan's flooded eyes replaced her answer and she turned.

I sat for a few minutes. I held Emily's hand in mine and stroked it now and then. Eventually I said quietly, "I've come to say goodbye, Emily." I stroked her hand again. "Have a good time with that Edward of yours. Oh…" I leant forward and whispered to her. "And I do think you've got a magnificent bust!" Emily smiled and fell into unconsciousness.

The next day I attended Emily once again. This time to certify her death - my final service to her.

Both Margaret and I went to Emily's funeral. It was a bittersweet occasion and her family and friends said their sad goodbyes, but I knew that Emily herself would be having a good time, enjoying being with Edward again. Maurice, judging by the few words he spoke, also knew it and that her hope was fulfilled.

After the service, a young man approached me with his hand held out. He looked the spitting image of Edward and I half expected him to be in a 1917 army uniform. "I think you must be Dr Hainsworth?" I nodded as he went on, "I'm Peter, Emily's son. She spoke a great deal about you, doctor, and Joan and I want to thank you for how you cared for her. It made a great difference."

I felt somewhat humbled by this gratitude and said, "I try to bring dignity in every person's life especially at the end, Peter, but with your mother it was slightly different. It was as if she was actually adding to my life through the way that she dealt with her own illness, rather than the other way round. She was a wonderful lady."

"She was, doctor. Joan and I have been very fortunate to have had her, and Dad, as our parents. Are you going to come along to the refreshments?"

"I'm afraid I can't, Peter. I have to get back to the practice. I have an evening surgery to take. Thank you all the same."

"Well, I'll tell you now then, doctor. Emily has left you something. She always said that you should have it and even put it in her will. It's that stone head in her hedge. Do you know it?" I smiled and nodded. Emily's magnificent bust. "We won't be doing anything with the house until the New Year so you don't need to rush to collect it."

We made the journey to Margaret's mother as often as we could. This would usually be on my half-day, a Tuesday afternoon, after I had finished my visits and snatched a quick lunch. Margaret's mother lived in the same house in which she had brought Margaret up. It was situated above a bank in Kirkburton, a village outside Huddersfield, and a visit there was a little like stepping into a museum. In fact, I think that is how Charles and Ruth regarded it, from the stone flagged floors, rag rugs and shiny black range cooker to 'Grannie' sitting in her Windsor chair, listening to her pre-war Bush radio.

We hadn't made that customary journey for some time and one was definitely overdue, so Margaret and I had carefully set aside a Tuesday a few weeks after Emily's funeral. I had learned that I had to protect the bits of free time that I had, otherwise patients and practice demands could easily nibble away at them.

The children were on half-term holiday so were being groomed for the outing. Charles had managed to stay clean and relatively tidy when he put on his coat to leave. I was tying up my stout outdoor shoes in the kitchen, when I heard the most almighty crashing sound, again and again. Ruth ran in. The banging stopped.

"What's that, daddy?" Ruth asked, alarmed.

Margaret walked in, "I think that's somebody at the surgery door, Eric. It sounds serious. Whoever it is seems to be trying to break the door down."

I didn't say anything. What if it was really important? It seemed like it. But it was my half-day and Tom and I had been very explicit in our correspondence to the patients about this. The other partner was always on duty and we had outlined the procedure for getting in contact with the duty doctor in an emergency. The banging, more urgent now, started again.

"Eric, do you think we should go?" Margaret asked. She was clearly concerned.

"No." But then I was suddenly filled with resolve. "Yes, we will. Some patients always do this. They won't come when the surgery's on and then expect me to see them when it is convenient to them. Charles, can you just go into the playroom to see who it is? Look through the net curtains in the bay window. You can see the surgery door from there. BUT don't touch the curtains, Charles." The playroom was the children's name for the Blunts' old sitting room, the one where I had waited before taking my first surgery. It was stripped of any furniture and carpets but contained the trunk full of dressing-up clothes and assorted cardboard boxes of objects waiting for a more permanent resting place. The children, when frustrated by the rain at not being able to 'play out', would go in this room instead. The bay window still leaked.

Charles approached his task as if he was a commando approaching enemy lines and disappeared. The banging stopped again, but the front doorbell started ringing. Incessantly. It sounded as if someone was leaning on the bell switch. How could a doorbell sound angry?

Charles returned. "It's that man from down the road, Mr Ramsbottom. The thin one, dad." Charles made his report importantly. "He's looked in all our windows and now he's at the front door. He hasn't seen me though!"

The ringing stopped. "Hum, Mr Ramsbottom. He knows very well that I'm not on duty on a Tuesday afternoon. I have told him over and over again. I don't think it'll be much, knowing him…" I started. I was still unsure what to do.

The ringing stopped and Charles disappeared again. When he returned, he reported that Mr Ramsbottom was walking down the path and leaving. I said, "Well, that's it then. We'll just let him get well away, then we can go."

"But what if it was an emergency, Eric?" Margaret asked.

"Oh well, he'll just have to do what everyone else does. He can telephone Tom. Mrs Bristow says he uses her 'phone all the time. No doubt I'll find out tomorrow." I was a little worried though, and this clouded our time at Margaret's mother's. I was determined to ask Tom the next day if Abel had been in contact with him with anything serious.

The following morning the weather matched my mood. Low grey clouds wrapped themselves around the house and made it feel alone. Sharp rain showers broke the incessant drizzle but couldn't dilute the gloom. Margaret noticed my silence during breakfast. "Eric, are you still thinking about Mr Ramsbottom?"

I nodded, "Yes, I can't get him out of my mind. What if it really was an emergency? I know that Abel always wants to get his money's worth out of me, as he says…"

"What? It's free now. He doesn't pay you anything!" Margaret was getting slightly agitated.

"Try telling that to him. I think he sometimes regards me as a personal servant. He tells me it's his right as he pays his taxes... but, even so, it could have been serious this time. Anyway, Tom's coming for coffee today so I'll talk it through with him."

I half expected Abel Ramsbottom to be the first one through from the waiting room at that morning surgery but he didn't appear then or at any time during it. I wandered through to the kitchen to wait for Tom to arrive and picked up the post that had been left by the telephone. I sorted through it, putting the ones I considered more important on top. There was one envelope that intrigued me in particular. It was the size of a personal letter and the address had been hand written, but it was for me alone. All other personal letters we received were for both of us or, sometimes, just Margaret.

I sat down and opened it first and drew out a small piece of cheap writing paper and read it quickly. "Cripes!" I said, uttering a word that I had picked up somewhere and couldn't get rid of.

Margaret was at the sink and looked round. "What's that, Eric?"

I re-read the letter to make sure. I didn't think it was a hoax. "Just listen to this. 'Dear Sir, I would be grateful if you could call at my address to examine my wife who has had a fall and does not appear to be able to walk. Yours truly, Mr Truman.' Well, what do you make of that? Extraordinary. Do you think it's genuine?"

"Let's have a look, Eric?" Margaret asked as she took it from me. I could tell that she didn't believe it either. "Goodness... goodness!" she said as she read it. "It isn't dated either."

I picked up the envelope. "Posted on Monday, two days ago. It can't be serious, can it?"

"You never know with these folk, but it sounds bad. But why send for a visit by letter?"

We heard steps outside and Tom's water-bedraggled face appeared at the window. He waved and walked in. He had come specifically to discuss duty times at Christmas but I wanted to talk about Abel Ramsbottom and, now, this mysterious letter.

Margaret had welcomed him and Tom entered, combing his wet hair and making darker grey splash marks on his light grey suit. "Hello, Eric. Is anything wrong? You seem a bit deflated." He sat and produced a cigarette packet and put it on the table in front of him.

"Coffee, Tom?" Margaret asked.

Tom nodded, "Yes, thanks, Margaret. Not Mrs Bartholomew again, Eric?"

"Ha! No, not this time, Tom. Do you know Abel Ramsbottom? He lives with his brother just down the road."

Tom nodded. "Yes, I know him well. I've had to visit once or twice and I know George found him difficult…"

"Difficult!! Anyway, did you get an emergency call from him yesterday afternoon?"

"No, why?" Tom had extracted a cigarette.

I related the whole story to him. Tom nodded his understanding all the way through the account. He blew out a lungful of smoke luxuriously. "You did the right thing, Eric. Don't worry about that. Abel will take a mile if you give him a fraction of an inch. George answered the door once when he was off duty to him, and I think all his problems started then. He's probably just trying to find out if he can do the same with you."

I was relieved and said, "Thank you, Tom. I spent our whole time at Margaret's mother's yesterday wondering if it had been a real emergency. But that's not all. Listen to this." I picked up the letter that was lying beside the cigarette packet and read it out.

"Hum," Tom mused. "That's something else, Eric. It could very well be serious. I know the Trumans a bit and they never come to us or send without a real reason. They are typical stalwarts. I think you'll like them. Once, they both had 'flu but when I asked how they were they both said, 'Oh, fair to middling!' They nearly died. I'd go there first, Eric."

"Yes, I was thinking about doing that. I don't think we'll be long this morning, do you, Tom?" My mind had already started to imagine various scenarios at the Trumans.

"No, but we have to think about Tommy Wilson. We cover for him at Christmas as well. When George was here, we took it in turns to do Christmas Days. We all do our morning surgery on Christmas Eve, and our own calls. We hold a short surgery on Christmas Eve afternoon. That's held by the Christmas Day doctor. However, from mid-day on Christmas Eve until mid-night on Christmas Day, only one doctor is on. Just being on duty, of course, on Christmas Day itself, no surgeries and only emergency visits …"

"Oh, I'll do it Tom. I can see that nobody would want to do Christmas Day, but I'm the most junior here. I might be lucky and not have any calls at all."

"Ha! Don't you believe it, Eric. It tends to be the elderly. They get excited and eat too much. And have you got any babies due? I bet they'd make an appearance."

I thought for a moment. "No, none are due over Christmas. Go on, Tom. I'll do it. Do you think Tommy will mind?"

"No, he'll be relieved. You'll get Boxing Day and the next day off. There's a short surgery on both those days, but I'll sort those out with Tommy."

We chatted a little longer and then Tom left. He was keen to do his visits before his half day and I was itching to get to the Trumans. They lived at the other end of the village, in an area called Ford. I pulled up outside a trim semi-detached house. It was still raining and totally miserable when I bounded up to the front door, knocked, turned the handle and attempted to push the door urgently open with my shoulder. I collided with the unyielding door with a mighty crash. I looked around, sure that my impact would cause jollity in the village in its retelling, if it had been observed. Fortunately, though, on this occasion my embarrassment had been secret. I stood back and looked through the windows to see if there was any sign of life. I heard footsteps.

"Oh, hello. Are yer tryin' to break in, lad?" a grey man said, half welcoming, half challenging as he rounded the corner of the house. He looked to be older than the seventy-five that his records had told me he was. He seemed to be bowed under the strain of life but his neat attire, finished off with a tie, showed that he wouldn't allow life's stresses to overwhelm him.

"Erm, Mr Truman?" I asked. The man nodded his affirmation. "You sent me a letter about your…"

"Oh, you're t'young doctor!" relief lit up the old man's face in a smile. "Ah'm glad you've come. Yer made a right clatter wi' t'front door. Yer won't get in there. We never use it and it's locked all the time. It makes more space in our front room like that. Anyway, ah was just getting Doris her breakfast. Come round to t'back door. Best get out o' this rain."

"Oh, is she all right now, Mr Truman? You didn't say in the letter what had happened." I was reassured that Mrs Truman was up and having breakfast.

Mr Truman carried on walking as he said, "No, doctor, she's just t'same though. She hasn't moved since it happened on Monday. Just mind t'step through the back door." We had reached the black door, which held a small panel glazed in bobbled glass. "Doris fell over it an' that's how she did it." He opened the door carefully and said, "Doris, it were t'young doctor making that din. He's here to see you."

I followed Mr Truman into the small kitchen. I could immediately see a slightly chubby woman lying on her back in most of the floor space. She had a pillow under her head and looked quite cheerful. Her body was covered with a blanket. "Oh, hello doctor. Do come in and make yourself at home." She said, "Ah'm sorry we had to send for you."

I squeezed in and closed the door behind me. Mr Truman had gone to the sink in front of the window. "Would you like a cup of something, doctor? T'kettle's on."

"No, thank you, Mr Truman. Well, Mrs Truman, you seem to have had quite a fall there." I knelt down by her head. "Tell me how it happened."

"Well, it was on Monday morning, just after breakfast and ah'd taken t'rubbish out. It was a bitter day and ah was rushing to get back in and ah tripped over that top step there. Ah kind of twisted it as ah fell. Ah heard a crack as ah hit t'ground and t' pain were bad. Really bad, doctor. It were pulsing wi' t'pain. Just here." Mrs Truman indicated the top of her right thigh. "Ah couldn't move. Cecil here tried to help me up but the pain was like… well, ah've never had it like that before. So, we sent for you."

"Erm, yes, you sent a letter. I got it this morning. I'm going to give you a brief examination, but I think you've broken your femur. Can I pull the blanket down and you can show me where the pain is?"

Doris Truman pulled up her dress to expose the thigh. It was swollen and bruised. The leg also looked misshapen. I felt around the swelling gently with my fingers but couldn't sense any abnormality through her tissues. "You can't move your leg, Mrs Truman?"

"No, and it hurts to try."

"I'm just going to move it very slightly…"

"All right, doctor." Mrs Truman bit her bottom lip in anticipation. I moved the lower leg gently and Mrs Truman groaned. I stopped immediately and pulled her dress down again.

"I'm totally sure that you have broken your femur, Mrs Truman. You'll have to go into hospital for an x-ray to be absolutely certain. They will deal with it there." I looked up at Mr Truman who had been watching the proceedings intensely from his position by the sink. "I'll telephone for an ambulance for you but I take it that you don't have a telephone here?"

"No, doctor. What would we want one of them things for, when we can send letters?"

"Dr Akroyd lives just down the road." Mr Truman nodded. "He's on his rounds at the moment but I'm sure that Mrs Akroyd won't mind me using theirs. I'll be back, though, to wait with you for the ambulance. They only take about twenty minutes to come up from Bradford."

"Oh, that's all right, doctor. We've waited all this time and twenty minutes is nothing."

Chrissey was in and, after a quick explanation, I rang for an ambulance. As Mrs Truman was being stretchered out, Mr Truman shook my hand and said, "Thank you, doctor, for coming so quickly! We knew you would if we had an emergency."

Soon after that episode the weather worsened and got much colder. Sleet showers kept the children firmly indoors. They normally could brave anything to get outside to play. The Craig-na-Hullie lights were on all the time to try and dispel the gloom. The last lingering leaves were whisked off the trees by the penetrating winds that lashed in gusts up the hill.

Sniffs and snuffles accompanied the conversation in the growing numbers in the waiting room for the surgeries. It was at one of these that I received an unexpected visitor - two, in fact.

The first entered after knocking firmly on the surgery door, after my "Next Please" buzz. I looked up to see the familiar figure of our vicar. I stood and said, "Oh, hello, Maurice. Is anything wrong? I never see you here."

"No, Eric. Just a bit of a cold," Maurice explained, his normal sonorous tones were dulled with a bunged-up nose. "I haven't really come to see you but I've brought the next patient along. It's Isaiah Shaw. I bumped into him up the village this morning and I asked him how he was. That was it. I got a litany of minor ailments. He then said that he hoped you'd be in church on Sunday, so that he could tell you about them. I'm afraid I got quite cross with him, Eric. In the end I pretended that I was on my way to your surgery and I almost dragged him along."

"Thank you, Maurice. I thought I had cured him of consulting me at any odd moment…"

Maurice smiled, "Oh, I don't think he will do that again, Eric. I can be very firm. Just ask Jean!"

I returned the smile. "I can believe it! Do you want to sit and have a consultation yourself?"

"No, Eric. Thanks though. Just got a touch of cold, that's all. I must get on. I'm sure that Jean sends her love to you both." With that Maurice left me to press the buzzer button to summon Isaiah.

As he entered without his usual unctuous smile, Isaiah said in a very husky voice, "Well, I've come to see you then, doctor." It was an obvious statement.

"Yes, so I see, Mr Shaw. Thank you for coming to the surgery for a consultation. I hope you'll attend surgeries like everyone else, from now on. I've just seen Mr Slighter, for instance…"

"I know, doctor. I came with him. I think I helped him get here. Between you and me, doctor, I don't think he'd have come if it wasn't for me. But…" Isaiah looked miserable and stopped.

"Well, I'm sure Mr Slighter would be grateful for your help. Why don't you take your coat off and sit down? You can tell me everything that's wrong." I smiled an innocent smile.

After composing himself carefully on the patients' seat, Isaiah coughed and harrumphed. "Well, actually, doctor, before that I'd like to apologise. I know I should have come here before and not spoken to you in the street and at church. It's just that I don't like being in the waiting room and everyone wondering what the matter is with me. I couldn't resist having those little chats with you when I saw you…"

I interrupted what seemed to be turning into a flow of contrition and confession. "Thank you, Mr Shaw. I understand completely. We'll start all over again with our relationship now that you know that the waiting room isn't so bad. What can I do for you today?"

Isaiah smiled for the first time. "Thank you, doctor. Well, since you ask, I've got a few things the matter."

Isaiah listed the symptoms of a typical cold with relish. I held up my hand to staunch the flow once again, "Mr Shaw, you've got a cold!"

"But I've got this bad throat, doctor. It won't go away," Mr Shaw's hoarse voice worsened. "I'm sure I need those antibiotic jobs."

"Oh, they only work against infections caused by bacteria, not viruses. Colds are caused by viruses. I'll just have a look at your throat to make sure." I depressed Isaiah's tongue to reveal a red throat but without any white spots. "Yes, I'm sure, Isaiah, but come back if it continues."

"Well, don't you need to examine me, you know, all over?' he asked in a voice that had suddenly been restored to normality.

"No, I can tell from here. It seems to be a bad cold, but asprin will help with your temperature. You can get some medication from the chemist for your sore throat and cough. A cold should then take two weeks to clear but if you take nothing it may last a fortnight!" I groaned inwardly. I seemed to be saying this rather a lot recently and the joke was wearing very thin on me. "By the sound of your voice, it seems to be getting better already."

"Oh, right then. I'll go…" Then realisation dawned in Isaiah's brain and he smiled. "Yes…yes. Well, thank you, doctor. That was helpful. And, erm."

"Yes?"

"Well, those headaches. They've gone. And I didn't find anything on my pillow!"

"Oh, I am pleased Mr Shaw." I had wondered if Isaiah would be angry at my silly diagnosis.

"So, it can't have been woodworm, then!" Isaiah Shaw looked at me for a minute before breaking into a massive smile.

There was still chatter in the waiting room, but I didn't press the buzzer when Isaiah had left. I opened the hall door and went through to the kitchen. Margaret was sitting at the table, reading the paper. I sat down.

Margaret looked up from the paper. "What on earth's the matter, Eric? It's not like you to come through from the surgery. And you look very pleased with yourself."

"Well, I've just had an early Christmas present! You'll never guess who from."

"No, Eric. But I can see you want to tell me."

"It was Isaiah Shaw and he came to apologise for his impromptu consultations. Amazing really. Oh, and Maurice and Jean send their love. He had dragged Isaiah to the surgery."

The first real snow hit two weeks later and, after the night when I was called out twice, I reflected on the advice that Alfred Clarence, the policeman, had given me as we chatted under the stars. I couldn't think what I could put in the boot of the car to put more weight on the rear wheels to aid their traction. However, as I was putting my bag into the boot, ready for my morning visits I saw the answer gleaming whitely in the dim corner of the garage. It was the WC pan, discarded during the refurbishments of the summer. That would be just the job, I thought, and quickly picked the thing up and placed it alongside my bag.

The first duty that always started my round of visits was posting the letters. Once again, I stopped the car in its regular spot outside the post office. I opened the boot to get the letters out of my bag and didn't close it again in my haste. In the moment that I took to reach the post box and return, the car had attracted two interested spectators who were looking at the strange object in the boot. One was Frank Dobson, the bank manager, whom I knew well enough to be on first name terms with. I didn't recognise the other man.

"Oh, it's your car, Eric," Frank said with a smile. We shook hands. "We've just been admiring your toilet. I must say I hadn't thought of that. It must be very convenient on your rounds!" He laughed – probably at his choice of words.

I blushed and looked in at the offending object, regarding it for the first time through the eyes of an onlooker. "Oh, it's not for, you know, erm …" I spluttered to a halt. "Well, it's just to give more weight in the snow…" All three of us looked around at the High Street, barren of snow and bathed in winter sunshine. "Well, you never know, you know," I stopped unable to complete my explanation.

"Well, ah think it's a grand idea, doctor," the mystery member of our trio added. "Ah wouldn't be embarrassed. An'yer never know when you're going to be caught short, do you? Ah can't think why someone hasn't thought o' that before." And he chuckled. I knew then that my peripatetic toilet would be the talking point of the village.

It was. Whenever I stopped the car, I had requests to see the wonder and two or three appeals to use it. I am sure that it brightened up that winter for the village no end. The toilet had to go. In its place I used four large stones from the back garden. I examined each one to ensure that their shapes were totally innocent and couldn't be confused with anything else, especially something that could elicit ribald remarks.

Thus prepared, we entered our first Christmas season in Craig-na-Hullie. Christmas Eve was full of excitement and the light morning surgery helped me to imagine a trouble-free Christmas Day, which I could enjoy with my family. I did have twelve home visits though. Most were repeat visits but four were new calls. Later in the afternoon, I fetched Margaret's mother from her house in Kirkburton so that she could join us for her one brief annual trip away from her own house and bed. My thoughts on the journey there were with my own father and mother who were still up in Cumberland winding up all their affairs there. They would be having a miserable Christmas alone with the tatters of their lives around them.

I held one more surgery that evening. Only five patients attended.

The children enjoyed laying stockings by a real fireplace, the first time they had done so in their young lives. We all went to bed before our normal bedtimes in preparation for what would be a very early start to the next day with all its excitement.

The bedside telephone jumped into raucous life at half past eleven. It brought a terrible reality to my anticipations: emergencies still happened. I grabbed the receiver rather grumpily. "YES," I shouted, and then brought myself under control, realising that whatever it was had severely disrupted a patient's sleep and those jangling rings of the telephone bell were their cries for help. "Doctor Hainsworth here. How can I help you?"

"It's Ian, doctor," a worried female voice sounded with barely controlled despair. "He's having another asthma attack. And it's bad. I'm sorry to disturb your Christmas, doctor. Ian didn't want me to but I've never seen it like this." I was sitting up now, all my senses awake. Ian worked at the mill and was a member of The Black Dyke Mills Band. He was an important cornet player, but his young life had been blighted by asthma. I had managed to get him one of the first metered dose inhalers in England, which had been developed in America, and it had been of enormous help. Ian had managed to keep playing his cornet.

"Has he used his inhaler, Iris?"

"Yes, yes, doctor. He's too bad to breathe in properly. Please come, doctor."

"I'm on my way, Iris. Keep Ian calm and sitting up. I'll be with you very soon." I went through my 'night call' dressing automatically as I searched my mind for an answer. The metered dose inhaler had really helped with Ian and Mrs Riley, the lady I had visited on the first night of the snow,

now had one. It had transformed her life. The only real option was to phone for an ambulance, but time was short. Ian could well be my first Christmas Day death. I imagined his young family waking up to that. I couldn't let it happen.

I switched the light on in the dark of the surgery to grab my bag. I was totally oblivious to the cold. In desperation, I opened the cupboard door to somehow draw inspiration from its random contents. Bleakly I looked in. And there it was, on the bottom shelf: an old and forgotten squeeze-bulb nebulizer, made from glass. The rubber squeeze-bulb propelled the drug into the lungs through the mouth. They weren't that efficient as the particles tended to be too large to enter the lungs, but I thought I would give it a try. I grabbed it. But I knew that I was clutching at straws.

Amazingly, though, the thing worked. My frantic squeezes just managed to get some of the drug into place through Ian's white, drawn lips. His breathing became slightly less of a deathly struggle. He could use his inhaler now, the drugs finally reaching the raging lung tissues. Iris watched through every laboured breath. She didn't move. She couldn't move.

Ian breathed more easily. His eyes regained life and hope and his body relaxed with relief. I stayed about ten minutes longer to make sure that he was through the attack, and then I stood to go. I looked at my watch. It was nearly one o'clock.

I smiled at Ian and Iris. "Well, Happy Christmas!"

Iris suddenly sprang into life. She dashed forward and hugged me. "Thank you, thank you, doctor. How can we thank you enough. You've given us the best Christmas present ever. Happy Christmas, doctor."

On my way home, Iris's comments rang in my head. What a wonderful job I had! I couldn't think of a higher privilege than to be able to give someone a Christmas present like that. It had also made my Christmas. And then a thought struck me. In all the pre-Christmas rush I had completely forgotten to buy a present for Margaret. All my elation evaporated as I imagined my confession being greeted with a teary acceptance. But then I had a brainwave. I knew what I could give her. I was suddenly totally sure she would love it.

I drove on past Craig-na-Hullie, glancing out of habit at the front room window. No newspaper disturbed it. The house itself, as well as its occupants, was asleep and at rest. I carried on over the hill and down to Emily's house to collect her magnificent bust.

I was surprised with Margaret's reluctance with her thanks but I had to admit that the sculpture resembled a lump of dirty stone from most angles ... and that it was her only present from me that year. The bust rested forlornly in the back porch for the rest of the day. However, Margaret kept sneaking through to have a look at it when she thought I wasn't watching. When we were climbing into bed, exhausted after all the jollity, she suddenly smiled and threw her arms round me. "I think I'm going to like her, Eric. Thank you. What do you think we should call her?"

I smiled in return. "Oh, I don't think that's in any doubt. I think she's Emily."

"Yes... yes. Emily it is. She can't stay indoors though. I think she can live at the top of the rockery and spend her days admiring the view. What do you think?"

"Yes, darling. That would be splendid!"

A few days later, we proudly positioned her overlooking the valley.

And so, Emily became a loved member of the family. Margaret talked to her as she gardened. From her vantage point Emily watched the arrival of a new decade. It was to be the decade during which the children grew up. She was there as the years passed. In the warmth of the summer sunshine, we would often relax there in the back garden and talk about our lives - the struggles and joys that we experienced – as we sat by her.

Emily

Printed in Great Britain
by Amazon